Anthony Giddens: An Introduction to a Social Theorist

Anthony Giddens

An Introduction to a Social Theorist

Lars Bo Kaspersen

Translated by Steven Sampson

Copyright © Lars Bo Kaspersen and Hans Reitzels Forlag A/S, Copenhagen 1995

Emglish translation copyright © Steven Sampson 2000

First published in Danish as *Anthony Giddens: Introduktion til en Samfundsteoretiker* by
Hans Reitzels Forlag A/S, Copenhagen, 1995

First published in English 2000

This English edition has been published with the support of Statens Samfunsvidenskabelige
Forskningsrad in Denmark.

2 4 6 8 10 9 7 5 3 1

Blackwell Publishers Ltd
108 Cowley Road
Oxford OX4 1JF
UK

Blackwell Publishers Inc.
350 Main Street
Malden, Massachusetts 02148
USA

British Library Cataloguing in Publication Data
A CIP catalogue record for this book is available from the British Library.

Library of Congress Cataloging-in-Publication Data
Kaspersen, Lars Bo.
 [Anthony Giddens. English]
 Anthony Giddens : an introduction to a social theorist / Lars Bo Kaspersen ; translated
by Steven Sampson.
  p.   cm.
 Includes bibliographical references and index.
 ISBN 0-631-20733-3 (hb : alk. paper) — ISBN 0-631-20734-1 (pbk. : alk. paper)
 1. Giddens, Anthony.   2. Sociology—Methodology.   3. Social structure.   4.
Sociology—Great Britain.   I. Title.

HM479.G54 K3713 2000
 301'.01—dc21
                                                                                    99-085968

Typeset in 10 on 12 pt Galliard
by Ace Filmsetting Ltd, Frome, Somerset
Printed in Great Britain by T. J. International, Padstow, Cornwall

This book is printed on acid-free paper.

Contents

Preface

This book is not another critical introduction to Anthony Giddens's sociology and social theory. It is, rather, an introduction with a critique. To add another book to the Giddens industry may seem futile and silly, but I do claim that this book is needed, because it is the first genuine introduction to the universe of Anthony Giddens's social theory and sociology. Several books "introducing" and debating Giddens have appeared since the late 1980s, but either they are quite advanced critical discussions of Giddens's work or they pretend to be introductory but do not succeed, because they all have the main aim of criticizing Giddens's work. It is perfectly legitimate to discuss and criticize Giddens (it is absolutely necessary!), but such a project does not always provide the best introduction for new students. This is exactly the purpose of this book: to introduce new students to Giddens's social theory, including his latest writings on politics, which are omitted in most other books.

Since the early 1970s, Giddens has criticized classical and modern sociology, but also contributed with his own constructions: structuration and modernity theory. Most recently, he has entered into politics. Giddens is one of the most productive sociologists of our time. Since 1960, he has published 33 books (authored, co-authored, and edited), approximately 85 major articles, and more than 250 minor articles and book reviews. In the wake of his considerable contributions to sociology and other social sciences are dozens of articles and books by colleagues discussing his work. Giddens is today a "global phenomenon," translated into many languages and read in almost all sociology curricula.

Giddens is an interesting sociologist who covers a wide range of interests. He manages to get to the center of sociological discussions and is therefore someone you must relate to. Unfortunately, his writing sometimes contains too many neologisms and difficult expressions, convoluted theoretical language, and very few examples. This makes him less accessible, which means that many potential readers are scared off from the beginning. In addition, he often presumes that readers are acquainted with a whole range of theories within social theory, philosophy, and sociology, automatically creating problems for students without this knowledge.

Such difficulties cannot be avoided completely and are, in a way, part of the learning process for those who are interested in social theory. Still, I find that Giddens's theoretical work makes an introductory book necessary. The purpose of this book is, therefore, to introduce his conceptual universe and its preconditions, so that new Giddens readers can start here. An introductory book cannot, of course, replace Giddens's own texts, but it can help to remove the worst obstacles to their understanding.

The primary target groups are undergraduates and graduates at universities and business schools, but sociology and social science teachers at high school level and in health care, social work education, and pedagogical education will also find the book helpful for an overview of Giddens's theories. One or two semesters of social science theory at university level are, however, required for comprehension of some of the chapters.

I have worked on Giddens for several years, and many people have provided support, advice and criticism. My interest was aroused almost fifteen years ago when I first read Giddens's book *Sociology – a Brief but Critical Introduction*. Later followed an intense period at the University of Sussex, and I am indebted to Gillian Rose and William Outhwaite for good and inspiring discussions about Giddens's theories. My master's thesis on Giddens, the basis of chapters 3 and 4 in this book, was completed at the Department of Sociology in Copenhagen, and I want to thank Tom Brock for great and lively discussions and Göran Djurfeldt for good and thorough supervision. At the University of California, Santa Barbara, Thomas P. Wilson, John Mohr, and Connie McNeely helped me through a bumpy Giddens period with their wit and humor. Throughout, Anne Binzer Sørensen and Morten Wiberg have been extremely helpful and contributed many ideas and critical comments. Thanks are also due to Anthony Giddens for help and willingness in connection with interviews and discussions of central themes in his production. The real reason this book was written is, however, the students at the Department of Political Science, University of Aarhus, who participated in my seminars, read working papers, and gave me ideas and criticism. Thanks to all. In the last phase of the book I owe special thanks to William Outhwaite, Poul Poder Pedersen, Mette Kjær, Keld Hosbond, Lisbeth Gudmand-Høyer, Anja Jacobsen, Carsten Jørgensen, Vibeke Boolsen, Erik Gudmand-Høyer and Anne Binzer Sørensen, who all read and commented on the manuscript. Thanks for the critical comments which were sometimes (mistakenly?) ignored. Thanks to

Steven Sampson for doing the translation and many thanks to Louise Eff for doing the bibliography and reading the manuscript. Many, many thanks to Annette Bruun Andersen for word processing, some translation and proof-reading. I am also grateful to the Danish Social Science Council, which provided financial support for the translation. Finally, thanks go to Hanne for her cooperation and tolerance – and to William and Vincent for all the challenges!

Please note that all references pertain to Giddens, unless otherwise stated.

Lars Bo Kaspersen
Copenhagen

Introduction

About the Man

Who is Anthony Giddens? He was born in 1938 in Edmonton, a north London suburb. He went to the local Minchenden grammar school, where he graduated with below average exam marks. Admitted to the University of Hull, where he originally wanted to study philosophy, Giddens found that the university's only philosophy teacher was on leave that year. He looked around for another subject and moved to psychology, but this subject could only be studied alongside sociology. It turned out to be a fortunate choice, as Hull at that time had a lively sociology department, led by the renowned Peter Worsley. Giddens became so inspired that in 1959 he graduated with a first class honors degree in sociology. Going on to the London School of Economics (LSE), Giddens received a master's degree for a thesis on the development of sport in England in the nineteenth century.

Although initially having planned a career as a ministerial civil servant, after his third semester at the LSE he was offered a lectureship at Leicester University, where he worked from 1961 to 1969. At Leicester, Giddens found himself among several of England's and Europe's foremost sociologists, among them Norbert Elias and Ilya Neustadt. During these years in Leicester, Giddens was also a guest professor at Simon Fraser University near Vancouver and at the University of California at Los Angeles. This meeting with North American radicalism in the crucial years of 1968 and 1969 became quite influential on Giddens, since he here witnessed social change with profound effects on contemporary societies.

In 1970 he went to Cambridge as a lecturer and fellow at King's College, becoming professor in 1985. Together with this Cambridge professorship, Giddens has also been visiting professor at various universities, including the University of California at Santa Barbara, where, until recently, he has resided during the cold, wet English winters.

In 1996, he left his job as a professor at Cambridge to become the new director of the London School of Economics. He has taken up this challenge with a lot of energy, appointing new staff and running a series of lectures called the Director's Lectures. Moreover, he has established a close link to the political world, partly by promoting the LSE's role in policy-making and partly by taking an active part in the New Labour project himself. The involvement in New Labour can be seen in recent publications, most notably *The Third Way – a Renewal of Social Democracy*, his contribution to New Labour's policies via the Institute of Public Policy Research, and in his being an occasional advisor to Tony Blair. One of his ambitions is strengthening the LSE intellectually and financially in order to transform it into "an institution that defines our time." In 1984 he was the co-founder of Polity Press. Since then he has been chairman and director of the company, which today is one of the most successful publishing companies in social science and humanities.

During Giddens's academic university career his teaching, research and publishing activities have been supplemented by his traveling around the world as guest lecturer. Despite this seemingly overwhelming work load, Giddens, until he became Director of the LSE, succeeded in writing nearly a book a year. While the quality of some of his work can be debated, the amount of Giddens's published work is incredible. His enormous production is made possible by a combination of a Protestant work ethic, a photographic memory, a great ability to concentrate, and modern technical aids.

However, Giddens's productivity as a writer is not the only thing that sets him apart from other academics. His eloquence and ability to express complex ideas in simplified form make him a superb lecturer. His extremely well structured lectures are always delivered fluently and without a manuscript. Since eloquent speakers can also be seductive, it behoves us to listen – and then to critically evaluate the content. Let us therefore examine Giddens's sociology more closely.

Giddens's Social Theoretical and Sociological Project

Giddens introduces his first book, *Capitalism and Modern Social Theory* (1971a), with the claim that "social theory stands in need of a radical revision" (1971a, p. vii).

According to Giddens, the paramount task of social theory and sociology is to understand and explain human action and social institutions.[1]

This goal cannot be achieved as long as social theory and sociology remain mired in theories developed a century ago. Sociology arose and evolved as a discipline at the end of the 1800s and in the early 1900s. The society which the first sociologists (Comte, Marx, Weber, and Durkheim) saw as their first task to investigate was immensely different from the modern, complex, and differentiated society we are experiencing at the beginning of the twenty-first century. Therefore, says Giddens, we must break with the classical sociological theoretical foundation. If we are to grasp the modern world, new concepts are needed. Giddens sees his task as undertaking this rethinking.

Giddens as Critic

Giddens develops this revision by carrying out a comprehensive study of classical and modern sociology, philosophy, and social theory. During the 1960s and 1970s he reviewed and analyzed the work of Karl Marx, Max Weber, Émile Durkheim, and Georg Simmel (Giddens, 1968b, 1971a, 1972a, b, 1978a). He then went on to criticize several of the major twentieth-century thinkers in sociology, anthropology, and philosophy, including Talcott Parsons, Robert Merton, Alfred Schutz, Erving Goffmann, Martin Heidegger, Jürgen Habermas, Claude Lévi-Strauss, Ferdinand de Saussure, Louis Althusser, Michel Foucault, Herbert Marcuse, and Ludwig Wittgenstein (1968a, 1976a, 1977a, 1979a).

Giddens finds several fundamental problems among the aforementioned theorists which reflect some of the classical questions in the history of social theory: "What is the scientific object of sociology?" Or, in other words, "What is it that sociology should study?" "What methods should be employed?" "Can we discover laws for human behavior analogous to the laws of nature?" "Is society an independent 'entity' that exerts force and limits on our behavior?" "Or is society simply the sum of human actions?"

The all-important problem for Giddens is the tension between the individual and society. Sociological theories can be categorized into two groups. First are theories where the individual and individual action define and constitute society. Here the individual and the individual's actions receive so much attention that the theory cannot conceptualize and explain the existence of social institutions. Second are theories where society consists of structures that have an autonomous existence independent of individuals. The structure of society and social systems are emphasized more than the individual's possibilities of action, such that the actors appear to be constrained by the structure.

The two categories of sociological theory raise major questions. To what degree is it possible for individuals to create their own lives and the frameworks for these? To what extent are we already constrained by the fact of being born into an already existing society? This conflict between the individual and society is often labeled as the dualism between actor (the acting individual) and structure (the surrounding society). Giddens criticizes the sociological analyses which tend to stress either social actors or social structures, and he has spent considerable effort in trying to reconcile the two differing perspectives on society.

Giddens as Constructor

Giddens claims that if sociology is to generate tenable and adequate analyses of modern society, the agent–structure dualism must be transcended. From the late 1970s through the 1980s he worked intensively on developing a theoretical foundation which takes account of this dichotomy. Giddens's radical revision leads in the first instance to the emergence of his own contribution to sociology, the theory of structuration, which in its most coherent form is presented in *The Constitution of Society* (1984a). Here he conceptualizes the relationship between the individual actor and the social institutions and structures by considering structures as both a means to and a result of actors' actions. When I speak English, for example, I already use my existing language structure, but I am also creating these language structures while I think and speak English. In this way, society is continually created in an ongoing process of structuration.

With structuration theory as the general theoretical point of departure, Giddens turned to concrete studies of modern society (1985a, 1990a, 1991a, 1992b, 1994a, b).

The Nation-state and Modernity

Giddens investigates the emergence and development of the modern nation-state in *The Nation-State and Violence* (1985a). Here he describes how the convergence of four crucial forces creates a unique development in Europe. The four forces are capitalism, industrialism, the development of the military and its association with the state's monopoly of violence, and the state's increasing surveillance capacity and thereby control over the population. The interaction between these "institutional clusters" creates a special state system in Europe, with its own dynamic. This state system evolves out of the mutual rivalries among states, ultimately leading to the emergence of the European nation-state, the liberal-democratic constitution, and a market economy. This state, with its associated institutional features in the form of surveillance, industrialism, and capitalism, comes to play an increasingly dominant role in our everyday life and the creation of the first global society in world history. Giddens describes this globalization process in *The Consequences of Modernity* (1990a), *Beyond Left and Right* (1994a), and the chapter "Living in a post-traditional society" (in 1994b). Giddens has subsequently developed his analysis by examining the consequences of modernity for the individual, identity, sexuality, and intimacy (*Modernity and Self-identity* (1991a) and *The Transformation of Intimacy* (1992b)). His central theme in these works is an analysis of the changes that evolve in interaction between the extensive social institutions and individuals in their day-to-day lives. As these titles indicate, the analysis focuses upon the individual level, where Giddens investigates the conditions for the development of the self and identity in modern society.

Giddens and Politics

In the 1990s Giddens moved beyond his role as a social theorist and analyst of modernity. He has become much more concerned with politics, including party political matters. Although he has never operated with a clear-cut distinction between sociology and politics, his recent publications are directly focused on politics (1994a, c, d, e, f, 1995a, b, 1996b, 1997, 1998a, b; Lloyd, 1997b). We can detect a shift of interest from a number of articles published in the British magazine *New Statesman and Society* and the book *Beyond Left and Right* (1994). Subsequently, he continued writing articles to *New Statesman* and the Sunday paper the *Observer*, and most recently he has published *The Third Way – a Renewal of Social Democracy* (1998a), which explicitly attempts to set up a new agenda for British, European, and world politics, mainly addressed to the center-left.

About This Book

The first three chapters of this book concentrate upon Giddens's social theory, followed by two chapters on his more sociological works. Chapter 6 focuses on his most recent work, directly related to political matters and party politics.

Chapter 7, another chapter focusing on his sociological work, contains an interview with Giddens where he discusses the post-traditional cosmopolitan social order and its increased violence and fundamentalism, but also the potential for a more democratic world order. Here he also presents the main ideas from one of his more recent books, *Beyond Left and Right* (1994).

Chapter 8 presents a discussion of Giddens's social theoretical and sociological project, as well as a critique of parts of his work. This chapter also provides a general assessment of Giddens's entire project.

The book also includes a bibliography of Giddens's production and the most essential secondary works and journal articles dealing with what could be termed the Giddens phenomenon.

Because of limited space, I do not deal with Giddens's empirical and theoretical studies from the 1960s and early 1970s on the classical sociological problem of suicide (1964b, 1965a, b, f, 1966b, 1970d, 1971b). During this period, Giddens also concerned himself with class analysis, both theoretically (1973) and empirically (1972d, e, 1974a, 1975a). While certainly interesting, the studies of suicide and class do not comprise a part of his overall project in the same way as his other studies.

Much of Giddens's sociological project, because it is so abstract, makes for difficult reading. Therefore, I have made an effort to introduce his conceptual universe in as simple a fashion as possible, without distorting or presenting his theories in too simplistic a way.

This book presents Giddens's work chronologically in order to demonstrate both the development and the continuity in his thinking. One drawback of such a presentation, however, is that the more difficult chapters must be placed at the beginning. Chapter 1, which presents Giddens's review and critique of the dominant theoretical orientations in sociology and social theory, deals with complex questions of philosophy and theory of science. While I have tried to define all the concepts and to avoid unnecessary jargon, the chapter may at times be difficult for readers unfamiliar with sociological theory. It should be mentioned, however, that if the chapter seems too difficult, or the problems lie beyond the reader's field of interest, the reader may go on to chapters 2 and 3, concerning the theory of structuration.

The first seven chapters try to fulfill the book's intention as an introductory text. In the beginning sections of chapter 8, however, I discuss Giddens's work in the context of problems in the theory of science. While the first sections demand a certain degree of background knowledge of philosophy and theory of science from the reader, I have included them because these crucial critiques are seldom presented in the debate about Giddens's sociology.

In general it should be noted that the book is written so that the individual chapters can be read separately. This has inevitably produced some overlap, but it also enables the reader to skip through the book and study those aspects of Giddens's work he or she finds most interesting.

Note

1   For Giddens the term social theory refers to questions that apply to all the social
    sciences. "These issues are to do with the nature of human action and the acting
    self; with how interaction should be conceptualized and its relation to institu-
    tions; and with grasping the practical connotations of social analysis . . . soci-
    ology [is] that branch of social science which focuses particularly upon the
    'advanced' or modern societies" (1984, p. xvii).

1

Anthony Giddens, the Positive Critic: the Dialogue with Classical and Modern Sociology

Theoretical developments do not take place in a vacuum but in a critical dialogue with existing theories. This chapter presents a summary of Giddens's discussion of several sociological and social theoretical positions that have inspired his subsequent work on structuration theory and his analysis of modernity. Giddens's polemic against an entire range of theoretical positions was conducted largely in the 1970s, although a few additional contributions appeared in the 1960s and early 1980s.

The development of a new theory for conceptualizing our own contemporary era, which is Giddens's main project, demands a theoretical foundation that not only explicates the nature of modern society but can also lead to a method for investigating this society.

In this light, Giddens presents several general theoretical considerations on the nature of society, including the relation between individual and society. This presentation entails a fundamental investigation of the core concepts within sociology, concepts such as society, agent, structure, system, time, and space.

Our purpose here is to show how the principal schools of sociology, with their points of departure in either positivism or hermeneutic philosophy, have attempted to understand society. Giddens is not particularly preoccupied by epistemological problems, i.e. how we should know society. Rather, he is interested in ontological questions, i.e. what the various social theoretical and sociological schools consider as being or existent. In other words, he is interested in what these schools see as constituting society. In general terms, society is the focal point, but there remains considerable disagreement as to the nature of society, what a society consists of, the relations between individual and society, and so on. Is a society simply the sum of the actions of the individuals, or does society exist independently of individuals? Giddens undertakes a critical study of these questions within the principal sociological traditions: functionalism, action theory, structuralism, and Marxism. According to Giddens, these four schools are dominated by two perspectives which emphasize either systems/structures or individuals' actions.

In his elaboration of these main problems, Giddens identifies a dualism which he finds to be an obstacle to the development of an adequate theory of society. The dualism arises because the two aforementioned perspectives have two contrasting views of the object and methods of sociology. In chapter 2, we examine Giddens's own theoretical contribution, the theory of structuration, more closely; structuration is an approach which attempts to transcend this dichotomy.

The Philosophical Basis of Sociology

Sociology evolved as an independent professional discipline in the late 1800s. Society and the concept of society became the object of sociological inquiry, but disagreement quickly arose in professional sociological circles as to the character of society, as well as about what kind of methods should be used to study it. Various sociological schools promote diverse views about what constitutes society, but the principal opposition is between functionalism on the one side and action-oriented sociology on the other. Functionalism, originally developed by the Frenchman Émile Durkheim (1858–1917), takes its point of departure in society understood as a system with its own independent existence. This system consists of more than simply the sum of individuals' actions. Action theory, with the German Max Weber (1864–1920) as its most important founder, focuses on the individual actor; here society is understood exclusively as the sum of individuals and their actions. The third of the great classical founders of sociology, Karl Marx (1818–83), is often interpreted as being within one of these two orientations; hence, Marx may be depicted as either a functionalist or an action theorist.[1] In their attempts to create a secure foundation for their respective science of society, the two major orientations try to garner support from various philosophies. On the one hand, philosophy attempts to provide answers as to how knowledge is possible, how true knowledge can be acquired, i.e. what methods are to be applied (epistemology and methodology). On the other hand, philosophy presents a solution as to how reality appears (ontology).

To put it very simply, Durkheim seeks inspiration primarily from the philosophical tradition known as "positivism," while Weber relies upon hermeneutics in the broad sense of the term. The two philosophies both present themselves as providing answers to the question of why the natural sciences have been and still are able to discover the laws of the world of nature in a scientific fashion and thereby produce scientific progress for the benefit of humanity. Both orientations also present solutions as to how the social and cultural sciences can achieve the same scientific character and thereby also generate progress.

The central controversy between positivism (the naturalistic tradition) and hermeneutics (the anti-naturalist tradition) revolves around the relationship between the natural and social sciences. The disagreement concerns the degree to which society can be studied in the same fashion as nature.

The positivists/naturalists assert that there is no fundamental difference between the object of natural sciences and the object of the social/cultural sciences. The characters of the world of nature and the world of culture are very similar, and one can therefore apply the same methods and concepts, such as species, to describe relations in both worlds. With a point of departure in sensory data, one should apply systematic methods to the construction of general laws for both the physical and the human worlds.

The hermeneutics/anti-naturalist school agrees with the positivists on natural science. In nature there occur connections between causally related phenomena, from which general laws can be developed. Here one can utilize so-called positivist methods with the collection of sensory data, i.e. phenomena which we can observe and register with our senses, and on this inductive basis generate laws.

Disagreement between the two philosophical orientations begins to occur when society becomes the object of study. The hermeneutics believe that society is a unique entity, in that it is created by human beings and is a product of human subjectivity and intentions. Society consists of human beings who act on the basis of cultural values, who have experiences, and who can always alter their behavior. Therefore, human behavior cannot be measured and recorded in the same fashion as, for example, the behavior of molecules. As a consequence, hermeneutics maintains that we can never derive general laws for human behavior. Rather, we must utilize totally different methods in order to understand human relations. Hermeneutics means the art of interpretation, and the basic method, therefore, is to interpret human activities so that we understand the motives and intentions behind them.

This conflict between positivism and hermeneutics, a conflict about method and epistemology, is discussed by Giddens in his *New Rules of Sociological Method* (1976a) and *Studies in Social and Political Theory* (1977a). In these two works he examines various strands of the two philosophies and the critique against positivism and hermeneutics during the twentieth century. Especially, he reviews and analyses dominant philosophical positions through the 1960s and 1970s, when the main criticism against positivism and the most naive hermeneutics developed. His concern with these positions may be seen as a process where he focuses on his own philosophical foundations.

From Epistemology to Ontology: Giddens's Philosophical Position

The critical review of positivism and hermeneutics helps Giddens to see that both philosophical tendencies are caught in a subject–object dualism which neither of them has the capacity to transcend. According to Giddens, none of the philosophies mentioned has been able to provide satisfactory answers to the question of how a subject can understand his or her environment (the object). There exists fundamental disagreement between the two philosophical positions around the nature of the social world, as well as which methods are to be applied to elucidating this world.

Giddens is in agreement with the post-positivist and recent hermeneutic critique which developed during the 1960s and 1970s (1976a, 1977a). We cannot create true knowledge that describes laws which can be observed, explained, and predicted. The scientific process cannot be considered as a unilateral relationship in which an observing subject which presents theories on the basis of observations. Science is not unilaterally a question of "erklären," of producing explanations. Science is a complicated interaction between interpretation and explanation. Hence, the distinction between subject and object (theory–data) becomes more diffuse and applies to both the natural and social sciences.

We can therefore find no solid ground for knowledge. As knowing beings, we cannot separate ourselves from that which we know. It is our encounter between our preconceived ideas and the present which creates the social reality. We are always "imprisoned" in a given tradition and a given horizon of meaning. When we "understand" our environment, we carry with us this framework of meaning. As knowledge is created in a process of interpretation having its point of departure in a given horizon of meaning, new knowledge will always be affected by this confrontation between tradition and history on the one hand and the concrete social reality on the other. Furthermore, this knowledge will to a certain degree always be relative. As human beings, we ourselves are participants in and producers of the social reality, and thereby possess a knowledge about it. The encounter between different horizons of meaning can entail a revision of our knowledge.

This aspect also means that such a theory is always critical. Here we are not thinking of Critical Theory in any Frankfurt School or Marxian sense. Rather, Giddens simply states that such an approach will always pose critical questions when the past and the prejudices in a specific horizon of meaning are confronted by the present. In this way, tradition can be called into question.

Giddens sees how the post-positivist critique and modern hermeneutics lead in the same direction. The ontological question replaces the epistemological question. Instead of focusing on how reality is to be understood, we must instead realize that we are a part of reality and that understanding takes place through our language and is thereby to a great degree a question of interpretation. Hence, it is the nature of reality which ought to be the central issue for philosophy and the various sciences.

Giddens thus applauds the "ontological turn" in philosophy, and his own position is therefore inspired by the post-positivist critique, and by the modern hermeneutists, chiefly Hans-Georg Gadamer (Giddens, 1982, pp. 1–17).

Giddens and Critical Realism

Giddens's attempts to downgrade the epistemological and methodological questions in favor of the ontological questions has many points of intersection with the critical realism of the English philosopher of science Roy Bhaskar, who, like Giddens, places ontology at the center.[2]

Giddens's use of Bhaskar and critical realism is not entirely coincidental. Critical realism is a philosophy of science which Giddens himself explicitly refers to as a possible point of departure for a social theory, although he at times deviates from it (Giddens, 1977a, p. 80, 1979a, p. 63, 1982a, p. 14). The very fundamental point of departure, where the nature of being and thereby reality obtains a prominent place, is the same, however, for both Giddens and for critical realism.

As formulated especially by Bhaskar, critical realism builds on a premise that the objects of science exist entirely independently of science and its activities. For Bhaskar, realism is not a theory of knowledge or truth, but a theory of being and of the nature of being (Bhaskar, 1986, p. 6). There exist real structures which exist and evolve independently of our knowledge. The earth moves in an orbit around the sun. If I drop my pen, it falls to the ground because of gravity. Tomorrow will see millions of people driving their cars to work. These structures and processes take place regardless of our knowledge of astronomy, gravity, or sociological theories.

Realism is a "common-sense ontology," which takes seriously the existing things, structures, and mechanisms, such that science can reveal them. To explain facts is not to relate them to universal laws but to identify the mechanisms which produce these facts (Outhwaite, 1987, p. 19). Science is a systematic attempt via thought to express the structures and events which exist and take place independently of the idea (Bhaskar, 1978, p. 250). These explanations can possibly reveal how conditions which we consider as facts are illusory; for example, when science proves that the earth revolves around the sun despite the fact that what we observe is the sun moving across the sky every single day (Outhwaite, 1983).

Bhaskar's realism is an attempt to describe reality as it is. The world must be understood as a complex arrangement of differently interacting structures and mechanisms which it is science's goal to describe and explain. This is a change in relation to positivism's emphasis on the *knowing* of reality and attempts to achieve certain knowledge by way of observation. Thus, we find a change from epistemological questions to ontological questions. Realism asserts that science is interested in the structures and mechanisms of *reality*.

Giddens distinguishes himself from Bhaskar's critical realism inasmuch as he maintains the clear distinction between nature and culture, which, as we have seen, stems from early hermeneutics. Bhaskar's lack of separation between nature and culture does not lead into the classical positivist model of unified science, however. Bhaskar does not commit himself to any special ontology or method.

Despite the close links to recent philosophers of science such as Kuhn and Hesse, to modern hermeneutics (Gadamer), and to the "critical realist" school developed by Bhaskar and others, it is not possible to precisely pinpoint Giddens's philosophical position (McLennan, 1984). Giddens does not find it fruitful to be able to choose between two strategies: he does not choose between trying to bring about a certain epistemology on a philosophical basis, or a clear ontology in the form of a sociological theory which says something about the nature of reality (Bleicher and Featherstone, 1982, p. 72). Instead, Giddens proposes a middle-of-the-road strategy where "critical salvos are fired into reality." These salvos consist of sociological theories and concepts and seek to describe pieces of the existing reality, e.g. the nation-state, the contrast between the traditional and the modern.

Even though Giddens would apparently like to avoid being placed in one of the two positions, it seems to me that in his later work he does in fact choose sides. His structuration theory is an attempt to construct such a social ontology and to make a statement about the nature of social life. In the next chapter we shall see how his analyses of classical and modern social theory and sociology are ultimately an attempt to choose from useful elements for his own ontology construction, what is called "structuration theory." However, here we present some of the critical considerations which create the basis for this.

Sociological Dualism: Action or Structure?

In the previous section we saw how Giddens identifies an opposition between subjectivism (hermeneutics) and objectivism (positivism) within Western philosophy.

Giddens's interest in the various philosophical positions is due to the major influence of philosophy on disciplines as diverse as biology, literary criticism, physics, and sociology. How philosophy views the world and the methods used to obtain knowledge of this world have directly affected sociological theory. Hence, both hermeneutics and positivism have functioned as the basis of legitimation for the main sociological schools. Hermeneutics and positivism have provided the philosophical foundation for sociology, in terms of both how to understand the nature of society and the correct method for studying society.

It is thus hardly surprising that, in his review of sociological theories, Giddens is able to identify a dualism which corresponds to the subjectivism–objectivism dualism in philosophy. In order to explore the nature of this dualism, Giddens undertakes a critical analysis of sociology's principal orientations: functionalism, structuralism, action-theory, and Marxism. Giddens's purpose is to evaluate the strengths of these theoretical traditions as a possible foundation for a social theory with which to analyze modern society. How do these four traditions treat the relationship between individual and society? How do they view and define an individual? What concept of society do they operate with? How do they account for social reproduction and social change? These questions comprise the main threads of Giddens's analysis of social theory.

In analyzing the dominant theoretical tendencies, Giddens finds a dualism which corresponds to the philosophical dualism. In sociology this dualism is manifested in the manner by which the four main tendencies employ either a system or an actor perspective on society (1971a, 1976a, 1977a, 1979a, 1981a, 1982d). Let us first examine functionalism.

Functionalism: from Comte and Durkheim to the Orthodox Consensus

While the intellectual roots of functionalism go back to Auguste Comte (1798–1857), it was primarily Emile Durkheim (1858–1917) who established a genuine functionalist orientation for sociology.

Durkheim derived his inspiration from Comte and from the Englishman Herbert Spencer (1820–1903), and it was the synthesis of these two thinkers that created the foundation for Durkheim's functionalism. For Durkheim, a society had to be understood as an independent thing, *sui generis*. The study of society had to search for the causes of social phenomena in social facts, not in the individual consciousness, which according to Durkheim belonged to the domain of psychology. A society could only be understood if it were viewed as a whole and as an autonomous thing, where the whole was greater than the sum of its parts.

From Spencer, Durkheim obtained the biological organism metaphor. Society was considered an organism, in which each individual part had its place and fulfilled a specific function so that the organism could reproduce itself. In addition to the biological metaphor, Durkheim also borrowed Spencer's distinction between structure and function. Durkheim posed the question of a given social phenomenon's function for the social structure. One example is Durkheim's first major work, *De la division du travail social* (*The Division of Labor in Society*) (1893), in which the main problematic was the function of the division of labor for the social structure. Within this problematic lay the implicit notion that society contains certain needs – just as a human organism has needs – which must be met in order for society to survive. Durkheim therefore concentrated upon analyzing how a given structure fulfills society's need for integration. Hence, he argued that the division of labor provides a new basis for solidarity and integration in a modern differentiated society. To the extent that the need for solidarity is not satisfied, pathological states such as anomie (absence of norms) will occur.

Durkheim became the chief inspiration for the next generation of functionalists, primarily the social anthropologists Alfred Radcliffe-Brown (1881–1955) and Bronislaw Malinowski (1884–1942) (Giddens, 1977a, pp. 97–8, 1984a, pp. 228–9).

Following its development within anthropology, functionalism experienced a renaissance within sociology. This occurred primarily in North America, where for the first time the United States became the center for theoretical developments in sociology, with Talcott Parsons (1902–1979) and Robert Merton (b. 1910) as the most prominent exponents. Compared to Radcliffe-Brown and Malinowski, Parsons and Merton developed a far more sophisticated form of functionalism. Merton, for example, refined the concept of function by distinguishing between manifest and latent functions: when the involved participants are aware and understand the consequences of their acts, we may speak of manifest functions, whereas latent functions are the unintended, unacknowledged consequences of certain social activities. The classic example for Merton is the rain dance of the Hopi Indians (Merton, 1968, pp. 118–21; Giddens, 1984a, pp. 294ff). The Hopi perform the rain dance with the intention that it will produce rain for their crops. This is the manifest function of the rain dance. Beyond this, the dance and the ceremony also have a latent function of reinforcing social cohesion and integration in Hopi society. According to Merton, the main objective of sociology is to describe the latent functions of various social activities and institutions.

Another element in Merton's functionalism is the distinction between functions and dysfunctions. Especially in modern industrialized society, several phenomena occur which do not contribute to societal integration. For example, theft and drug abuse can be seen as dysfunctional, inasmuch as they work against integration in society.

During the 1950s and 1960s, the functionalism of Merton and Parsons was the dominant theoretical tendency in sociology. Functionalism was the tendency which set the agenda, and on which everyone had to take a stand. It was a situation which Giddens sees as an orthodox consensus within sociology (1984a, p. xv). The dominance of functionalism lasted until the late 1960s, when new, especially Marxist, trends began to exert their influence.

Giddens's critique of functionalism

The polemic against functionalism, for so many years the dominant trend in Anglo-American sociology, is essential for Giddens. Hence, in order to proceed, he first had to deal with functionalism.

In 1976, when Giddens published his most comprehensive critique of functionalism ("Functionalism: apres la lutte," reprinted in Giddens, 1977a), he was of the conviction that the battle against functionalism was either won or in any case close to being decided. In Giddens's opinion, the weaknesses of functionalism are so numerous that it should be clear that it cannot constitute a foundation for a useful sociological theory. With the renaissance of functionalism in the 1980s, Giddens has subsequently modified this view (1982h, 1989a, pp. 697–8). Nevertheless, despite the reemergence of functionalism in new, more sophisticated garb, Giddens has maintained his principal criticisms (1982h, 1989b, pp. 260–2, 1990e, pp. 307–10).

Giddens's critique can be summarized in three major points:

1   Functionalism's distinction between a dynamic and static perspective.
2   Functionalism's assertion of systemic needs.

3   The underemphasis on the human actors, and its inability to account
    for purposeful human behavior.

The first point focuses upon functionalism's problems in explaining social
change. The primary concerns of functionalism are the investigation of the
functions that must be carried out in order for a system to be maintained.
It is precisely the emphasis on system maintenance that prevents the theory
from explaining why systems change. The theory is unable to combine an
explanation of a social system's development over time – the dynamic perspective – with a given society's structure, the static perspective (1979a,
pp. 198–9).[3]
    The next criticism against functionalism is especially critical for Giddens:
functionalism asserts that social systems have varying needs which must be
met by different social institutions in order for society to reproduce itself.
Giddens emphasizes that functionalism here takes a wrong turn, inasmuch
as social systems do not have needs or do not have to fulfill functional
demands. Giddens reserves the concept of need exclusively to human actors. As an example of such a functionalist perspective, Giddens uses Marx's
theory of the reserve army in the capitalist economy. Capitalism has its own
needs which can be fulfilled by various functions in the system. A reserve
army evolves because capitalism needs a reserve labor force and a group to
keep down wages. Such an explanation is vacuous, says Giddens (1977a,
1981a, 1990e, p. 308), for no social institutions arise, persist, or disappear
because society needs them. "They come about *historically*, as a result of
concrete conditions that have in every case to be directly analyzed; the
same holds for their persistence or their dissolution" (1981a, p. 18).
    Giddens's third critique concerns functionalism's failure to explain hu-
man action (1976a, pp. 94–6, 1977a, pp. 106–9, 1981a, pp. 17–18). Here
he offers a general critique of functionalist thinking from Durkheim to
Parsons and Merton. He sees the functionalists as viewing human actors as
cultural dopes: people appear as puppets controlled by the social system
without any independent will. Stated in another way, functionalism emphasizes systemic and organismic perspectives at the cost of the actors'
extended skills and knowledgeability. People's actions and individuals' free
will disappear in the system.
    With Durkheim the problem arises in his definition of society, which
appears as an independent totality entirely distinct from the individuals.
People are born into an already existing society which sets specific frameworks for their possibilities of action. Durkheim never succeeds in specifying this tension between the system's dominance over the individual and
the individual's possibilities for action. Instead, Giddens says that Durkheim
conflates physical constraint with social constraints, such that they both

obtain the same constraining and coercive character toward the individual. Society constricts the actor's freedom of movement, and the actor thus disappears under the yoke of the oppressive system (1979a, p. 51).

Merton attempts to go further with the problem by distinguishing between manifest and latent functions. Until Merton made these distinctions, functionalism had found it difficult to explain the consequences of actions which had not been intended, desired, or expected by the acting individuals.

What is problematic, however, is that Merton uses the concepts of unintended consequences and unacknowledged consequences as synonyms. The two terms contain an important difference, having major implications for a theory of social action. There is a difference between acting with *knowledge* of the occurrence of a given outcome and doing something where one *intends* a certain outcome. Giddens points out that failure to distinguish between these two situations would entail an incomplete analysis of the intentions, causes, reasons, motives, etc. which humans possess when they act, and thereby an unsatisfactory explanation of social action (1977a, pp. 106–9).

Durkheim and Merton suffer from the same problem: they lack an adequate incorporation of the human actor into their theories, and they do not provide theoretical reflections on the aspect of action generally.

Summarizing, Giddens finds functionalistic thinking to be incapable of constituting a foundation for sociology. The static character of the theory, the gaps in its explanatory model, and the deterministic character of the system make functionalism inadequate as a theory of society. Giddens's solution is discussed in the following chapter. First, we shall examine his relationship to structuralism.

Structuralism: from Saussure to Lévi-Strauss and Derrida

Structuralism is a generalized designation for several different theories within philosophy and other disciplines, among them linguistics, anthropology, sociology, history, psychology, and literary criticism. Giddens connects a range of different theorists to structuralism, including Ferdinand de Saussure (1857–1913), Claude Lévi-Strauss (b. 1908), Roland Barthes (1915–80), Michel Foucault (1926–84), Louis Althusser (1918–90), Jacques Lacan (1901–81), Jean Piaget (1896–1980), and Jacques Derrida (b. 1930) (1979a, pp. 10ff, 1987b, pp. 195ff). Although several of these thinkers never considered themselves structuralists, Giddens sees them as having certain common features which derive from structural linguistics as formulated by Saussure. Giddens's critique concentrates primarily on Saussure, Lévi-Strauss, Althusser, Foucault, and Derrida. The focus in this chapter, however, will be limited to his presentation and critique of Saussure.

Like functionalism, structuralism traces its roots back to Durkheim, but it evolved primarily within linguistics, where especially Ferdinand de Saussure appears as the leading figure. Saussure's basic concepts also obtained subsequent popularity within the social and human sciences, foremost within anthropology, with Claude Lévi-Strauss as their chief exponent.

Saussure was opposed to the linguistic research at that time, whereby language was considered as consisting of words which were to be analyzed separately. For Saussure, the key aspect was the very structure of language and not its individual parts. Saussure himself did not use the concept of structure, but spoke of a system. The concept of structure was first added to linguistics by the Russian linguist Trubetzkoy. Nevertheless, the two concepts of structure and system are analogues. It is language as an independent system, what Saussure calls *la langue*, which constitutes Saussure's approach to studying language. As such, Saussure distinguishes between language as a system and actual speech, *la parole*. The system of language is a social institution, which is not immediately created by the individual language user. When we are born, there already exists a language which we learn and use. Language is a social relation, and thereby contrasts with speech, which is related to the individual. The language system therefore becomes fundamental for Saussure, as it is precisely the existence of a language (*langue*) consisting of signs and codes which is the prerequisite for the individual person to be able to communicate.

The language system consists of signs. A sign has two sides, which constitute a unity. Saussure calls one side the word, the sound image (*le signifiant*), what in the terminology of the Danish linguist Hjelmslev is called the expression (Hjelmslev, 1961). The other side is called the concept (*le signifié*) or the content(Hjelmslev, 1961). The sign is thus a unit of expression and content (sound image/concept). Saussure's work with the double character of the sign challenges the traditional view of language as consisting only of expressions. Saussure asserts that the expression *chair*, for example, can only be considered as a sign because it is related to or is the bearer of a content, a concept, that of chair. The expression I use when I speak stands in an interdependent relationship to a concept. It is thus the contrast between the expression "chair" and the concept "chair" which defines the sign. "Chair" as an expression and "chair" as a concept are not based on any natural relation. It could just as well be another expression which bears the meaning of the concept "chair". In this way we have elucidated another important element in structuralism: the arbitrary character of the sign. The arbitrary relation between expression and content means that this relation and thereby the sign is socially and historically constructed. The connection between the two sides is based upon a social norm or convention which is not given in advance, but is the result of an unconscious and collective creation.

The specific relationship which appears between, for example, the expression "green" and the content/concept "green" evolves only because the sign stands in opposition to other signs. Saussure here states that the unity is determined by the differences (*les différences*). With a traffic light, it is not the colour green which determines whether we can walk or drive onward. It is the difference between green, yellow, and red which gives meaning. The signs only acquire their identity or continuity insofar as they are differentiated from one another as oppositions or differences within the totality that is *langue* (Giddens, 1979a, pp. 11–12). This can be illustrated by the example of a London to Glasgow train which departs each day at 12 o'clock. While the train may depart at the same time on any given day, it does not necessarily depart with the same locomotive, personnel, coaches, and passengers. Nevertheless, this train has an identity based on the fact that its departure time is always the same. It is precisely here that this particular train distinguishes itself from other trains in the rail timetable.

It is this emphasis on constituting signs via confrontation and on their arbitrary character which marks Saussure's argument that language must be considered an independent system *sui generis*, i.e. independent of individual speech acts.

Giddens's critique of Saussure's structuralism

Giddens presents several criticisms of Saussure and other structuralists. Here we shall discuss only one of them.

Giddens takes issue with Saussure's implicit claim that a system is only defined by the internal opposition among the individual signs. Saussure does not acknowledge that there is a hidden hermeneutic problem in the relation to the meaning of the signs. The signs obtain meaning not only in relation to each other, but also because they enter into and are interpreted in the daily practice of human beings. Our 12 o'clock London to Glasgow train has, according to Saussure, a special identity, as it distinguishes itself from other trains by leaving at exactly 12 o'clock. However, says Giddens, the train's identity cannot be specified independently of the context in which the sentence is used. Such a sentence is always used in a practice. When Saussure affirms this train's special identity, he assumes the viewpoint of the traveler. Seen from the traveler's perspective, the 12 o'clock London to Glasgow differs from the next train an hour later. For the train mechanics, who repair the stock of passenger coaches, it is not the departure time which gives the train its identity. When the train needs to be repaired, it makes no difference whether it departs at 12:00, 1:00, or 2:00. For the mechanics, it is perhaps the composition of the motor's components, the factory in which they were produced, the type of train, and its date of fabrication which give it a unique identity. Hence, the train which departs at 12 o'clock does not constitute a special sign which distinguishes it from other signs in a system. The 12 o'clock London to Glasgow train becomes a special sign only because it is interpreted within a specific context by specific, individual actors. When, as part of their practice, people interpret signs within a specific context, it helps to break the closed character of the system. The signs now obtain a connection to the world of objects and events outside the system.

Structuralism has a problem which resembles that of functionalism: the theory recapitulates a sign *system*, but ignores the *action* aspect. The interpretation of the signs and, hence, the creation of the sign system take place among language users and in their practice. When the practice is not taken into consideration, there is no possibility of understanding why the language system changes.

As described above, Giddens also concerns himself with other structuralists, among them Lévi-Strauss, Foucault, Althusser, and Derrida (1979a, pp. 28–45, 155–160, 1982d, pp. 215ff). While their work will not be dealt with here, it is Giddens's view that several of the critical points mentioned here also apply to these four theorists (see, for example, 1984a, p. 217).

Action Theory from Weber to Ethnomethodology and Symbolic Interactionism

The term action theory covers a variety of theoretical schools, which tend to focus on the individual – the human actor – as their key unit of analysis. To utilize the designation "action theory" is to a certain extent misleading, since other theories, such as functionalism, also concern themselves with actions and their consequences. In contrast to functionalism and structuralism, however, the point of departure of action theory is not the system or the structure in its entirety, but the individual, who is regarded as the basic building block of society. Society consists only of the sum of individuals and their actions. Society and the social structure, therefore, are not a thing external to or independent of the individuals, as is the case, for example, with Durkheim.

Most action theories build upon a hermeneutic-philosophical foundation, where understanding, interpretation, and empathy (*Verstehen*) are the point of departure for understanding human beings and, hence, society. Human beings are unique in that they act on the basis of subjective motives, values, and intentions. Sociology can only explain the cause of these actions if it utilizes interpretation of, understanding of, and empathy with the individual's life-world.

It was Max Weber who became the bridge-builder between hermeneutic philosophy and sociology, especially because he introduced the concept of *Verstehen* into sociology. Weber's action sociology is not Giddens's primary concern, for he views Weber's "interpretative sociology" as possessing a number of weaknesses and inherent logical problems (1977a, pp. 179–82). Instead Giddens emphasizes several other theoretical orientations – language philosophy, hermeneutics, phenomenological sociology, ethnomethodology, and symbolic interactionism – all of which focus upon the individual actor and on various aspects of action.

Here I discuss ethnomethodology as an example of the action theories Giddens discusses. The leading theorist within ethnomethodology is Harold Garfinkel, whose main work, *Studies in Ethnomethodology*, appeared in 1967. Like Parsons, Garfinkel is interested in the problem of social order. Unlike Parsons, however, Garfinkel does not take his point of departure in society as a system with its associated institutions. Social structures and the social order do not exist outside ourselves. The social order is constantly being produced in our actions, including in our conversations with each other. For Garfinkel, then, human beings and our daily activities become the key focus of understanding. The social order is created via our actions, where we apply a range of methods, procedures, and practices which are taken as given. Ethnomethodology means "methods which people apply in informal contexts." Garfinkel maintains that, consciously or unconsciously, we are continually applying these methods, and they are seen as "reflexively accountable." By reflexivity he means the process of which we are all part when we use our thoughts and actions to construct our social reality. When we say "Hi" to someone on the street, we are seldom conscious of the great reflexive work which takes place among ourselves and the person we are greeting. Only at the moment when the other person turns his or her back or does not return the greeting do we become aware that we have attempted to create or construct a specific social reality and that this attempt has failed. By "accounts" Garfinkel means the process whereby people provide explanations or narratives of actions and situations and thereby contribute to making the world comprehensible. Ethnomethodologists attempt to analyze people's accounts and the ways in which accounts are given or received (or rejected) by others. Hence, ethnomethodological studies focus especially on conversations. If I get home too late and explain to my wife why, thereby attempting to construct a situation in order to make it understandable to her, she can either accept or reject my explanation. Such a situation would constitute the field of interest for ethnomethodology, as it is an instance of an "accounting practice": my explanation and my wife's acceptance or rejection represent an example of how such a conversation contributes to creating the social order. In other words, the events of our day-to-day life are reflexively accountable, as people are able to reflect on their actions and then offer to others an account or explanation of these. An insight into the shared reflexivity and the reciprocal offering and acceptance of accounts makes possible an understanding of why our daily life, which may otherwise seem so chaotic, constitutes a social order (1976a, pp. 35ff).

Giddens's evaluation of ethnomethodology and action theories

Giddens applauds the ethnomethodologists' focus on the reflexive actor, who by providing explanations of his or her acts helps to produce these actions and thereby constitutes the social world. Yet Giddens finds the ethnomethodologists' concept of reflexivity too narrow, in that ethnomethodology concerns itself primarily with the structure of conversation and its contribution to the social order. For Giddens, reflexivity is extended to our ability to constantly reflect on our activities. Moreover, this entails that we incorporate knowledge about ourselves and that we thereby possess the capacity to alter our actions. Giddens praises Garfinkel for the great emphasis placed by ethnomethodology on human knowledgeability and skills. However, in its negligence of superordinate social structures and institutions, ethnomethodology retains a fundamental problem. The strong focus on conversation and the behavior of individual actors prevents development of a theory which can account for the structural aspects, i.e. the reproduction of social practices across time and space.

In sum, it can be said that Giddens appreciates the contribution of action theories to social theory and sociology insofar as the various schools of thought call attention to the social world as being understood as produced and reproduced by creative, knowledgeable, and active human subjects. The constitution of the social world as meaningful, accountable, and understandable is conditioned by language as a medium for practice. The action theory tradition (at times called interpretative sociology) furthermore maintains that a sociologist who undertakes an analysis draws upon the same concepts and enters into the same process as the layperson in his or her daily activities. When social behavior is described, hermeneutic abilities are used to penetrate the frames of meaning. These frames of meaning are utilized by laypersons themselves when they construct and reproduce the social world. In this way, all of us end up acting like sociologists.

While noting these positive and important contributions of action theory to modern social theory, Giddens cites several problems, all shared by the various theoretical perspectives within action theory. Their focus on meaning occurs at the cost of people's practical involvement in material relations (certainly people do not produce nature, but we nevertheless create our material conditions of existence on this basis, and in our interaction with nature we transform it and thereby our own conditions of existence). The actors within action theory are ultimately free floating in a world which they can form according to their own wills. What is lacking is a connection between action theory and the significance of institutional structures for the action. Another problem is the tendency to explain all human behavior in terms of motives, norms, and values. In this connection, action theory is unable to account for the relationship between social norms and power. According to Giddens, action theory never asks the question: "Who controls, determines and forms the social norms?" (1976a, pp. 155–6).

Marxism: Action or Structure?

Marx and Marxism also become the object of Giddens's interest. Giddens treats Marx in three contexts. In *Capitalism and Modern Social Theory* (1971a), Giddens was one of the first sociologists in the Anglo-American world to reintroduce Marx as one of the classics of sociology following the prolonged dominance of functionalism. In Giddens's period as critic of sociology through the 1970s, Marx and Marxism are studied in relation to the tension between the actor and the structure/system (1976a, pp. 98–104, 1979a). In the 1980s, Marx and historical materialism are subjected to an analysis which focuses specifically on the Marxist understanding of history and on the power dimension in Marx (1981a, 1985a).

Here we shall briefly touch on Giddens's reading of Marx in connection to the problem of resolving the dualism which affects social theory and sociology.

In Marx, Giddens identifies the same tension between a strong emphasis on the human agent and an emphasis on society, the latter understood as a structure which regulates and governs people's actions. In his early writings, such as *Theses on Feuerbach*, Marx focuses upon the human agent and praxis. Unlike animals, says Marx, humans cannot simply adapt themselves to their environment because they do not possess the necessary natural instincts. Rather, human beings enter into a creative interplay with their surroundings and must to a greater degree control them rather than simply adjust to the given. Hence, humans change themselves through changing the world around them in a continual and reciprocal process (1976a, p. 100). Marx calls this process praxis. According to Giddens, however, Marx never really succeeded in working out the implications of these ideas. Here in fact lay the core to a theory of praxis which could have formed the basis for a unified conceptualization of the practice- and action-oriented aspect with structural/institutional conditions. Instead of developing a specific linkage between actor and structure, Marx's later works show him immersed in a study of modes of production, i.e. the general social structure.

The works of the mature Marx, as mentioned, focus on structural conditions and especially on the role of the economic structures. The latter are given so much weight, however, that the human agent and human consciousness appear to be determined by the economy.

Giddens sees the same dichotomy as prominent in the later Marxists: these include Marxists such as Lukács and Paci, who interpret Marx in a phenomenological, action theory framework with emphasis on praxis, as well as thinkers like Althusser, who emphasizes the importance of structural conditions for human activity. Regarding Althusser, Giddens claims that he is a functionalist in disguise, as ideology for Althusser seems to be inherent within the structure. Hence, the human subject also appears as being governed by societal ideologies, thus causing the disappearance of the agent's freedom of action (1979a, pp. 52–3).

Having identified the existence of this dualism in Marx and in Marxist thinking, Giddens finds himself unable to accord Marxism the dominant role it had held through the 1970s. Marxism cannot constitute a viable foundation for social theory and sociology.

Functionalism, Structuralism, Action Theory, and Marxism: Summarizing the Sociological Dualism

In his analysis of classical and modern sociological theory, Giddens demonstrates the existence of a dualism consisting of the opposition between theories that emphasize society's systemic aspects and those that emphasize actors and agency. Despite this problem, however, Giddens maintains that the various theoretical systems all contribute with insightful points and concepts. None of the respective theories, however, has the capacity to bridge the two positions. Functionalism and structuralism remain locked into a structure/system position, where the individual is overlooked and the system/structure is seen as an external, given reality. Among the action-oriented sociologists, says Giddens, the situation is just the opposite: society remains the sum of individual decisions and acts. Action theory has major problems explaining the existence of social institutions and social norms. It culminates in a position where the individual is claimed to be the only existing entity, and where, as a result, all social phenomena can be explained only in terms of the individual. Furthermore, action theory often reduces actions to the production of meaning and thereby ends in an idealistic, subjectivist position. Even though the individual is at the core of the theory, most action theories operate with an unreflected concept of individual and actor (1984a, pp. 219–20).

In his critiques of functionalism, structuralism, and action theory, Giddens has thus created the foundation for his own theoretical work. He attempts to establish the much needed linkage between the individual actor and the social structure. As we shall see in the next chapter, he retains various points from the theories reviewed here, but these are extended, redefined, and supplemented by elements from other social science theories.

From Philosophy to Social Theory and Social Ontology: Concluding Comments

Giddens thus points to several dichotomies in the dominant philosophical and sociological theories (see figure 1.1). Within philosophy there exists a dualism between an objectivist (positivism) and subjectivist (hermeneutic) position. As these philosophies are utilized as a foundation for sociological theories, there exists a corresponding dualism between the structural perspective (functionalism/structuralism) and the actor perspective of action theory.

This is a very simplified and schematic overview of the dualism problematic. The theories' main sources of inspiration are a much more complex network of effects from various sociological theories and philosophies. For example, ethnomethodology did not simply originate from Weberian action sociology. Equally important is the inspiration from American pragmatist philosophy. Moreover, the Frankfurt School sociologists have derived much of their inspiration from Freud, while Weber was not only inspired by hermeneutic philosophy. There are also some links to positivism.

Giddens's Response to the Philosophical Dualism: the Double Hermeneutic

In relation to philosophical dualism, and taking his point of departure in hermeneutics, Giddens maintains that there exists a fundamental difference between nature and society. Nature exists independently of our

The philosophical level

Dualism:	objectivism	subjectivism
Philosophical orientation	positivism	hermeneutics

The sociological level

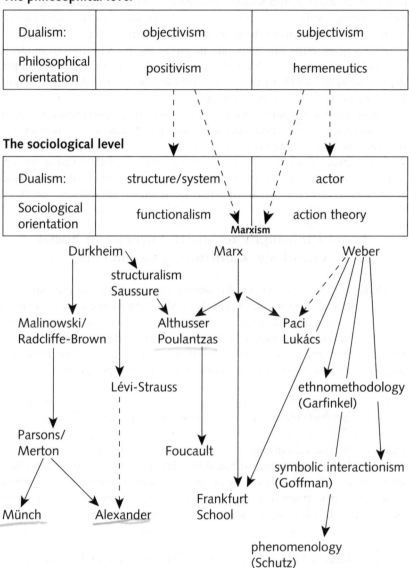

Dualism:	structure/system	actor
Sociological orientation	functionalism	action theory

Figure 1.1   The dualism problem in philosophy and sociology.

knowledge about it. Nature obeys its own laws. Society, in contrast, is produced by humans and therefore has no existence independent of that of its members.

Giddens asserts that when nature and the human world are studied and subjected to scientific analysis, both natural and social scientists employ the hermeneutic method. But whereas the natural scientist utilizes concepts developed by research to investigate nature, this is not the case for the social sciences: "The hermeneutics of natural science has to do only with the theories and discourse of scientists, analysing an object world which does not answer back, and which does not construct and interpret the meanings of its activities" (1982d, p. 12).

Within social science we can speak of a *double hermeneutic*, as the researcher observes and interprets a reality which is already interpreted by the laypersons who themselves constitute the researcher's object. Hence, there is a logical bond between our everyday language and the more technical, scientific terminology used by sociologists and social scientists in general. The relation between these two languages takes place in a dialogue between sociology, which interprets the activities of laypeople, and the laypeople who draw on sociological concepts for use in their daily practice. Sociologists researching criminality develop concepts such as deviant, stigmatization, and labeling. Criminals themselves can thereby use these concepts to construct accounts or explanations of their own behavior. In this way concepts and theories, i.e. interpretations, circulate back and forth between the social scientist and his or her target group. It is this interpretative process which Giddens terms the double hermeneutic process.

The Separation of Philosophy and Sociology

It is not only the dichotomies within both philosophy and sociology which create problems in relation to the development of a coherent theoretical foundation. The separation between philosophy and sociology is also a critical problem, asserts Giddens. Thus, his *Central Problems in Social Theory* begins with the following quotation from the French philosopher Merleau-Ponty: "Philosophy and sociology have long lived under a segregated system which has succeeded in concealing their rivalry only by refusing them any meeting-ground, impeding their growth, making them incomprehensible to one another, and thus placing culture in a situation of permanent crisis" (Merleau-Ponty, quoted in Giddens, 1979a, p. v).

Giddens is aware of the way in which philosophy has functioned as a foundation of sociology. Philosophy has preoccupied itself with the general philosophical and scientific-philosophical problems, notably concerning

epistemology. The eternal rivalry among various epistemological positions
has failed to generate a fruitful result. Besides, philosophy has obtained a
virtual monopoly on these discussions and thereby created an artificial division of labor whereby philosophy provides the true theory of knowledge
and method, and various disciplines (sociology, biology, etc.) assume the
task of studying their respective fields. Giddens sees this separation as extremely unfortunate, as the philosophical and sociological considerations are
closely connected and virtually inseparable. One cannot undertake epistemological judgments without connecting them to a reality and a field of
study. Conversely, one cannot study society, heavenly bodies, or biological
organisms without fundamental reflection on how these should be known,
and on the necessary methods connected to achieving this knowledge.

Giddens believes that recent developments within philosophy and sociology are proceeding in the right direction, as both are beginning to approach each other. In his discussion of the relationship between philosophy
and sociology/social theory he points out that social theory (and sociology) has become more philosophical and more preoccupied by epistemological questions. Conversely, philosophy has also become more
sociologically oriented (1987a, p. 53). Giddens applauds this rapproche-
ment and believes that social theory and sociology will be in serious difficulty if social theorists do not come to grips with philosophical problems
(1984, p. xvii). This involvement must not proceed too far, however, in
that social theory must not be driven to the point where it can be accused
of being more speculative than empirically founded. Giddens emphasizes
that social theory involves the analysis of issues which spill into philosophy,
but is "not primarily . . . a philosophical endeavour" (1984, p. xvi). While
he accepts these close ties to philosophy, Giddens maintains that social
theory must be justified on its own terms.[4] The implication, therefore, is
that social theory and sociology are not independent scientific disciplines
with discrete boundaries, but instead are characterized by an intersecting
field of contact to philosophy.

The close bonds to philosophy are problematic, as they link sociology to
epistemology. Giddens is aware of the difficulty in constructing a sociological theory upon an epistemology which avoids both subjectivism and
objectivism. He realizes the difficulty of developing a sociology which avoids
being anchored in either hermeneutic or positivist philosophy. This is an
unsolved, perhaps even unsolvable, problem of philosophical character.
Giddens's solution, therefore, is to push epistemological questions into the
background and allow ontology to step out into the limelight.

> Significant as these may be, concentration upon epistemological issues draws
> attention away from the more "ontological" concerns of social theory. . . .

> Rather than becoming preoccupied with epistemological disputes and with the question of whether or not anything like "epistemology" in its time-honoured sense can be formulated at all, those working in social theory, I suggest, should be concerned first and foremost with reworking conceptions of human being and human doing, social reproduction and social transformation. (1984, p. xx)

Based on his analyses in the 1970s, Giddens concludes that we must develop an alternative to the frozen positions which exist between philosophy and sociology and the various dichotomies within each of them. Giddens's main objective thus becomes that of establishing a social theory which can serve to mediate between subjectivist (hermeneutic) and objectivist (positivism) positions within both philosophy and sociology.

If we are to move beyond the present stalemate within philosophy and sociology and avoid the aforementioned dualism, we must, instead of discussing *how* to know social reality, focus on the *existing* reality (ontology).

Giddens's solution to these problems becomes the theory of structuration, which is a contribution to a social ontology. Social ontology connotes an attempt to develop a set of concepts which can describe the social reality. The next chapter examines more closely how these concepts are brought together to constitute this social ontology.

Notes

1 When the political-ideological dimension is included, Marx and historical materialism are often depicted as being in opposition to both Weber and Durkheim.
2 Critical realism is a general term for a realist philosophy which is especially prominent in Britain. Roy Bhaskar stands as the leading representative of this philosophy. Other key figures include Russell Keat, John Urry, Rom Harré, and William Outhwaite.
3 See chapter 3 for a more detailed critique.
4 Here lies a contradiction hidden in Giddens. Social theory cannot be an autonomous science distinct from philosophy and at the same time be closely connected to philosophy. For further discussion of this point see Kaspersen (1992a, pp. 85–86).

2

Giddens as Constructor: the Theory of Structuration as Response to the Dualism of Social Theory

In chapter 1, I discussed how Giddens pointed to the dualism between subjectivist and objectivist positions within philosophy and sociology as the decisive obstacle to the construction of a stronger theoretical foundation for sociology. This and the following chapters examine Giddens's theoretical solution to the dualism problem: the theory of structuration. The focus here will be on Giddens's key concepts – agent, action, structure, and system – and chapter 3 deals with the implications of structuration theory for our understanding of social change.

The theory of structuration evolved in a critical dialogue with the four main tendencies within sociology: action theory, functionalism, structuralism,

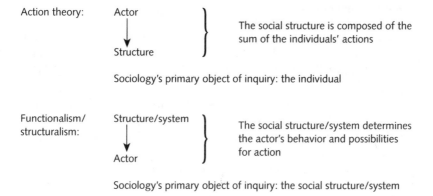

Action theory:

Actor
↓
Structure

} The social structure is composed of the sum of the individuals' actions

Sociology's primary object of inquiry: the individual

Functionalism/
structuralism:

Structure/system
↓
Actor

} The social structure/system determines the actor's behavior and possibilities for action

Sociology's primary object of inquiry: the social structure/system

Figure 2.1 The actor–structure relationship in traditional sociological theory.

and Marxism. As stated, Giddens sees action theory as having remained in a subjectivist position, which means a failure to explain the social structures and the conditions for action. Similarly, functionalism and structuralism do not adequately account for agency, the fact that individuals possess a will and contribute to changing these structures. The functionalist and structuralist positions therefore result in a determinism which overlooks the fact that social structures are not only constraining but also enabling (see figure 2.1).

The dialogue with these theories leads to the theory of structuration, which is Giddens's attempt to resolve the tension which exists between individual and society. Giddens's most comprehensive presentation of structuration theory is his *The Constitution of Society* (1984a), and the discussion that follows builds primarily on this monumental work. Structuration theory should not be considered only as a sociological theory. It is also a social theory which covers the entire field of social and human sciences.

As pointed out in chapter 1, Giddens's point of departure is that social science must abandon the eternal and endless epistemological discussion as to how reality should be known. Instead, it should focus on the ontological questions of how to conceptualize reality. For Giddens this means a conceptualization of the human being, of human doing, of the reproduction and transformation of social life. Hence, the first prerequisite for a new social theory that goes beyond the dualism is a change from epistemology to ontology. The second precondition for the project's success is the development and redefinition of concepts. "The attempt to formulate a coherent account of human agency and of structure demands, however, a very considerable conceptual effort" (1984a, p. xxi). This conceptual effort is a pervasive feature of Giddens's work and a necessity. Thus an important part of the structuration project is a redefinition of concepts and the construction of neologisms.

Structuration theory utilizes a deconstruction and redefinition of the basic concepts of agent, action, power, structure, and system from action theory, functionalism, and structuralism so as to create the foundation for a new social ontology. Giddens develops and redefines the concepts so that the traditional actor/structure dualism is instead conceived as a *duality*, which means that the structure no longer determines individuals' actions. Conversely, the social structure is not simply the sum of individuals' actions. Society is viewed as a *structuration process*, whereby human actions simultaneously structure and are structured by society. When Mary is in school, she is *qua* her actions helping to produce and reproduce the school as an independent system, and at a higher level the entire educational system. At the same time, when she acts, she draws upon the school's and the educational system's set of values and rules. The school as a structure is, therefore, not something which exists external to her. The school and the educational system as a set of rules and values are both a means and an outcome of her actions. This condition is labeled by Giddens as a duality of structure or as social practice.[1] Understanding social practices is for Giddens the key to achieving insight into the production and reproduction of social life. Hence, social practice becomes for Giddens the field of study for social theory. Yet how do we determine the concept of social practice?

Social Practice

The basic domain of study of the social sciences, according to the theory of structuration, is neither the experience of the individual actor nor the existence of any form of societal totality, but social practices ordered across space and time (1984a, p. 2). This exposition of structuration theory concentrates upon two of Giddens's theses:

1 Social practice is constitutive of social life. Social practice constitutes us as actors and embodies and realizes structures.
2 As a result, social practice is the mediating concept between agency and structure, between individual and society.

The entire project in *The Constitution of Society* consists of defining social practice. The concept is defined in a long theoretical movement in which the concepts of agent, power, action, structure, system, and time–space are redefined so that they come to constitute practice. Giddens's contribution

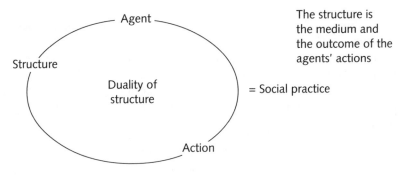

Sociology's object of inquiry: social practice

Figure 2.2 The theory of structuration: from actor–structure to social practice.

lies precisely in defining the concepts in terms of each other, such that they *together* can define practice.

In contrast to Durkheim, Giddens asserts that sociology does not concern itself with the already given universe of objects, but with a universe which is continually being constituted, produced, and reproduced by active acting subjects. He maintains that social practice constitutes us as actors and simultaneously embodies and realizes structures. Actor and structure thereby become two modes of considering the same relations: social practice (see figure 2.2).

As mentioned, the development of the concept of social practice is a continuous process in *The Constitution of Society*. The book can be seen as an attempt to refine the concepts of practice and structuration, as Giddens first applied them in *New Rules of Sociological Method* (1976a) and *Central Problems in Social Theory* (1979a).[2] It should be mentioned, however, that Giddens does not see structuration theory as a decidedly coherent *theory*. Rather, he considers it to be an approach containing several different concepts which operate as tools to open and elucidate social life.

I now examine the process by which Giddens defines social practice as the mediating concept between action and structure. For Giddens, this process starts with the agent.

The Concept of the Agent

As social practice is Giddens's key concept for transcending the actor/structure dualism, he takes upon himself the task of defining the individual elements that together constitute social practice in such a way that they all contain both a producing and a reproducing aspect, i.e. both an agency dimension and a structure/system dimension. The specific concepts are thus defined so that the action perspective does not obtain priority over the structure perspective or vice versa. In other words, all the individual elements (agent, action, structure, system, etc.) possess the same double property: they unite an element of agency and structure.

Giddens's structuration theory takes its point of departure in the concept of agent. A redefinition of the agent and the agent's activity is essential. The problem with the existing theories of system and structure, as discussed in chapter 1, is that the agent appears only as the bearer of structures, which means that the actor's own free will and knowledgeability are overlooked. It is therefore essential for Giddens to understand the agent as knowledgeable. "A conception of action . . . has to place at the centre the everyday fact that social actors are knowledgeable about the conditions of social reproduction in which their day-to-day activities are enmeshed" (1982d, p. 29).

The agent is knowledgeable, with a knowledge of most of the actions he or she undertakes. This wealth of knowledge is expressed primarily as a *practical consciousness*. When I ride my bicycle, I do not need to explain the underlying physical and anatomical process involved. I speak English without any knowledge of linguistic theory or formal rules of syntax. Nevertheless, I am able to carry out these activities entirely without any conscious reflections about them. The vast majority of our day-to-day activities are very routinized. We get up in the morning, shower, eat breakfast, brush our teeth, pack our lunch, and so on. These actions have nearly ritual character. Giddens emphasizes that we have great knowledge about these actions, but this knowledge is seldom formulated explicitly (or, as Giddens calls it, discursively). It is a tacit knowledge. Our knowledge entails that we know how to act. We know the rules for behavior, and we know the sequences of actions. When the alarm rings in the morning, we turn it off. We get out of bed and then go to the bathroom, etc. We just act, almost automatically (if not half asleep!). Our actions are routinized and automatic, and they take place at a level of practical consciousness. This practical knowledge and/or consciousness comprises most of our activities and is one of the most central, though often the most overlooked, levels of consciousness an agent possesses.

The agent's practical consciousness is an unknown area for most of sociology and social science. Only among phenomenologists and ethnomethodologists in the sociological and social psychological disciplines can we find a detailed treatment of the nature of practical consciousness.

Whereas the level of practical consciousness encompasses the knowledge which we cannot immediately account for, the situation is different for our *discursive consciousness*. A discursive explanation means that we explicitly express an activity; for example, how and why we ride a bicycle. Such an explanation may operate at several levels. Asked about my bike riding, I can respond that I am on my way to work, I can provide an anatomical/physiological explanation, or I can declare that I bike because I am opposed to automobile pollution.

By emphasizing the agent's knowledgeability, Giddens emphasizes that systems and structures do not act behind the back of the actor. The voluntaristic element, i.e. the element of will, is strengthened by the agent's discursive capacity. Discursive reflexivity around the action, besides enabling us to provide explanations, connotes the possibility of changing our patterns of action.

The boundary between the discursive and practical consciousness is permeable and can be altered (see figure 2.3), but discursive consciousness refers to the understanding/knowledge which the agent achieves by reflecting upon his or her actions. Reflection may occur with the aid of

Discursive consciousness

Practical consciousness

Unconscious motives/cognition

Figure 2.3   Discursive and practical consciousness.

others or as an autonomous act. Discursive consciousness is most often triggered when we reflect upon a specific act, or when someone else asks us to account for a specific sequence of acts; for example, why I left the office early yesterday. The agent is able to verbally express and explain an action that has taken place, and this also creates an opportunity to alter future behavior.

Not all motives for action can be found at the conscious level. Therefore, in contrast to many action theorists (including the phenomenologists and ethnomethodologists), Giddens operates with an *unconscious level* which involves actions caused by unconscious motives. The unconscious includes knowledge that is suppressed or appears in distorted form. Whereas the boundary between discursive and practical knowledge is permeable, there exists a genuine barrier between these types of consciousness and the unconscious motives which, due to repression, inhibit discursive formulation (1984a, p. 49). All three levels are important, but practical consciousness appears to be the most critical in order to understand social life. Compared to unconscious motives and discursive consciousness, practical consciousness operates to rehabilitate larger amounts of implicit knowledge which the social sciences often overlook. This tacit knowledge of the agent is especially important for the maintenance and reproduction of social life.

Agency

The understanding of the agent as knowledgeable is closely connected to Giddens's reformulation of the concept of agency in his theory of structuration. In contrast to a great deal of classical sociology, Giddens does not consider action as a series of combined discrete acts. Rather, agency is a processual concept. Agency must be understood as a flow of events which stream through life in an infinite fashion, an incessant process analogous to processes of cognition and understanding which continue to run through our heads. "The notion of agency connects directly with the concept of *praxis*, and when speaking of regularized types of acts I shall talk of human *practices*, as an ongoing series of 'practical activities'" (1976a, p. 75). Agency is a flow without starting or endpoint. It is a structuration process. It only gives meaning to speak of isolated acts at the very moment when the agent thinks back to a concrete event or where others ask about a concrete act. Drinking coffee in the morning only becomes a unique act when I reflect upon my breakfast and morning coffee. When I reflect discursively upon an activity, the act appears in my consciousness, and only here is it meaningful to speak of agency as a specific event.

The understanding of agency as a process stands in contrast to most action theorists and to the view of Anglo-American action philosophy, which sees actions as unique, distinct elements, each having an underlying cause, purpose, intention, or motive. Ethnomethodology (Garfinkel) and phenomenology (Schutz) approach, however, a perspective similar to that of Giddens. Consequently, Giddens can obtain inspiration on this point from these two theorists.

Instead of understanding intentionality (i.e. the agent having a purpose and a motive for an action) as a concrete cause of a given action, Giddens emphasizes that intentionality must also be seen as a process. The vast majority of actions are purposive, the intentional being an inherent element in all human behavior.

All actions which the agent undertakes through his power to intervene in the world are carried out with a knowledgeability and consciousness, often a practical consciousness. When this flow of actions is undertaken by the agent (and simultaneously becomes an inherent part of the agent), several subjective, reflexive processes occur in the agent. The entire action process, including the agent's subjective aspects of the process, are summarized by Giddens in his model of the agent (see figure 2.4). I will initially

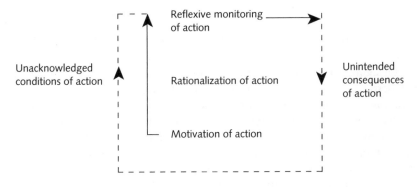

Figure 2.4 Agent and agency.

ignore the unintended consequences of actions and the unacknowledged conditions of action. The core of the model (the three levels in the middle) represents some aspects of the agent's subjectivity, processes which are embedded in the agent's body and cognitive activity. The three elements – reflexive monitoring of action, rationalization of action, and motivation of action – are not expressions of states, but processes which take place inside the agent and which are maintained, enacted, and repeated infinitely by the agent.

The *reflexive monitoring of action* and rationalization of action are closely connected and virtually impossible to distinguish. Reflexive monitoring of action tends to occur as part of the agent's practical consciousness. The agent constantly undertakes a reflexive monitoring of the flow of activities in which he or she participates. The reflexive monitoring of action refers to the intentional or purposive character of human behavior. It is a routine feature of human conduct. The agent continually evaluates what he or she does, how others react, the circumstances under which the action takes place, and the setting of interaction. When I buy food at the supermarket, I participate in a complex sequence of activities (which for Giddens include both my thought processes and my body as a single entity) where I continually register the physical environment, the time, the other customers, the clerk at the cash register, etc. I regulate my activity in relation to these circumstances, take cues from the actions of other actors, avoid upsetting the stacks of canned tomatoes or bumping into other customers with my shopping cart, and so on. These are routine activities which we normally do not consider especially problematic, but Giddens demonstrates how extremely complex such a course of activities really is. The reflexive monitoring of action is a necessary element when we act. Without it we would be unable to function in society.

Reflexive monitoring of activities takes place constantly, and agency is therefore nothing exceptional. The vast majority of human activities are routinized and recursive.

Like reflexive monitoring of action, the *rationalization of action*, the second of these subjective processes, takes place primarily at the level of practical consciousness. This process should not be confused with the ability to provide discursive explanations to specific actions. Rationalization of action occurs as a process whereby the agent maintains a tacit understanding of the grounds for his or her activities. Whereas reflexive monitoring of action concerns the intentional part of the action processes, rationalization of action primarily concerns the ability and the competence to evaluate the relationship between the action and its reason. In this way the agent also evaluates his own and others' competence. As stated, this rationalization occurs continually and always as something we simply take for granted: we do not generally ask about actions that are regular and normal for a given culture. Only at the moment when a rupture or a lapse occurs in certain routines do we inquire about or explicitly consider (discursively) the reason for the result of a given action or ask about the intention behind this action.

These many routines, monitored reflexively and rationalized, help to give the concept of agent and agency a reproductive character. Repeated day in and day out, these actions are extended for the same reasons in time and space and therefore contribute to the daily creation and recreation of society. They give society a structural/system-like face.

Whereas we find no clear division between reflexive monitoring of action and rationalization of action, we can clearly distinguish between these and *motivation of action*. The concepts of monitoring and rationalization of action are directly connected to the very moment where the flow of social action takes place. In contrast, the concept of *motivation of action* refers more to the potential for action. The majority of daily practices are not directly motivated, but take place, as mentioned, primarily as routines. Motives appear most often only in special situations where, for example, routines are breached.

Why do knowledgeable agents undertake these actions? What kind of unconscious motives are the indirect cause of these actions? To elucidate this problem, Giddens takes his inspiration from psychology, especially from Erik H. Erikson (1902–94) and Sigmund Freud (1856–1939). Giddens's point of departure is the child's development of identity. In order for the child to be able to develop an identity, a basic security system is created. The basic security system facilitates avoidance of anxiety and preservation of self-esteem. The system consists of several unconscious mechanisms which protect against anxiety-producing or anxiety-provoking stimuli, including mistrust, shame, doubt, and guilt. The mechanisms are unconscious, especially because they evolve before the child acquires language.

Inspired by R. D. Laing (b. 1927), Giddens calls this system *ontological security*. It continues into adult life and helps to control diffuse anxiety and self-esteem. Several strongly positive and especially predictable routines in relation to the mother create ontological security in the child. The effect of these routines in adult life is that most of our activities – day-to-day routines – provide us with a feeling of security and trust. These activities, says Giddens, are unconsciously motivated routines that reproduce our ontological security. We need this security to avoid those situations in which we are exposed to extreme anxiety and to maintain our self-esteem.

The three levels in Giddens's stratification model of the agent appear as recursive activities. As previously mentioned, Giddens views actions as purposeful and intentional, but it is extremely important to point out that the concepts of intentionality and rationalization of action imply that the agent is not conscious – practically or discursively – of all the consequences of his or her actions. On the contrary, Giddens emphasizes that recursive activities have unintended consequences. For example, I speak English with the intention of being understood by those who listen. The unintended consequence of this action is that I simultaneously reproduce the English language. The concept of unintended consequences, taken from functionalism and from Robert Merton, is important, because it introduces the reproductive character of action. It is via this concept that Giddens approaches the aspect of structure. Giddens maintains the value of the concept, but emphasizes that it must be separated and removed from all functionalist explanatory models.

As shown in figure 2.4, the unintended consequences become preconditions for new actions; hence, it is clear that, for Giddens, action and agency are not rationally considered discrete acts with an expected result. History, therefore, is not a rational progressive process with a specific goal. The course of history changes constantly in the most unpredictable way precisely because our actions have unintended consequences which again constitute the basis for future actions. The agent's knowledgeability is always limited by the unacknowledged conditions of and the unintended consequences of action.

Power and Agency

Another element in Giddens's theory of agency is its connection with power. Giddens takes it as given that the agent is a human being with transformative capacity, i.e. with the power to intervene or to refrain from intervention. In other words, the agent has the potential to be able to act differently. Agency does not refer to "the intentions people have in doing things, but to their capability of doing those things in the first place" (1984a, p. 9). Thus, agency has to be related to power rather than to intentions. To act is to exert power. "To be able to 'act otherwise' means being able to intervene in the world or to refrain from such intervention, with the effect of influencing a specific process or state of affairs" (1984a, p. 14).

Furthermore, Giddens emphasizes that power does not characterize a specific type of behavior but is part of all action. As part of the concept of agency, power concerns

> the capability of actors to secure outcomes where the realization of these outcomes depends upon the agency of others. The use of power in interaction can be understood in terms of the facilities that participants bring to and

mobilise as elements of the production of that interaction, thereby influencing its course. (1979a, p. 93)

Interaction always contains relations of both autonomy and dependence.
Even though we may find ourselves in a situation of dependence, we will
always possess some resources that can help alter the activities of our superior. Even in a lord–peasant relation in feudal times, where the power relation appears to be entirely in the lord's favor, the peasant has the opportunity
to exert counterpower. Peasants can cheat in the payment of tithes or reduce their labor intensity when they work the lord's land. Giddens calls
this the dialectic of control (1984a, pp. 16, 374).

In the case where the dependent agent is no longer able to act otherwise,
he or she will cease being an agent. This serves to emphasize the importance of power and transformative capacity to Giddens's concept of agent
and agency.

Agent and Agency: a Summary

Ontological security, practical consciousness, reflexive monitoring of action, and rationalization of action give the agency concept a recursive character, thereby providing both the concepts of agent and agency with a
reproductive dimension. These elements help to explain why the same patterns of action are repeated and create the foundation for a social order.
The concepts of transformative capacity, discursive consciousness, unintended consequences, and unacknowledged conditions of new actions are,
however, aspects that may change existing routines.

For example, the unintended consequences of action help to create the
foundation for new action because they are unacknowledged conditions of
new actions. This is an aspect of the agency concept which leads to a structure level (a social objectivity), while simultaneously retaining a voluntaristic
element, in that the unintended consequences also enable change.

In this way Giddens succeeds in redefining the traditional concepts of
agent and agency, such that they form a part of a social practice having
both an actor and a structure element.

Structure, System and Structuration

As with agent and agency, Giddens also tries to redefine the concept of
structure. Giddens distinguishes between *structure* and *system*. Each day
throughout the year, for example, London's buses drive through the city

streets along the same routes; the passengers enter, buy their tickets, sit down, and get off at their respective stops; these actions are all continually repeated and reproduced. Giddens terms such a pattern of actions a *social system*. Social systems consist of relations between actors or collectivities reproduced across time and space, i.e. actions which are repeated and therefore extend themselves beyond an individual act. Social systems are therefore social practice which is reproduced, and from which emerges a pattern of social relations.

Structures, in contrast, are characterized by the absence of acting subjects. Structures have only virtual existence, in that structures exist only as a possibility and have not actively manifested themselves. It can be seen that Giddens's concept of structure is to a great extent inspired by structuralism.

> To say that structure is a "virtual order" of transformative relations means that social systems, as reproduced social practices, do not have "structures" but rather exhibit "structural properties" and that structure exists, as time–space presence, only in its instantiations in such practices and as memory traces orienting the conduct of knowledgeable human agents. (1984a, p. 17)

From this quotation, it can be seen that structure exists only in practice itself and in our human memory, which is used when we act. For Giddens, the concept of structure does not exist as an external condition. Structures appear only in our memory traces when we reflect discursively over a previously performed act. In other words, structure does not exist as such; rather, it is being continually recreated *qua* the agent, who draws on the same structure (or, more correctly, structural properties) whenever action occurs.

In order to avoid the view of structure as an external constraint which determines and thereby limits our actions, it should be emphasized that structures are both enabling and constraining. Structure, or what Giddens prefers to call structural properties, consists of *rules* and *resources* which the agent utilizes in the production and reproduction of social life, and thereby also the structure. Rules and resources are the medium by which the agent acts. Inspired by the linguistic philosopher Wittgenstein, Giddens states that rules must be very broadly understood as the techniques and formula which, deeply rooted in our tacit practical consciousness, are used in the action. For Giddens, the concept of rule refers to procedures of action, to aspects of practice. Rules are procedures which are applied in the performance and the reproduction of the social practices, and they operate as formulas that tell us "how to go on in social life" (Wittgenstein, quoted in Giddens, 1984a). The concept of resource is closely linked to power as the medium by which the agent can exert transformative capacity (see chapters 3 and 4).

The agent, agency and structure are thus linked together. For Giddens, structure cannot be viewed as something external, as outside of the agent. The traditional concept of structure dissolves and becomes at the same time the means to and the result of the agent's social practice.

Here we arrive at *the duality of structure*, a concept which lies at the core of structuration theory, and the concept of practice. *Duality of structure* succeeds in transcending the dualism between action theory and functionalism/structuralism. "Structure is both the medium and outcome of the practices which constitute social systems" (1981a, p. 27). In this way the structure–actor relation is no longer viewed as a dualism but as a duality. The concept of duality of structure links the production of social interaction, conducted by knowledgeable agents, with the production of social systems across time and space.

The replacement of the traditional concept of structure with a conception of structure as structural properties consisting of rules and resources entails that structure for Giddens is no longer deterministic, but is now both enabling and constraining. Take the example of language. When I speak English, I utilize certain rules that enable me to formulate myself understandably. At the same time, I reproduce these rules and thereby the structure of the language. Language enables me to express my desires and intentions, but when I find that my motives/desires cannot be expressed in words, language becomes constraining. Similarly, the English language can be constraining if I meet someone who is not an English speaker.

The criticism of structuralism and functionalism has centered on exactly the determinism implied by the structure/system concept. Structure is here an external constraint that limits the individual's possibilities of action. This problem seems to disappear in Giddens's duality of structure, for the concept of structure itself is placed within the knowledgeable agent. At the same time, Giddens avoids voluntaristic reductionism by maintaining the reproducing character of agency in the form of structural properties.

By maintaining that structure consists of rules and resources that are applied in every action, Giddens succeeds in avoiding the trap of Parsonian functionalism. Giddens embeds values/norms (rules and resources) within the agent, whereas Parsons places them in the structure/system. Parsonian values and norms are outside the agent and control and constrain the agent's possibilities of action.

The duality of structure lies at the core of Giddens's concept of practice and thereby also his social ontology. Society is understood as a social practice, which via a process of structuration constantly produces and reproduces society.

Structure and System: a Clarification

In an attempt to further refine his concept of structure, Giddens differenti-
ates between structural principles, structures and structural properties
(1984a, p. 185).

1 Structural principles are principles of organization of societal totalities;
 for example, capitalism and representative democracy are two important structural principles in the Western world.
2 Structures are rule–resource sets, involved in the institutional articula-
 tion of social systems.
3 Structural properties are the institutionalized features of social systems
 stretching across time and space.

To describe what Giddens means by these three concepts, I will use one of
Giddens's own examples.

If one considers the structures in a society, the most fundamental structural level will consist of certain *structural principles.* In other words, they
are the most fundamental and, simultaneously, the most abstract principles
for a specified society's organization. Giddens mentions that capitalist society's central structural principle is the separation of state (politics) and market
(economy). The repeated production and reproduction of this principle
distinguishes the capitalist system from other social totalities, such as the
feudal system.

In his attempt to concretize and clarify the structural principles, Giddens
employs the concepts of *structures* or *structural sets.* An example of modern capitalism's structural set is the following process:

private property: money: capital: labor contract: profit

I can utilize my private property rights to procure money, which can be
invested in labor, which ultimately leads to the procuring of profit. In this
very process I draw upon rules and resources that enable the sequence of
actions to take place.

The third concept, *structural properties,* Giddens defines as institutional
features of social systems. Here Giddens means social practices which are
reproduced across time and space. The division of labor in modern society
is an example of one of the system's structural properties. The division of
labor is an institutional feature, as various social practices placed in various
geographic spaces produce goods at different points in time, which together constitute a pattern of practices. High technology is produced in

the Western World, raw materials are extracted in the Third World, etc.

As mentioned, Giddens distinguishes between structure and system. He views social systems as the activities of human agents situated in various contexts, these activities being reproduced across time and space (1984a, p. 25). Social systems consist of relations between actors or collectivities that are organized as regularized social practices and continually produced and reproduced (1979a, p. 66). Social systems, therefore, are not independent of the actor, but created by social practice. In the widest sense, one can say that social systems refer to reciprocal dependent action. Social systems must be seen as very different with reference to their degree of systemness, and we seldom find social systems that possess the kind of internal unity shown in biological systems (1984a, p. 377).

Giddens uses the term society as a special type of social system. Sociology has traditionally conceived society as a closed, demarcated system. This is due especially to the functionalist legacy, which brought with it the biological organism thinking, where systems are viewed as closed cycles. Moreover, modern sociologists often implicitly equate society with the nation-state, something Giddens finds unacceptable. According to Giddens, society is simply one system among many others. Society simply has special characteristics, which make it stand out more than other systems. In principle, a system in Giddens's theory is constituted by all actions that are reproduced. A society as a system contains interaction between actors or collectivities which are institutionalized and extended in time and space. Regarding the concept of society, Giddens also states that society distinguishes itself from other social systems because "definite structural principles serve to produce a specifiable overall 'clustering of institutions' across time and space" (1984a, p. 164). Giddens uses the concept *structural principles* primarily to distinguish between various types of society. More generally, he mentions certain key aspects that must be present before we can speak of a society:

1 A connection between the social system and a specific "locale" or territory. By "locale," Giddens means a physical region connected to a specific environment of interaction. "Locale" has specific boundaries that make interaction more concentrated within these boundaries.
2 The existence of normative elements, which entails claims to the legitimate occupation of the "locale." For example, Jewish people refer to various historical arguments to assert their claim to Israel.
3 The widespread feeling among members of society that they possess a common identity, although only vaguely specified.

An important feature of the individual society or societal totalities, as Giddens terms them, is that they always exist in a context that includes other societies. Societal totalities are woven into a network of what Giddens calls intersocietal systems. Intersocietal systems are social systems that cut across any kind of demarcation line that might exist between societies (1984a, p. 375). Hence, we can consider England as a society and a system, but this society consists of an infinite number of systems, which crisscross England and, moreover, cross traditional national borders. The pound sterling, for example, is used in only one specific society called the United Kingdom, but other economic and for that matter political and cultural systems are not bound to this society. They enter into other, at times larger, intersocietal systems (this is elaborated in chapter 3).

The Time–Space Dimension in Theory of Structuration

Other aspects of the theory of structuration that will be briefly described in this context are time and space, concepts which traditional sociology often treats in a stepmotherly fashion. Here, too, Giddens emphasizes that sociology must be re-evaluated, inasmuch as all social systems, which are constituted by social practices, are embedded in time and space.

According to Giddens, a genuine conceptual effort is needed to incorporate time and space into the theory of structuration because it is not sufficient just to add the two concepts to the theory. In order to explicate how time and space are constitutive of our being, he reconceptualizes time and space by drawing upon, among others, the German philosopher Martin Heidegger and the Swedish time-geographer Torsten Hägerstrand.

Time–space relations enter into the most stable forms of social reproduction as they do to moments of social change. Inspired by Heidegger, Giddens argues that time–space relations "expresses the nature of what objects are" (1981a, pp. 30–4). In other words, there is an irreducibly temporal character to human existence. Like Giddens, Heidegger is concerned about ontological matters, and central to Heidegger is the relationship between ontology and time. Time expresses the nature of human beings. Human beings are temporal and their meaning is found in the temporal character of human existence (Urry, 1991, p. 162). But it does not stop here. Social practice does not only occur in time. It involves three forms of temporality (Giddens, 1984, p. 35). One is the *durée* of daily life, the reversible time of continuously returning events and routines, of practices repeatedly returned to on a daily basis. "Daily life has a duration, a flow, but it does not lead anywhere . . . time is constituted only in repetition." The *durée* of day-to-day life at every instant intersects with the *durée* of the lifespan of the individual, which, in contrast, is irreversible time. This "being towards death" is a human condition. This is an experience of finitude. "This is death, to die and know it." These two forms of *durée* or temporality are interrelated with the "*longue durée* of institutions which is the 'supra-individual' *durée* of the long term existence of institutions, the reproduction of institutions and institutional time" (Giddens 1984a, pp. 35–6, 1979a, p. 96). This is reversible time.

> The reversible time of institutions is both the condition and the outcome of the practices organized in the continuity of daily life, the main substantive form of the duality of structure. It would not be true ... to say that the routines of daily life are the "foundation" upon which institutional forms of societal organization are built in time-space. Rather, each enters into the constitution of the other, as they both do into the constitution of the acting self. All social systems, no matter how grand or far-flung, both express and are expressed in the routines of daily social life, mediating the physical and sensory properties of the human body. (1984a, p. 36)

Social systems are both temporally and spatially binding and time–space constitutive. By this he means that those actions that constitute and are constituted by the social system produce the space in which social practice takes place. At the same time, the social system also binds the actions to a specific temporal-spatial context. When we consider the Manchester Business School as a social system, this system is time–space binding on the social practice which takes place within the system. Students and teachers come to the school each day, do their homework for the next day's lectures, participate in visits to local businesses, and attend school parties. As all the social practices of the affected agents (students, lecturers, and administrative staff) are linked to the Manchester Business School, this school becomes a "locale," which means that all their actions and practices take place in the same space. The school as a specific social system determines the time interval for the actions: classes are held each day at the same time of day, and there is a two-year or three-year program of study. In this way, the school structures a process whereby a student spends precisely two years or three years there, and further determines which years of his or her life a student will spend at business school. Conversely, the continuity in all the daily routine actions undertaken by students, teachers, and administrative personnel at the business school constitutes the school as a system and thereby also the space in which the social practice takes place.

Every form of interaction entails either presence or absence in various combinations. In face-to-face interaction the two agents are placed at the same time and place. Taking inspiration from Goffmann, Giddens terms this form of interaction co-presence. The action takes place at a specific locale and in a delimited time period. With time–space distanciation, social interaction can take place in the same space, but not necessarily in the same geographical locale. This has become more and more common as means of communication have extended their range from handwritten messages to fax and Internet. These communication methods make it possible for people to interact despite their geographical absence. In order to analyze these matters, Giddens draws upon Hägerstrand's time–geography.

The constitution of society through time–space situated practices is closely interrelated with his conception of the human agent. The human agent is purposeful, with a bodily involvement and a mental activity, who is characterized by "presencing" and enabling presences and constraining absences. As we previously saw, Giddens conceives the agent as a continuous being, a being continuously coming-to-be of presence, or "presencing." Agency and action are not seen as single sequences or single acts. They are a flow of being. Intentions and practices of human beings dialectically emerge out of and into one another as part of the temporality and spatiality of existence (Pred, 1990, p. 123). Consequently, the time–space categories are crucial to Giddens's understanding of being and the constitution of social life. Society cannot properly be conceptualized without the time–space dimension. Time and space are the very core of his social ontology.

The Theory of Structuration and Empirical Research

Since structuration theory is so abstract and complex, it may be useful to illustrate some of the theory's concepts in a concrete empirical context. Giddens himself attempts to do this by discussing various studies which elucidate specific aspects of a concrete analytical field from a structuration perspective (1984a, pp. 288ff).

Structuration theory entails two approaches to empirical research. They consist, respectively, of an *institutional analysis* and an *analysis of strategic conduct*.

An institutional analysis concerns primarily those structural properties that are the reproducing features of social systems. The analysis of strategic conduct focuses on how the agent draws on these structural properties (rules and resources) in the constitution of social relations. According to Giddens, every concrete societal analysis ought to contain an analysis of both the structure and the actor level. The two analytical levels are two elements in a core (structure duality), and therefore cannot be separated. For practical reasons, however, one must choose one as point of departure. Hence, the institutional analysis must be placed in "methodological brackets"; for example, while one carries out the analysis of strategic conduct

(1984a, p. 288). In this bracket, the institutionalized properties of the environment of interaction are retained as a given, but not a determinant for the actors' behavior. The analysis simply concentrates on the actions of specific agents.

Giddens demonstrates an analysis of strategic conduct using Paul Willis's *Learning to Labour*, a work considered to be inspired by structuration theory (Willis, 1977). Willis's study is a sociological/ethnographic analysis of a group of boys in a school in the English Midlands. Willis followed the group at the beginning of the 1970s in their final year of school. He shows how these working-class lads (which is what they call themselves) develop their own counterculture in the school system, where they oppose the school's value system and authority structure. Their counterculture functions as preparation for their role on the labor market as unskilled workers.

What is decisive for Giddens is Willis's point of departure. Willis considers the lads to be agents having extensive discursive and practical knowledge about their school environment. In addition, their culture of resistance has some unintended consequences which help to reproduce general features of capitalist/industrial society.

Willis illustrates how the boys are able to formulate their view of authority relations in the school, and how they react to these. Their discursive knowledge seldom results in any clearly explicit formulations, but in a form of humor, sarcasm, and irony. The boys are also very conscious of the practical level. As they often actively run up against the authority relations of the school system, they have a well developed ability to react to the very points/places where the system/persons are weakest. For example, they know exactly how to respond to the teachers if caught breaking the rules and asked to change their behavior.

Willis thus provides a clear description of what Giddens calls the dialectics of control. Although the boys are formally subordinated to several authorities, they nevertheless possess considerable power. They understand that the more often the teachers and the school emphasize disciplinary problems and exert sanctions, the more clearly the relations of authority have weakened. The boys turn this situation to their own benefit and therefore reveal a power which many sociological analyses have overlooked.

In their social practice, structural properties (rules and resources) are utilized. The rules and resources used in the immediate context of action in everyday life are linked to their practical and discursive knowledge. Giddens points out that it is also necessary to add an institutional perspective to the analysis, something Willis touches upon only in passing. Giddens therefore examines more closely the rules and resources that are more general and are connected to a broader understanding of the embeddedness of the boys' activities in time and space.

As mentioned, the boys' opposition to the system and their role in the school have unintended consequences, which maintain and reproduce the conditions that both constrain and enable their actions, e.g. private property, money, capital, educational advantages, job opportunities, labor contracts, and industrial authority structures. These conditions then become unacknowledged conditions for future action. Here we arrive at yet another element of the structure duality. These unacknowledged conditions are both the condition for those actions which the lads can undertake and the consequence of these same actions.

In this way, the boys' social practice is connected to features of the society and the state system in general. Their actions are placed in a larger perspective as the medium by which the external society's conditions and structure are realized. Societal conditions, therefore, do not mold the agents in a passive way.

Conclusion

In this review of the key concepts of structuration theory, I have illustrated how Giddens attempts to dissolve the dualism in social theory by a total reformulation of the concepts of agent, agency, and structure, and the time–space understanding of the duality of structure. Taken together, the redefinition of these concepts describes the social practice which is for Giddens the decisive concept if we are to understand the production and reproduction of social life. This social practice, in the form of the duality of structure, transcends the traditional dualism between action and structure, between subjectivism and objectivism.

In the next chapter we take a closer look at some more specific aspects of structuration theory. There I review some of the core concepts as they apply to an analysis of social change.

Notes

1 It should be noted that according to the *Oxford English Dictionary* duality is a synonym for dualism. Consequently, the change of terminology from dualism to duality does not in itself solve the problem (Hekman, 1990, p. 164).

2 It should also be mentioned that while Giddens uses "structuration" in his book on class theory, *The Class Structure of the Advanced Societies* (1973), it is not in the same sense as in his subsequent work on structuration theory.

3

The Theory of Structuration: Studying the Social Order and Social Change – Breaking with Evolutionism

The two preceding chapters have explained how Giddens develops structuration theory as a constructive contribution to modern social theory. Structuration theory is a social ontology, i.e. an attempt to conceptualize social reality as consisting of human social practice, or, in Giddens's own words, "human being and human doing, social reproduction and social transformation" (1984a, p. xx). A social theory that builds upon a social ontology of this kind is a boundary-transgressing theoretical project which breaks down the barriers among traditional disciplines such as sociology, political science, history, anthropology, and geography. The study of social order and social change is a general feature of these disciplines. For Giddens the study of the social practices that constitute and are constituted by time and space is equally central to all these disciplines. The study of social change over time has traditionally been viewed as the domain of the historian. In the same fashion, the spatial dimensions of society have been the province of geography. Giddens seeks to break down the boundaries between these fields: the theory of structuration is thus a general theory for conceptualizing society and social development. In this chapter we shall examine how Giddens uses the time and space concepts of structuration theory to break with other theories on social development and social change, especially Marxism and functionalism. The later part of the chapter discusses Giddens's theoretical reflections on the study of change.

Challenging the Evolutionistic View of Social Change

For Giddens, structuration theory is an attempt to bring about a social ontology which can create the foundation for a sociological analysis of modern society. This requires a theory that accounts for what society is, how society evolves, how it is reproduced, and how it is transformed. This part of structuration theory, what we can call the historical-theoretical aspect, is developed most fully in two of Giddens's works from the early 1980s: *A Contemporary Critique of Historical Materialism* (1981a) and *The Constitution of Society* (1984a). The English sociologist David Jary has noted that the objective of incorporating a theory of history into structuration theory is "to provide a theoretical and empirically based analysis of past, present and possible future societies that can replace both historical materialism and social evolutionary theories, each of these being seen as possessing serious weaknesses, not least their dependence on functionalism" (Bryant and Jary, 1991, p. 116).

The point of departure for Giddens's historical-theoretical considerations is the polemic against Marxism and historical materialism, and what Giddens himself terms the social evolutionary theories, primarily of the functionalist type (Durkheim and Parsons, but also Herbert Spencer). His critique of the evolutionistic aspects of these theories can be summarized in the following points:

1 Many evolutionary theories regard historical development as a natural process where simple organizational forms are replaced by more complex ones. Giddens attacks this view by arguing that these classifications are untenable, mainly for empirical reasons. Much research has shown that so-called primitive or simple societies possess complex and evolved languages, kinship structures, and the like.

2 The evolutionists consider societies to be closed entities isolated from the many systems of which these societies are a part. Giddens argues that it is necessary to include these external systems in order to understand the significance of change in the individual societies (compare the concept of intersocietal systems).

3 Many evolutionists view historical development as linear, such that certain types of societies replace each other gradually. This view of history ascribes to the individual societies properties that predetermine the society's development. Giddens believes this to be the case with Marx, who views societies as being based upon modes of production that succeed each other in a law-like fashion. Marx speaks of the primitive com-

munist, ancient, feudal, capitalist, socialist, and, finally, communist mode of production, where history ends. Giddens rejects Marx's evolutionism and asserts that no society proceeds through a fixed, predetermined evolutionistic trajectory; history consists of an open project without end (without a telos).

Like that of the American sociologist Talcott Parsons, Giddens's perspective for understanding the construction and development of society is "the problem of social order." However, Giddens redefines the problem of order. Parsons saw sociology's prime task as the study of how society can exist in a stable fashion over time despite the conflicts and differentiated interests among society's members. For Parsons, the opposite of social order is disintegration, and consequently social control for him became an important element in the maintenance of social order. Giddens criticizes Parson's conception of the problem of order, because it is founded upon a notion of society and the individual as two opposing poles. Giddens attempts to resolve this problem (1979a, pp. 102–3). Instead of setting up order against disintegration, he places order as opposed to chaos or formlessness. Giddens understands social order as the social practice that maintains social actions and activities, so that these are produced and reproduced as social systems across time and space. "The problem of order" therefore turns into an investigation of how social actions are reproduced and become systems, of the degree of systemness, and of the character of the system. This requires an analysis of how social systems bind time and space, something very critical for Giddens. In other words, the problem becomes: what types of social actions and interactions can take place such that a social systems evolves and is reproduced? The crucial difference revolves around whether social interaction is primarily face-to-face interaction, i.e. at the same time and in the same space (presence) (or in the same locale), or whether interaction takes place in different locales/spaces and perhaps even at the same or different points in time (absence). Many Iron Age societies were characteristically dominated by social interaction that took place at the same place (the same space and locale, in this case the village) and at the same time. The village constituted the primary social system. The Western world entering the twenty-first century is a social system where much of the social interaction takes place in different locales or spaces and at different times. In order to characterize such different forms of social interaction, Giddens uses the concept of "*time–space distanciation*," i.e. the extension of social systems across time and space. This concept is important for his understanding of history, as different levels of time–space distanciation specify the kind of social system and society that evolves (see figure 3.1).

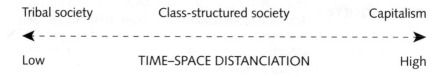

Figure 3.1   Time–space distanciation (after Giddens, 1981a, p. 157).

Giddens thus characterizes society in terms of low or high time–space distanciation. In tribal society, virtually all interaction is face-to-face, i.e. at the same time and in the same space, and consequently tribal societies have an especially low degree of time–space distanciation. In contrast, the high degree of time–space distanciation in capitalist society expresses the fact that a large part of our interaction and communication takes place across time and space, facilitated by modern technology, e.g. airplanes, telephone, fax, computer networks, and television.

The concept of time–space distanciation must be seen in close connection with the concept of *structural principles* (see chapter 2). All social systems and thereby societies possess structural principles that bind the system together. Giddens expresses it as follows: "Structural principles can thus be understood as the principles of organization which allow recognizably consistent forms of time–space distanciation on the basis of definite mechanisms of societal integration" (1984a, p. 181).

Figure 3.2 illustrates various types of societies classified primarily according to which structural principles bind together social systems across time and space, and by the level of their time–space distanciation. On this background and according to very specific structural principles, Giddens selects three main societal types with three different solutions to the problem of order, or what Giddens calls "*societal integration.*"

Tribal societies, which include hunter-gatherer and smaller agrarian societies, are structured around tradition and kinship as the most important binding elements. Tradition is a governing principle in the sense that the actors act in relation to specific types of convictions and specific types of practices embedded in custom.

A tradition is respected because it is a tradition (1981a, p. 161). The tradition itself implies that the behavior is repeated without further reflection, because the action has to a certain extent been institutionalized by repetition over a long period of time. All communication and societal organization takes place in the horde, the tribe, or the village. Giddens calls these organizations "locales," i.e. the settings within which "systemic aspects of interaction and social relations are concentrated".

TRIBAL SOCIETY

Tradition (communal practices)
Kinship
Group sanctions

[Fusion of "social" and "system" integration]

Dominating locale organization: band groups or the village.

CLASS-DIVIDED SOCIETIES

Tradition (communal practices)
Kinship
Politics-military power
Economic interdependence (low lateral and vertical integration)

[Differentiation of "social" and "system" integration]

Dominating locale organization: symbiosis of city and countryside.

CLASS SOCIETY (CAPITALISM)

Routinization
Kinship (family)
Surveillance
Economic interdependence (high horizontal and vertical integration)

[Differentiation of "social" and "system" integration]

Dominating locale organization: the "created environment".

Figure 3.2 Summary of structural principles of various societal types (after Giddens, 1981a, p. 159).

The next types of society are called *class-divided societies*. In using this label, Giddens distances himself from Marxism, which uses the class concept in the analysis of all societies. Giddens rejects the notion that the class struggle should be a dominant feature of this societal type, which would include city-states (Athens, Florence), agrarian empires (Egypt), and feudal societies of different types (e.g. France around CE 1000). Classes exist in these societies, but there is no actual class struggle, and it is not the major driving force in history.

Tradition and kinship are still important structural principles and are of great importance for societal integration. In contrast to tribal society, however, social interaction across time and space is now more common than ever, because the time–space distanciation has increased. This is due partly to the development of written language and improved means of transport, which mean that communication no longer has to be face-to-face. According to Giddens, the change in time–space distanciation is crucial to the initial development of state formations. In particular, written language makes possible the emergence of a state administration, tax collection, and jurisdiction (see chapter 4). Another decisive structuring principle in the state's development is the town–country relation, in which a division of labor evolves such that the town enters into a symbiosis with the countryside, partly through the exchange of goods and partly through tax collection. The town becomes the dominant "locale" in which the state and the state apparatus are anchored. As the state's possibilities for extended control over the population are reduced, especially in the rural areas, tradition and kinship still constitute essential structuring principles for most people's everyday life.

In these societies the division of labor takes on a different character than in tribal societies, where it is primarily gender specific. In the class-divided societies a division of labor is established both within the town and between town and country. This creates new forms of economic interdependence, which also help to integrate the social relations into a more fixed system. The same is true of the military power which, especially in the great imperial empires such as Rome, is the means by which the empire is integrated so that it appears as a consolidated social system.

The final type of society is *class society*, which includes the modern capitalist nation-states. Despite a certain connection between the state and the economic institutions (e.g. via the state's taxation of enterprises), the general separation of politics and economy is a critical principle in the structure of these societies. Another characteristic is the relationship between capital and labor. Giddens supports Marx on this point, but unlike Marx focuses more on how societal integration in the nation-state (the dominant "locale") is achieved by the monopoly of the means of violence and by the state's extended ability to control and penetrate the population's everyday life via surveillance and collection of information.

Both the state and the capitalist mode of production structure people's daily lives, which means that tradition and family no longer constitute the fundamental, integrating elements. The "locales" in which face-to-face interaction takes place are converted to a manufactured or "created environment" (1984a, p. 184). A total urbanization of the entire society occurs insofar as all environments where interaction takes place are artificially created by people for people. The division of labor is now no longer a question of internal divisions of labor between town and countryside. In class societies the division of labor is globalized, which further underlines the time–space distanciation.

Giddens emphasizes that the classification is only a typologization of various existing societies. The intention is not to describe a trajectory of development.

I have here discussed how different systems bind together time and space. As described in my review of the concept of system in chapter 2, social systems that can be characterized as societies exist only within intersocietal systems. The fact that all systems are part of a network of other systems means that the interaction between the various systems always affects the individual systems (societies) and molds these in a many-sided interaction with the social processes embedded in the individual systems. Giddens is aware that society and states are not closed systems, which challenges the traditional view of the state and of society in sociology. Chapter 4 illustrates the consequences of Giddens's views for the understanding of the actual construction of states.

Based on his identification of various types of society, Giddens has categorized certain corresponding intersocietal systems. Figure 3.3 shows that various types of societies (and states) have coexisted in different types of systems. Tribal societies have constituted the longest period in human history. In a world dominated by tribal societies, it is only possible to speak of very fragmentary systems. Genuine interaction is rare due to the low level of time–space distanciation. The imperial world systems, in contrast, are larger and more coherent; the Roman Empire, for example, interacted with other empires, numerous city-states, and various tribal societies such as the Germanic tribes. Yet this system is far from global. Genuine globalization first occurs with the consolidation of capitalism and the modern nation-state. For the first time in history absence in space is no longer an obstacle to societal integration and coordination at the global level. The broken lines in figure 3.3 indicate that the enormous industrial and military capacity of the capitalist societies has gradually eroded most of the tribal and class-divided societal types.

The foregoing discussion of society and societal systems is included in order to illustrate how Giddens's structuration theory comprises an alternative to evolutionist and functionalist views of history. With his typology of societies based on structuration theory, Giddens attempts to break with evolutionism. His main complaint against evolutionism is its built-in unfolding mechanism of change, the focus on endogenous causes of change, its fixed developmental stages, and the idea that change always entails adaptation to new circumstances (1984a, pp. 228–36). Giddens therefore formulates his own view in the following fashion: "In explaining social change no single and sovereign mechanism can be specified; there are no

Society	Intersocietal systems
Tribal societies	"Prehistorical" and fragmentary systems
Class-divided societies Tribal societies	Imperial world-systems
Capitalist societies Class-divided societies Tribal societies	Early capitalist world economy
Capitalist societies State socialist societies Developing countries ┌─────────┐ │ Class-divided societies │ │ Tribal societies │ └─────────┘	Present-day capitalist world economy

Figure 3.3   Intersocietal systems (after Giddens, 1981a, p. 168).

keys that will unlock the mysteries of human social development, reducing them to a unitary formula, or that will account for the major transitions between societal types in such a way either" (1984a, p. 243).

The theory of structuration thus takes its point of departure in a view of history understood as an open project without fixed paths of development. History cannot be reduced to individual causal explanations. Societal development is conditioned by an infinity of causes which must always be seen in a specific context. Let us examine more closely Giddens's other conceptual apparatus for understanding social change.

Analysis of Social Change

The first part of this chapter has shown how Giddens, with the aid of concepts such as structural principles, time–space distanciation, and "locale," distances himself from the evolutionistic theories of history. This section examines other aspects of Giddens's theoretical reflections on the study of social change. Whereas the foregoing discussion described his reading of history, this section deals more specifically with his considerations and concepts of social change.

An analysis of social change necessarily requires a definition of the concept. Giddens avoids such a definition, which is not surprising, as social change is a complex and difficult concept. While all social activities imply change, this is not what is normally thought of when questions of social change enter the agenda. As formulated in Giddens's terminology, we tend to think of how social systems – understood as relations which are produced and reproduced by various types of actors (individuals, organizations, states, etc.) – "anchored in time and space" change over time. It is this type of social change with which Giddens is preoccupied and which forms the basis for his discussion of the problem.

When we analyze social change, the duality of structure compels us to take account of the level of the strategic conduct (the actor aspect) and the institutional level (the structure aspect), although one can place a methodological bracket around one of these (see chapter 2).

Let us begin by considering social change in relation to the actor/agent.

When the individual actor acts, it is often based on what Giddens calls practical consciousness, which indicates that a great many actions take place in a rule-like fashion and virtually as a routine, thus simultaneously producing and re-producing the structures that are the means and the outcome of the action. It should be pointed out that, for Giddens, reproduction connotes only the repetition of the same actions and structures – not necessarily their invariability. Change can also occur even when actions are reproduced, as actions often have unintended consequences resulting in social change. For instance, John gives George a friendly slap on the back but fails to notice that George is holding a cup of coffee, which then spills all over George's shirt. That George spills his coffee is an unintended consequence of John's action. To take another example, an individual peasant improves his plow in order to increase his harvest. Other farmers take up the idea, and the improved plow becomes the standard within agriculture, with major consequences as a result.

Not only do the unintended consequences of the agents' actions contribute to changes of structures and systems. The agent's ability to comprehend various conditions in life can also mean that the agent changes his or her patterns of action. This can occur when the agent's consciousness moves from the practical to the discursive level. The degree of discursive consciousness can be linked to occupation, education, and social position. Higher education can entail more resources and thereby more power to

act. Both the amount of resources and the degree of discursive consciousness can contribute to alterations in social practice. Part of my daily practice is drinking milk. I open the refrigerator in the morning, pour the milk
into the glass and drink. This occurs every day as a routine and constitutes
a part of my practical consciousness. One day I may read an article about
the many advantages of organic milk. I may reflect about my own choice of
milk and switch to organic milk. I can become more aware of the advantages of organic milk and act upon it because I have become discursively
conscious of my previous routines, and because I have the available resources to alter my practices, which in this case means the money to buy
the more expensive organic milk. This example shows that our reflexive
ability and discursive consciousness influence social practice and eventually
change it.

When the agent acts, he draws on various structures which are both the
means and the result of the actions of the actors. The actions can be structured in social systems, and for Giddens it therefore becomes important to
investigate how the actors' interaction is bound together in and with a
system. It requires an examination of the structures upon which the actor
draws and which bind the actor to the system. The binding factors consist
of the following elements: meaning and communication structures (signification), structures of control and power (domination), and structures of
legitimization. These structures, which contain some rules and resources,
are used by the actor in every action, and the decisive factor in relation to

1   S (signification)

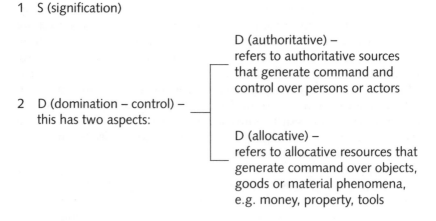

2   D (domination – control) –
     this has two aspects:

D (authoritative) –
refers to authoritative sources
that generate command and
control over persons or actors

D (allocative) –
refers to allocative resources that
generate command over objects,
goods or material phenomena,
e.g. money, property, tools

3   L (legitimization)

Figure 3.4   Dimensions of structure (after Giddens, 1979a).

1	S-D-L:	Symbolic order (modes of discourse)/ ideological institutions (church, media, schools)
2	D (authoritative) -S-L:	Political institutions
3	D (allocative) -S-L:	Economic institutions
4	L-D-S:	Jurisdiction/law/modes of sanction

S = Signification
D = Domination
L = Legitimation

Figure 3.5 Classification of institutions (after Giddens, 1979a, p. 107).

an analysis of social change is to examine more closely how these binding structures are reproduced and transformed. The three or four structural dimensions used in every action can be depicted as shown in figure 3.4.

The distinction is only analytical, as all four structures (four, because the domination–control dimension is divided into two independent levels) are inherent in all systems and are both the means and the product of the actions of actors. A student, Maria, who attends classes at the university, draws on these four structures. Language and communication are pre-requisites that enable her to enter the building, find the right classroom, participate in the class discussion, etc. Maria has the power to control her environment to such a degree that she can pay for the bus ticket, gain admittance to university, participate in school activities, and the like. All these social activities require that she can control both authoritative and allocative resources. The legitimization element refers to the norms and sanctions to which she necessarily partly allows herself to be subordinated, and to which she may partly contribute when she acts. For example, Maria agrees to pay for the bus trip, accepts that the teacher conducts the class, and so on. In other words, she uses communication, power, and legitimation in all her actions.

Consequently, an analysis of social change must always explain how the composition and type of these four elements changes.

A study of the actor's strategic conduct, such as the above-mentioned university situation, emphasizes the actor's use of these structures. However, if we seek to examine the changes in the institutional dimensions[1] more closely, it is necessary to focus on the outcome of the actions at the system level. This can be done by investigating the three structural levels – meaning/communication, power, and legitimation – at a superordinate institutional level. The three/four types of structures are embedded in certain institutions that correspond to the content of the structures, namely the political, ideological, economic, and juridical institutions.

On a general level, the model illustrates how a sociological analysis of social change at the system level could be conducted. The four institutions are mutually dependent and cannot be analyzed in isolation.

The model's many letter combinations, while they may appear confusing, represent Giddens's attempt to avoid every form of determinism and reductionism. If one undertakes an analysis of the transformations in Eastern Europe, for example, one can begin with the political institutions (D(aut)-S-L). Politics cannot be discussed without relating it to other institutions. Therefore, D is followed by S-L. Ideological, juridical, and economic changes must necessarily be incorporated in order to avoid reductionism, which is to say that only one factor, the government's decisions, for example, can be identified as the cause of the comprehensive social transformation process. Giddens would thus oppose citing Gorbachev's political reforms in the USSR as the cause of the revolutions in USSR and all of Eastern Europe. This is only one of many causes. The factors would include the USSR's poor economy and ideological changes, such as increasing distrust of the system and widespread defeatism.

In line with his critique of evolutionism, Giddens does not cite one of the model's dimensions as the only driving force in historical development. The interaction between the four dimensions is critical for understanding the transformation process in the former USSR. Giddens emphasizes that a concrete analysis must result in knowledge about the level of differentiation in various institutions. An investigation of the symbolic order entails a review of religion, science, art, ideologies, and cultural flows with their associated institutions. These are then related to the economic institutions and so on.

Analysis of Larger Systems

We have now examined the four structural levels that must necessarily be included in an analysis of social change. In the following, I discuss that portion of Giddens's conceptual apparatus which has been developed to analyze social changes in larger systems. In his analysis, Giddens develops five conceptual tools:

- structural principles;
- episodic characterizations;

- intersocietal systems;
- time–space edges;
- world time.

I have previously discussed the significance of *structural principles* for understanding the construction of society. For example, the lineage in tribal societies and the relationship between capital and wage labor under capitalism are essential structural principles which help to bind these systems together. When social change is discussed in relation to social systems, therefore, it is important to determine which structural principles dominate, and the extent to which we can observe social changes in a society's structural principles.

The concept of episode denotes a specific aspect of social life where a number of actions or events can be viewed in such a way that we can speak of a beginning and an ending. Here we may speak of a specific sequence (1984a, p. 244). The concept of episode can identify sequences of change "affecting the main institutions within a societal totality, or involving transitions between types of societal totality" (1984a, p. 244). As an example, Giddens cites the analysis of state building because the concept of episode can be used here to "cut into history" and decode and identify specific elements which mark the start of the changes and trace a process of institutional change (1984a, p. 244). For example, the 1938–45 period in German history can be characterized as an episode, as it marks a change in one of society's main structural principles. The distinction between state and market, hitherto a dominating principle, disappears. In reality, the state's war economy suspends the market. After 1945 a new society evolves in which state and market are again separated.

As mentioned previously, a system understood as a society or a state can never be considered in isolation, and Giddens therefore brings up the previously mentioned concept of *intersocietal systems*. The concept requires that state formations be studied in the context of different state systems. Giddens emphasizes that the incorporation of intersocietal systems and external processes of change must not occur at the cost of the internal processes that take place within the state's boundaries. Therefore, change processes that affect a given system but originate outside it must always be juxtaposed with the changes that take place within the limits of the system. These processes must be seen as a mutual interplay. For example, the dissolution of the USSR must be seen as both a result of external pressure, where the spiral of military rearmament process undermined the country's economy, and a result of internal social changes marked by the appearance of new political-ideological ideas.

The concept of *time–space edges* is developed to elucidate how the coexistence of various types of societies in an intersocietal system can entail social change. Time–space edges refer to the forms of contact that occur between structurally different societies; for example, the coexistence of empires with the city-state or modern capitalist society's coexistence with tribal and/or class-divided societies. Even these edges or points of contact between various societies are potential or actual expressions of social change (1981a, p. 23).

The *world time* concept is developed to illustrate the necessity of studying social changes in a temporal and historical context. Two apparently very similar social processes can develop very differently and have different consequences if situated in different points in time in the historical development. Giddens thus wants to say that all forms of social change must necessarily be seen conjuncturally (1981a, p. 23, 1984a, p. 251). By this he means the "interaction of influences which, in a particular time and place, have relevance to a given episode" (1984a, p. 251).

Processes of development, when anchored in two different conjunctures, can be totally different, even though the result is apparently the same. States such as France, Norway and the United States are today considered as modern capitalist nation-states, but their paths to this stage have been quite different.

Giddens's attempt to understand social changes contextually is closely connected to the idea of the agent with human reflexivity.

> If all social life is contingent, all social change is conjunctural. That is to say, it depends upon conjunctions of circumstances and events that may differ in nature according to variations of context, where context (as always) involves the reflexive monitoring by the agents involved of the conditions in which they "make history." (1984a: 245)

The contextual understanding of social change is a fundamental aspect of Giddens's theory of social change. Here he seeks to prevent reductionism, in the sense that one driving force is selected as the prime mover of history. By emphasizing that explanations of social transformation must always be contextual, he rejects the idea that society contains laws which can be generalized across time and space. Explaining the development of the French state and the transition to liberal democracy is not synonymous with explaining the development of democracy in other European states.

Conclusion

This chapter has discussed the implications of structuration theory for the study of social change. Giddens's theory of structuration is an attempt to avoid the evolutionism that has dominated most sociological theories, especially Marxism and functionalism. Giddens rejects the idea that society proceeds through certain developmental stages in a linear fashion. Social life, he says, is contingent, and social change must therefore always be seen in a specific context – a conjuncture. Moreover, Giddens criticizes sociology for conceptualizing societies as isolated, distinct entities in which processes of social change caused by interaction with other systems are largely ignored. Hence, for Giddens, social change becomes the result of an infinite number of social processes. This implies that explanations of social transformation must always be historically specific and incorporate many causes. Thus, explanations which attempt to reduce complicated social processes to single explanatory models must be rejected.

The next chapter continues the discussion of social change, showing how Giddens studies concrete processes of social change in the European state system.

Note

1   Giddens defines institution as the more extended features of the social system, i.e. the practices with the greatest time–space distanciation within a social system (1984a, pp. 17, 24).

4

Giddens's Theory of the State: the Nation-state and War

A neglected aspect of Giddens's sociology consists of his ideas on the theory of the state. An analysis of modernity, which is his overall objective, requires theoretical reflections on the modern state, as it is the modern, globalized nation-state which is an essential and unique feature of contemporary society. Hence, during the 1980s Giddens devoted much of his work to problems of the state in general and the development of the European nation-state in particular. Developing a coherent theory of the state and state forms was hardly Giddens's initial objective. His considerations on the character of the state were meant to be only one element in his general effort to understand modernity. However, the unintended consequences of these reflections evolved into a sophisticated theory of the state and its developmental processes.

This chapter examines Giddens's work on the state more closely, focusing primarily on his general considerations on the state and the processes of change which take place in the European state system from the time of the traditional state forms to the modern nation-state. By way of introduction, let me first present the problematic of the state as it is viewed in classical sociology.

The State, War, and Classical Sociology

Giddens investigates the state problematic among several classical sociologists, such as Marx, Spencer, Durkheim, and Weber, concluding that none of them succeed in developing a coherent theory of the modern state (1985a, pp. 22–31). This is, first, because they focus primarily upon the concept of society and not on the concept of the state. Second, the poor theory of the state must be seen in the context of sociology's general neglect of military aspects and war in the development of state and society.

For Giddens, the state and violence are intimately connected. In classical sociology, the problem of violence is isolated as an internal social problem, with violence linked to the maintenance of society's social order. The fact that violence and the means of violence are rarely related to the problem of warfare and interstate relations must be seen in relation to the sociological conceptualization of society. Here society is seen as an isolated, demarcated unit. Giddens points out that society, understood as a special system, is always a part of other systems (intersocietal systems), just as society itself is penetrated by an infinite number of subsystems. This conceptualization of systems has implications for Giddens's concept of state and society, which is now conceived within a larger system of societies and states (see chapter 3), whereby society is now no longer conceived as a closed entity.

The conceptualization of state and society as closed entities has further consequence for the analysis of social change. Such an analysis often takes its point of departure in changes which take place within the boundaries of society and the state. In other words, explanations of change processes rely primarily on endogenous factors. Marx speaks of class struggle and the development of the forces of production; Durkheim of the division of labor, population density, and population volume; while Weber cites religion as an essential factor in explaining decisive processes of change. However, classical sociology overlooks the significance of the relations between states, including violence, war, and the development of the military in their analyses of the emergence of capitalism and industrialism. Here the classic traditional understanding and analysis of social change reveals itself to be poorly developed.

Giddens's Concept of State

Giddens finds it necessary to develop an alternative concept of the state which incorporates the importance of the means of violence. Such a state concept is presented in his *A Contemporary Critique of Historical Materialism* (1981a) and *Nation-State and Violence*, the latter having the subtitle, *Volume Two of A Contemporary Critique of Historical Materialism* (1985a).

As the two titles indicate, Marxism is the impetus for Giddens's thinking on the state and violence. The point of departure for Giddens's polemic with Marxism is the concept of power, which he finds undeveloped in historical materialism. For Marx, power is linked to the class struggle, and in focusing on the economic conflict between the owners of the means of production and the propertyless Marxism becomes – in Giddens's view – economistic-reductionist.

For Giddens, this particular notion of power makes Marxism incapable of dealing with the state and with violence. In Giddens's theoretical universe, power is something perpetual and omnipresent, being linked to the concept of actor (see chapter 2). Inspired by Parsons, Giddens believes that power is the capacity to achieve outcomes. Power is exercised and expressed via resources, and these resources are seen as a medium, constantly being used by actors (individuals, organizations, and collectivities) when they act. As mentioned previously, the actor draws upon two types of resources: allocative and authoritative. Allocative resources refer to dominion of human beings over the material world. Authoritative resources refer to the possibility of dominating and having power over other people or actors – the social world itself. How much power, and how it is exerted, is thus conditioned by the existence and use of allocative and authoritative resources.

Giddens criticizes Marxism for focusing primarily on the development of allocative resources, i.e. the forces of production.[1] According to historical materialism, the development of the forces of production has decisive importance for the formation of different types of society and their processes of change. Giddens thus sees historical materialism as reductionist and evolutionist. The reductionism consists in the notion that economic factors are regarded as the prime mover of societal development. Evolutionism reveals itself in the circumstances that the development of the forces of production automatically pushes the societal types into a specific trajectory of development.

Giddens's project is to break with reductionism and the thesis of a single prime mover of history. Consequently, he rejects the solution of replacing allocative resources with authoritative resources as the point of departure for understanding societal development. Such a solution would simply entail replacing one causal factor with another. Giddens instead emphasizes that an analysis of societal development must examine the interplay between allocative and authoritative resources and the actual composition of these two types of resources. Furthermore, Giddens investigates the importance of the composition of resources for the constitution of social systems and the social dynamics of change. In the next section, I review Giddens's analyses of various state forms, focusing attention on the composition of the two types of resources.

As the basis for his own concept of state, Giddens seeks inspiration from the German philosopher Hegel, from Durkheim, and above all from Max Weber. The influence of Hegel and Durkheim on Giddens is not treated here (see 1985a, pp. 17–22), as it is Weber's definition of the state which is most important for Giddens's own theory of the state.

For Weber, the state is a unique organization which distinguishes itself from all other types of organizations. Weber's definition of the state contains three main elements: (a) the existence of an administration able (b) to sustain the claim to the legitimate monopoly of control of the means of violence, and (c) to uphold that monopoly within a given territorial area. While Weber incorporates both the means of violence and the territorial aspect overlooked by Marx and Durkheim, Giddens nevertheless sees Weber's concept of state as too general, it being applied to all state forms throughout world history. Since Weber's definition is created on the basis of an analysis of the modern state, it cannot be generalized to include all other state forms, Giddens claims. Here Weber commits a fallacy, as the state apparatus only lays successful claim to the monopoly over the means of violence in the modern nation-state, and only here does a correspondence exist between the state's administrative apparatus and the territorial boundaries. Giddens, therefore, defines the state as a political organization whose rule is territorially ordered and which is able to mobilize the means of violence to sustain that rule (1985a, p. 20).

Here, Giddens distances himself from Weber on the question of the legitimacy of the means of violence and the state's claim to monopolize the means of violence. Giddens claims that it is only in the era of the *nation-state* that legitimacy and monopoly are maintained. With his analysis of Marx, Durkheim, and Weber as a backdrop, Giddens concludes that the best point of departure for the development of a state analysis must base itself upon a redefinition of Weber's concept of state.

Giddens's State Forms

Giddens's general state definition thus lays the foundation for his analysis of the emergence of the modern state. The aforementioned state definition is general in the sense that it includes the most general common features of all state forms, which according to Giddens have existed and still exist. The general definition of the state form, therefore, is broken down into specific subtypes, such as the absolutist state and the nation-state. Giddens juxtaposes these state forms in order to point out similarities and differences among them. He asserts that states do not undergo an evolutionary development, and in relation to the discussions of modernity his main purpose becomes that of demonstrating a radical break, of which the rise of the nation-state is an indication.

Figure 4.1 describes Giddens's state forms in his classification of society. As shown in the figure, state formation does not exist in tribal societies. The question, therefore, is why we find state formations in certain types of society and not in others. Hence, certain conditions must be present in

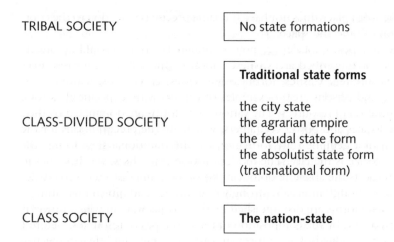

Figure 4.1 State forms positioned in various societal types.

order for a state to exist in a certain type of society. As this problem must be linked to key theoretical elements in Giddens's work, I will expand on this point in the following discussion. First, it is necessary to grasp some fundamental concepts of structuration theory.

In structuration theory, an actor (and here we do not distinguish whether the actor is an individual or an organization) is synonymous with possession of power, or, to use Giddens's terminology, transformative capacity. The scope of power and the possibility of utilizing it are determined by the character and amount of resources present. As mentioned above, there exist two types of resources: allocative and authoritative. Every state formation is conditioned by the organization and development of these two types of resources.

The resources are not possessed by the individual actor but are features of all social structures used by the actors in the further production and reproduction of the system. The existence and combination of allocative and authoritative resources makes possible the development of a state apparatus with a territorially ordered dominion, and which possesses the means of violence for the maintenance of such domination. The nature of such a state and the extent of its power can only be determined by further analysis of the specific composition of the allocative and authoritative resources.

As Giddens has set up the problem, there must necessarily be a center in which the two forms of resources are concentrated. Giddens calls this center a power container. This power container must be located in a specific locale in the social system. Giddens prefers "locale" over "place," as he finds that the word place does not have the same precise connection to the coordination of time and space.[2]

Specific types of locales are power containers, which should be understood as circumscribed areas where allocative and authoritative resources are concentrated. Castles, fortifications, cities, enterprises, nation-states, schools, and prisons are all examples of centers with a specifically strong concentration of resources. The various state forms are dominated by their unique locales and power containers, which are the preconditions for the creation of a genuine state formation. In the traditional state forms, the decisive locale is the city. The modern nation-state, however, becomes in many respects the absolute dominant power container as a territorially demarcated (though internally strongly regionalized) administrative unit.

The state forms are distinguished by the various ways in which power is generated, and by the composition of the two types of resources. Before I examine the individual state forms in order to determine their respective locales and the specific character and composition of their allocative and authoritative resources, I shall briefly describe the general factors that lead to the generation and development of power and its positioning in a power container.

Power containers generate power chiefly via the concentration of allocative and authoritative resources. The creation of allocative resources is determined by the level and accessibility of technology in society. Compared to the technology in ancient Egypt, the existence of our era's high technology entails greater possibilities to create and develop allocative resources, e.g. foodstuffs, housing, weapons, and better and more advanced means of production. The degree of concentration of the allocative resources is conditioned by factors which generate authoritative resources. Certain prerequisites must be present in society for the development of the authoritative resources, i.e. those resources which imply that a society can control its population. For example, surveillance is such a prerequisite. A technology, e.g. a written language, is necessary so that society can collect information about the population. The amount of information and the possibilities for storing it are crucial for controlling and governing population groups above the tribal level. It is only when written language evolves, in class-divided societies, that possibilities for power concentration essentially increase. Written language creates the foundation for legislation which can be codified and extended, and for the evolution of the tax collection system. This does not occur in tribal societies, where state formations have not evolved. For these reasons Giddens concentrates exclusively on: (a) traditional state forms in the class-divided societies; (b) the absolutist state as a transitional type; and (c) the modern national state.

The Traditional State Forms

The city as power container

Traditional state forms are often divided into the following categories: city-states, feudal systems, patrimonial states, nomad empires, and centralized, bureaucratic empires.[3] Giddens consolidates these into two ideal types: the city-state and the great agrarian empire.

In both state forms, the city is the decisive power container. However, this does not mean that the city is a coherent administrative center as such, for it enters into networks with other power containers, e.g. castles and landed estates. The relation between town and countryside is a predominant structural principle in the traditional state forms, and the relation is essential for the development of the power of the state. Most of the population lives outside the towns and is therefore not directly subjected to the state's surveillance and control. States with a high degree of administrative concentration and military autonomy are often found in city-states, where the city itself is the center of the state.

The use of systematically collected information is fundamental to the development of an organization. Information and knowledge create administrative power, which is synonymous with control over time and space. Administrative power expresses itself only if the coded information is used for the surveillance of human activities. To a certain extent, this occurs in city-states, but never so intensively as in modern organizations. The traditional states tend to be unable to control the population in daily life to the same extent that we now experience state power, with its omnipotent control and surveillance over us from cradle to grave. The traditional state intervenes into local matters to a only small degree, and, in contrast to the modern state, the central power (perhaps even a misleading term in this context) has no ability to exert domination and control over the population in terms of ideology, law, politics, and economics. Local customs, traditions, and religions continue to exist, as long as taxes are paid.

Traditional states: politics and economy

It is possible to speak of a genuinely dominant/ruling class in the traditional societies, the aristocracy. This class has great influence over the state apparatus, where it occupies all functions. The state, personified in the ruling figure, has extensive, often despotic, power over the population. However, the state can in no way control or rule like the modern state, which penetrates our entire everyday life. The authoritative resources in the traditional states are too few.

As mentioned, Giddens finds traditional state forms within what he calls the class-divided societies. These societies contain classes, but the class struggle is not a driving force in societal development. Giddens's conclusion derives from the assumption that the traditional state forms have two main classes: the landed aristocracy and the peasants. Their conflicts never fundamentally threaten the social order: peasant rebellions are few and sporadic and not organized in the modern sense. According to Giddens, this is because the peasants' only weapon – stopping agricultural production – is difficult to apply, because mass rebellion would threaten their own livelihood.

This leads to a description of the relationship between politics and economy, where Giddens is ambiguous. The economic and political spheres are depicted as being both separated and fused. The two spheres are separated in the sense that the state – the political level – rarely intervenes directly in the economic sphere, especially because the state does not possess adequate authoritative resources to do so. The local peasant often lives undisturbed by what takes place in the political center. The fusion of the two spheres is due to the domination of the ruling class in both the political and economic spheres. This contrasts with the capitalist society, in which the owners of capital do not necessarily possess the political power.

A further characteristic of the traditional states is the lack of fixed national boundaries of sovereignty. The great agrarian empires such as Rome and China had what Giddens calls frontiers, in contrast to the nation-states' fixed and demarcated territories demarcated by borders. The city-states, in contrast, are more demarcated and homogeneous, as the territory is more limited.

It can therefore be concluded that traditional states have a fragmentary character, with restricted administrative authority and no fixed borders, and hence a relatively weak integration compared to modern states.

A final important aspect concerns the development of military power. Giddens emphasizes that war, understood as armed struggle between groups where physical violence is used by or on behalf of one community against another, has been a prominent feature of all human societies. In band and tribal societies, war exhibits a very small degree of specialization. Not until the traditional states do we observe the evolution of a specialized military agency, with a moderate form of industrialization of the means of warmaking. Innovations in arms technology as well as an increasing degree of organization of the military apparatus can be observed, but the power holders never succeed in developing a genuine monopoly of the means of violence. Only in the city-state does this seem to occur to a certain degree.

Despite the increasingly rationalized and industrialized conduct of war, it is difficult for the traditional states to maintain the domain of sovereignty and actually draw borders around a fixed territory. This is, despite the improved military technology of the time, due to poor military organization, reinforced by even more primitive means of transport and communication, which make it difficult to maintain large armies for prolonged periods and over long distances. Building large armies is also a problem for the power holder himself, as the army can turn against him. The army, however, is an absolute necessity for the maintenance of the state. Without an army, the state would disintegrate, because of either attacks from the outside or internal collapse.

Traditional state systems

Giddens emphasizes the significance of the military for the maintenance of the state. Because states always exist in intersocietal systems with other states, there is an ever-present latent or manifest threat from other parts of the state system. This is a pervasive feature which is accorded great significance in the development of the various state forms.

Giddens specifies four non-modern types of intersocietal systems: (a) a system of local tribal cultures (hunter-gatherers/settled agriculturalists); (b) city-states, often port cities; (c) feudal state systems; and (d) larger imperial state systems (where smaller states or tribes exist in the periphery). These types of intersocietal systems have coexisted and replaced each other in a process full of contingency, and therefore cannot be considered the outcome of a linear evolutionary development.

Giddens emphasizes two types of state systems: the empire and the city-state. The use of military power was the constituting aspect of empires. They appeared, furthermore, as the result of war and/or conquest. Whereas modern nation-states are embedded in the international economic system and are deeply dependent on it, the empire was far more self-sufficient. Virtually all trade and production took place within the frontiers of the state.

The city-state's survival was highly dependent on trade and the import of goods, which meant greater vulnerability to external threats. Hence, city-states employed considerable resources for their defense, thus constraining the possibilities of maintaining agriculture at a sufficient level. Slavery was thus a necessity.

Absolutism

Geopolitics and military changes

Absolutism must be regarded as a traditional state form. However, it signifies a break and thus constitutes a transitional form on the path toward the nation-state. The state form itself reflects both an internal change in the state's organization and a transformation in the external state system. Giddens defines the absolutist state as "a formation limited to some two centuries or so in Europe [with a] political order dominated by a sovereign ruler, monarch or prince, in whose person are vested ultimate political authority and sanctions, including the control of the means of violence" (1987a, pp. 170–1).

The state form and the state system which evolved under absolutism were created by the simultaneous occurrence of several events. Giddens emphasizes the significance of geopolitics to the development of the state from the 1500s to the beginning of the 1800s. Geopolitics views political conditions in light of the states' relative geographical positions and in relation to strategic points, such as access to trade routes. Geopolitics helps us to understand developments in the relations between states from the 1500s, with the dominance of Spain and Portugal, until France gradually established itself as the leading Great Power. This development is absolutely fundamental for understanding the internal development of the states.

Discussing other significant factors in the development of absolutism, Giddens emphasizes the military domain, where three developmental features have influenced the emergence of the absolutist state: (a) military technological changes; (b) development of administrative power within the armed forces; and (c) the development of European sea power.

CHANGES IN MILITARY TECHNOLOGY

Among changes in military technology, Giddens cites reforms in the army structure. The armies of the Middle Ages consisted primarily of knights who served the feudal lord in return for the land given to them. This entire system changed radically from the 1500s. Mercenary soldiers (the Swiss, for example, had large armies for rent) now became the army's decisive element. In contrast to heavily armed knights on horseback, the mercenary soldiers were often foot soldiers armed with weapons. They were very mobile and superior to the medieval knights.

Developments in arms technology proceeded rapidly. The invention of guns, ammunition, foresights, cannons, and new types of fortifications created an arms gap of major dimensions between Europe and the rest of the world.

Arms technology also stimulated an emergent capitalism. The same was true of the new mercenary structure. Large sums of cash were now required, as it was no longer adequate for the belligerents to fight for honor and Christianity. War became a question of who had the most money, and when the money was exhausted, the soldiers went home or went over to the enemy. Possessing large financial resources was therefore of crucial importance. This was one reason for the need for more effective tax collection, and a more efficient taxation system required a currency system. This also contributed to stimulating capitalism. The old system based upon payment-in-kind prevented economic growth and dynamic capitalism.

ORGANIZATIONAL CHANGES

Possessing the latest, most advanced weapons was not enough. The organization of the army was just as important, and a certain degree of professionalization of the army therefore took place. France was the first country to have a standing army (still consisting of mercenary troops). Furthermore, for the first time in history, the army was no longer the foundation for internal order. The altered jurisdiction, the development of criminal law and an incipient police force are indications of a separation of the defense against external enemies and the maintenance of internal order. "The existence of large standing armies and the progression of internal pacification are complementary expressions of the concentration of the administrative resources of the state" (1985a, p. 113). Both elements increase the expansion of administrative power.

One of the many organizational changes in the military was the establishment of military academies intended to educate, train, and discipline soldiers and officers. A specialization occurred whereby the tasks of both officers and soldiers were divided into "specific, regular sequences of single activities." Work programs and organizational diagrams were introduced in order to make groups more effective and disciplined. Giddens draws parallels between this development in military training and subsequent changes in the state bureaucracy and in the industry. Giddens's thesis is that the organizational changes in the army became a model for society's other organizations. Hence, he claims that this reskilling and deskilling of army personnel can be seen as a form of Taylorism centuries before Taylor's "scientific management" entered the industry.[4] Furthermore, it should be mentioned that the size of the armies exploded: France, for example, had about 400,000 men under arms around 1700.

Those states which did not understand how to exploit the technological innovations and combine them with organizational changes did not develop an adequate capacity to defend themselves and at times were overrun by stronger state powers.

SEA POWER

The development of European sea power was also integral to the emergence of the absolutist state. England, Holland, and later France overtook Spain and Portugal as the leading sea powers. They took advantage of technological developments, such as improved ships with more advanced weapons, as well as seafaring and navigational techniques, all of which enabled Europe to develop and maintain a world empire.

Absolutism as organizational form

These geopolitical and military changes brought with them a comprehensive change in traditional state forms and the state system in which they were embedded. Before examining the changes in the state system itself, I shall briefly summarize those aspects which Giddens sees as characterizing the absolutist state as an organization, and which are especially linked to the changes in the external state system. The expansion of the absolutist state organization is simultaneously based upon the development of allocative and especially authoritative resources.

Giddens cites three main characteristics of absolutist organization.

1   *The state's administrative power becomes centralized and extended.* For the first time an administrative and bureaucratic apparatus with a salaried civil service staff is created. This bureaucracy was most developed in France, the pinnacle of absolutism. The French prime minister J. B. Colbert, in the course of rationalizing the tax collection system, developed both central and local civil service systems, thereby marking a break with feudalism. However, there still exist significant differences compared to the bureaucracy in the nation-state, since the absolutist state has limited power to create a total centralization.
2   *Development of a new type of jurisdiction.* As a stronger bureaucracy was constructed, a far more universalized legal system could be implemented. Three changes in the juridical system should be mentioned from this period. (a) An increasing number of statutes are enacted, and as a new feature they apply in an impersonal fashion to all persons regardless of their position in society. (b) The content of legislation changes, one of the most important changes being that private property can now be

distinguished from the public domain. This change supports the growth
of merchant and manufacturing capital. (c) Criminal law and methods
of sanctions also undergo change. Earlier, local authorities had largely
carried out the sanctions themselves, just as local custom came into
force if the law had been violated. During the absolutist period a larger
portion of the criminal law and sanctions is controlled by the state.

3   *Changes in tax procedures.* Tax collection is developed and made more
effective. This is a necessity, as the states are involved in an increasing
number of military conflicts which are expensive, since war is based
largely on mercenary troops. In this connection early capitalism is given
an impetus. The states have a direct interest in simulating capitalism, as
it generates greater tax revenues.

Changes in the state system

During the absolutist period the European state system underwent drastic
changes. The feudal state system, of course, created the background for
this transformation process, whereby the fragmented war-making princely
states and small kingdoms were consolidated into fewer units with pyra-
midal state structures. These created new and more demarcated territories.

A fundamental change from earlier state systems was the mutual recognition between states. Giddens claims that recognition of others' legitimate
right to autonomy was unique in European state history. As examples, he
cites the creation of borders, the development of diplomacy as a means for
this mutual recognition, and the creation of what he calls the discourse of
balance of power. The discourse of balance of power became a shared principle which all states referred to and used as a basis for power politics in Europe. Here the foundation was laid for a legitimation and ratification of the
international state system, as the states accepted each other's existence. The
states were thus no longer allowed to forcibly place other states under their
own administrative systems or laws; in short, outside intervention was forbid-
den (1985a, p. 87). In practice, the consequence was that some states intervened and became winners, while others lost territory or totally shattered.
Despite the existence of the concept of balance of power as a leading principle in European power politics, the risk of war had certainly not lessened.

From this examination of the development of the absolutist state, we can
observe the central role played by the state system, war, and the military in
explaining the transition from an absolutist to a nation-state form, and the
internal construction of these state forms. In this concluding section, I will
describe, on the basis of the absolutist state, how change is treated in connection with the state problematic.

Giddens is unequivocal in his explanations of the emergence of the absolutist state. The political level, here understood as war and military development, is the decisive driving force.

> Various main features of European state development were shaped in a decisive way by the contingent outcomes of military confrontations and wars. . . .
> It was war, and preparations for war, that provided the most potent energizing stimulus for the concentration of administrative resources and fiscal reorganization that characterized the rise of absolutism. Technological changes affecting warfare were more important than changes in techniques of production. (1985a, pp. 111–12)

Thus, it is clear, not least as a result of the many wars in Europe during the 1600s and 1700s, that military development is the critical factor in explaining social change on a general institutional level during this period.

The Modern Capitalist Nation-State

The significance of war for the development of the nation-state

As his point of departure for the discussion of the nation-state and the consolidation of capitalism from 1800 and onwards, Giddens emphasizes the close connection between military developments, capitalism, and industrialization. The interaction between civilian industrial production and military production is fundamental to the development of the modern state. Giddens particularly emphasizes the improved communication methods as an important aspect of the industrialization of the military, which simultaneously affected the rest of society; for example, the railroad, the steamship/steel ship, the telegraph, and later the telephone. These factors signified a total change in the form of war and the organization of the army; logistics, for example, were markedly improved. Developments in communication as well as the more general industrialization of the military were at the same time a driving force for capitalist development, inasmuch as private companies were carrying out a considerable share of military production in domains such as food supply, clothing, and boots. At the same time, these technological improvements made it possible for the growing capitalism to reach a greater market. In other words, the existence of allocative resources affects the development of authoritative resources, and vice versa.

The military involvement of the states was a life-and-death struggle which placed very specific demands on the construction of the state if its survival was to be assured. In terms of its organization, the state had to ensure a defense which was adequate to avoid defeat. The development of new constitutions, with their associated citizenship rights, must be seen in this context. The old form of defense relying on mercenary troops was no longer effective, and we now observe a new and extremely important element of the modern state: general conscription.

Giddens is very much aware of the connection between conscription, citizens' rights, sovereignty, and nationalism. Citizenship rights are Giddens's point of departure: "If the sovereign state is inherently a polyarchic order, in which citizenship rights are the 'price paid' by the dominant class for the means of exercising its power, citizenship in turn implies the acceptance of the obligations of military service" (1985a, p. 233). The nation-state and the conscription-based mass army appear and develop as a tandem pair, and as a result many groups of citizens are allocated citizenship rights and citizenship within a territorially demarcated political society – a state.

It was France (and later the United States) which in 1793 first introduced general conscription and along with it citizenship. The specific connection between conscription, citizenship rights, and control over the armed forces varied from one state to another. In France citizenship was developed as a way to actively create feelings of national loyalty; the conscripted soldiers thereby exhibited a will to fight which far exceeded that of traditional mercenary soldiers. The new soldiers now fought as Frenchmen for the nation and associated rights.

The period from the beginning of the 1800s exhibited this close connection between war, military and defense reforms, and citizenship rights as a specific feature of the development of the nation-states. This evolution continued after the First World War, conditioned only by the war's actual form and outcome. The United States' entry into the war on the side of the Allies, the United Kingdom's choice of Germany as its principal enemy instead of France from about 1900, and the Versailles Treaty itself (the peace treaty following the end of the First World War) all contributed to the well known outcome.

Another factor that might have changed the development of the nation-state was a strong Socialist International. As we know, however, the Socialist International collapsed and the revolutions in Germany and Russia were decisive for the development of these states. The USSR's continued process of creating a nation-state, which contradicted the idea of socialist internationalism, subsequently had tragic consequences. The USSR became the world's greatest fortress of a totalitarian character.

War and its outcome cemented the connection between the independent sovereignty of the states, citizenship, and nationalism. This was demonstrated particularly in the Versailles Treaty, which contained the idea of states' rights to sovereignty and the principle of plebiscite, which states had found it necessary to introduce if a strong, national, and loyal army was to be established.

The element of conscription and the industrialization of war meant great demands for soldiers and labor, thus giving wage laborers a strong negotiating position in certain industrial sectors. Women also began to enter sections of the labor market from which they had been excluded. These developments contributed to the formation of an increasing number of trade unions, and the framework was created for the subsequent development of "the institutionalization of class conflict" (1985a, p. 236–7).

Mass production technology and the intensive rationalization of industry, stimulated and reinforced by the First World War, became accepted by the workers, something which would hardly have occurred in peacetime. In this way, industrialization was further supported, to which can be added the massive application of science to technological innovations in the military, and subsequently in industrial mass production. Much scientific progress was created during the First World War in the conduct of war, e.g. the development of tanks and aircraft, but it was only after the war that these developments seriously came to benefit industry and civilian pursuits.

The Second World War saw the culmination of science and technological applications for military purposes. The atomic bomb, rocketry, and advanced weapons systems were developed and put into mass production. The most important technological innovations of the war have since had a decisive influence on economic and social life, e.g. jet traffic, telecommunications technology, and information technology.

The Second World War was also significant for internal political conditions; in the United Kingdom welfare state reforms and economic and social rights appeared in the wake of the war. Giddens also emphasizes that the appearance of liberal democracies in West Germany and Japan was not endogenously conditioned. Defeat in the war and, especially for Japan, the United States' intervention undermined the foundations of the old power elite.

The nation-state as power container

I have already mentioned several key aspects of the nation-state: fixed borders, extended administrative control, and the permanent existence of class conflicts as a result of the capital–wage laborer relation. Whereas the most important power containers in the earlier state forms were the towns, the nation-state now fulfilled this role. The combination of increased surveillance, control by the state power, monopoly of the means of violence via control over the army and police, intensified industrialization, and the expansion of capitalism in society resulted in an increased concentration of allocative and authoritative resources in the nation-state. Giddens summarizes the distinguishing features of the nation-state in four dimensions:

1 A strong development of surveillance potential by the state, including the collection of information, definition of deviance, totally extended legal jurisdiction, and so on. The entire population is now subordinated to the control of the state, and the state has the capacity to penetrate, monitor, and control the population's everyday life. Time–space distanciation has increased, especially as a result of technological innovations in transport and communication.
2 Expansion of military power and monopoly over the means of violence. The state has the monopoly of violence both as concerns internal pacification (police) and in the conduct of war in relation to other state actors. Moreover, war becomes industrialized, with major consequences for civil society.
3 Capitalism and with it the development of class society and class conflicts. The workplace becomes a key locale where allocative and authoritative resources are accumulated. The development and consolidation of private property, where the right to own the means of production, including labor power, leads to total capitalization. Capitalism and private property are separated from political institutions.
4 Industrialism as an independent dynamic force, which causes an unprecedented radical transformation of nature. A mechanization of production takes place and manufacturing production begins to dominate. According to Giddens, industrialism and not capitalism enables collection and centralization of the labor processes in one place (in the enterprise, at the factory).

After this characterization of the nation-state as a power container with a unique composition of allocative and authoritative resources, Giddens defines this state form. For Giddens, the nation-state is a state form "which exists in a complex of other nation-states, is a set of institutional forms of governance maintaining an administrative monopoly over a territory with demarcated boundaries (borders), its rule being sanctioned by law and direct control of the means of internal and external violence" (1985a, p. 121). It is important to point out that this state form is European in its origin. Only in Europe do these four dimensions come together in a unique fashion. In the second half of the twentieth century, the specifically unique European state form becomes globalized, and it is therefore only with the nation-state that we obtain a global state system. Globalization of the nation-state system is one of the dimensions that constitute the characteristics of modernity. This is discussed in chapter 5.

Conclusion

This chapter has focused on Giddens's theoretization of the state. Breaking with evolutionism, Giddens develops his own typology of societies, in which his Weber-inspired concept of state is embedded. Giddens develops his concept of state by placing it in a historical perspective. In addition, the state is conceptually embedded within a state system which obtains decisive influence on its internal relations. As the state system's significance for the individual state's development is heavily emphasized, the relations between states, including war and military development, obtain a more important role in Giddens's analysis of the emergence and development of the state. In emphasizing war as a significant element in a process of social change, Giddens breaks with classical sociology's focus upon endogenous explanatory models. The state as a social system reproduces and changes itself as a result of both the state's interaction with other states and the everyday practice of the actors within the state and society. The state is created and developed in a structuration process, a process which involves the external and internal relations of the state. A part of this structuration process is constituted by the practice of the people and other actors, where they draw upon the rules and resources available in the state and to society.

Giddens's analysis of the emergence of the modern state is a study in processes of social change. It serves as an illustration of how structuration theory can be applied to the study of social change.

Notes

1   The forces of production include the tools and technologies for the production of material necessities and the people who carry out this production.

2   Giddens defines "locale" as "settings of interaction, including the physical aspects of setting – their 'architecture' – within which systemic aspects of interaction and social relations are concentrated. The proximate aspects of settings are chronically employed by social actors in the constitution of interaction" (1985a, pp. 12–13).

3   Patrimonial states are formations from the Middle Ages where state and state power derive from the princes' inherited property and right.

4   As a management consultant, Frederick Winslow Taylor developed the principle of scientific management in 1911. Taylor studied industrial work processes and proposed that each labor process be divided into a series of individual operations in order to identify the "one best way" to be used by all workers. Each task could then be done more precisely and quickly.

5

The Analysis of Modernity: Globalization, the Transformation of Intimacy, and the Post-traditional Society

It is *the* task of "sociology," as I would formulate the role of that discipline at any rate, to seek to analyse the nature of that novel world [in] which, in the late twentieth century, we now find ourselves. *(Giddens, 1985a, p. 33)*

To understand our contemporary society's special character is one of sociology's most important goals. As mentioned above, Giddens's sociological project must be seen as a continued attempt to comprehend the uniqueness of the modern.

Giddens draws the contours of an analysis of modernity at the conclusion of *The Nation-State and Violence* (1985a). However, it is not until the 1990s that he presents a genuinely coherent diagnosis of contemporary society which incorporates an analysis both of the uniqueness of the institutions of modern society and of the specific characteristics of the modern individual, our self-identity, and our mutual relations. This contemporary diagnosis appears in *The Consequences of Modernity* (1990a), *Modernity and Self-Identity* (1991a), *The Transformation of Intimacy* (1992b), *Beyond Left and Right* (1994a), and the chapter "Living in the post-traditional society" (1994b). This chapter reviews Giddens's analysis of modernity, which extends from a general discussion of society's institutions and their rapid transformation to the implications for the individual and the mutual interaction between institutional and personal relations.

What Is Modernity?

Giddens claims that the modes of social organization which evolved in Europe from the beginning of the 1600s, and which have since become globalized, are unique compared to the modes of life of earlier eras. According to Giddens, these organizational forms, and thereby modernity, evolve through the interaction among a number of institutional dimensions, these being capitalism, industrialism, surveillance, and control of information by the nation-state, and finally the development of military power, including the successful monopoly of the means of violence and the industrialization of war. For Giddens, in order to understand and conceptualize our contemporary society, we need a new sociological theory capable of grasping the complexity of this interaction.

What distinguishes the traditional social orders from the modern? Giddens emphasizes primarily modern society's dynamic character. Modern society changes with a unique pace, scope and intensity. Premodern civilizations have also experienced change, but these are incomparable with the strength and scope of the changes the world has undergone in the past two hundred years. Another important feature of our era is the presence of modern institutions. The nation-state, the modern political system, highly mechanized and highly technological industrial production, wage labor, commodification (i.e. the fact that everything was made into a commodity, including labor), and urbanization are mentioned as unique to our civilization.

What creates this dynamic? The most dynamic aspects of modernity can be summarized in three points, which are pervasive themes in Giddens's analyses of modernity. These are: (a) separation of time and space; (b) the "disembedding" mechanism; and (c) modernity's reflexive character. Each of these dynamic aspects is discussed further in the following section.

Time–Space Separation

The greater part of the social interaction which now influences our everyday life no longer takes place at the same time and in the same place. Whereas previously the home and the village constituted the most important place, the entire family is now dispersed in time and space. Father works in a neighboring town, where he sells furniture for export to Germany. This selling is done by telephone and telefax. Mother, a health visitor, drives around visiting patients, but she is, via her mobile telephone, in continual contact with the leader of the 24-hour care service. Their young son attends the sixth grade and works with databases in geography, where he collects information about Ghana's roads, ports, and railways. Their daughter, in her second year of high school, is currently on a school trip to Rome. Another older sister is working as an au pair in California but is in frequent contact with the family by telephone and e-mail. Such a family is not unusual in our time, but would have been inconceivable just a few decades ago. Since time has now become standardized and globalized, the family members can interact with each other and with the surrounding world without difficulty. The father can agree upon a date and time for meeting, and regardless of whether he is dealing with companies in Germany or Colombia, it is possible for all parties to meet or phone each other at the agreed time, as time has become a globally standardized entity.

Not only is the concept of time being changed and emptied; the concept of space is also undergoing transformation. Our space has expanded markedly with new technological measures. We can be in the same space, but not necessarily in the same locale. This factor has been the driving force, for example, behind the modern rational organization, which has been able to connect the local and the global in new ways. A modern company can function only because it has been possible to break the time–space connection. The precondition for the optimal operation of a modern enterprise is its ability to coordinate many people's actions even though they are separated in both time and space. The company must be able to coordinate production, distribution and marketing, as well as its activities in relation to its suppliers, etc. Efficiency is created by several people acting in concert toward a specific goal, but not necessarily at the same time or in the same place (or, in Giddens's terms, the same "locale").

The concept of space is also altered by the extremely detailed mapping of the globe. Everyone agrees on Sweden's geographical location in Europe. In other words, we are in the same geographical space and have the same cosmography, the same conception and description of the world. If we agree on a meeting in Manila, there is no confusion about the place. Manila's location is fixed in our spatial conception, regardless of whether the meeting participants come from China, Denmark, or Canada.

Disembedding of Social Systems

In the early societies, before extended time–space separation, the institutions and actions of society were embedded in the local community. This condition has changed because social relations can no longer be limited to the local community, but are lifted out of the local interaction context by certain disembedding mechanisms. This process is closely connected with time–space separation, which to a large degree is its precondition. Disembedded activities contribute to a strong increase in time–space distanciation. Giddens distinguishes two types of disembedding mechanisms, both of which contribute to the development of modern institutions: (a) symbolic tokens and (b) expert systems. Together they are called abstract systems. The symbolic tokens are media of exchange which make up an independent system and which circulate between individuals and institutions. Money is one example of a symbolic token. Money is a means of placing time in brackets, as it functions as a means of credit. Money in your hands represents a value that can later be used to purchase new goods. Symbolic tokens, in this case money, also fracture the notion of space, as their standardized value enables agents who never meet physically to carry out transactions. In other words, they lift transactions out of their special transaction environment and create new patterns of interaction across time and space. Money is a means of time–space distanciation.

Another example of an abstract system which is also a disembedding mechanism is the expert systems which surround us in our daily lives. When I take the bus, I enter a large network of expert systems, including the construction of the bus, the construction of roads, and the traffic control systems. Without possessing knowledge of how these systems are constructed I can take the bus without complications: I need only the money for the ticket (which is another expert system) and I must know the destination. The expert systems also help to move social relations from one given context to another. The many expert systems and symbolic tokens increase my radius of action, such that with a bus and some money, I can move freely around in contrast to earlier, when we were bound to a local community. Such a disembedding mechanism also requires a time–space separation. The mechanism extends social systems across time and space. The bus schedule is an example.

The bank is another example of an expert system which helps to move and recombine social relations from a local context into new patterns of interaction which take place across time and space. In order to increase its share of the market, the bank expands with a network of branches. Opening a new branch draws upon a professional expertise which can be transferred and applied to other branches so that a national and global network of branches can be established. The expertise is passed on to local bank employees who implement it in a new local practice. This expert system operates as a disembedding mechanism, in that it produces a knowledge of bank operations which can be systematized and codified and therefore used in an infinite number of other cases. This enables a given bank practice to be extended across time and space (Cassell, 1993, p. 28).

The Reflexivity of Modern Society

Reflexivity is the third contributing factor in our society's profound processes of transformation. Giddens takes this concept from the American sociologist Harold Garfinkel, but redefines it in the process. Giddens identifies two forms of reflexivity. One is a general feature of all human action. When we act, we constantly undertake a "reflexive monitoring of action" (see chapter 2). The other type of reflexivity, however, and the focal point here, is unique to modernity. Modern society is experiencing a reflexivity process at both the institutional and personal levels, and this is decisive for the production and change of the modern systems and modern forms of social organization.

What is the nature of this reflexivity, and why is it connected precisely to modernity? Giddens defines reflexivity as our – i.e. institutions' and individuals' – regular and constant use of knowledge as the conditions for society's organization and change. The firm undertakes market surveys in order to establish sales strategies. The state conducts censuses in order to establish the tax base. We watch gardening programs on television in order to become better gardeners.

This increased reflexivity is made possible especially by the development of mass communications. The development of written language set off this process, but the subsequent rapid growth in the development of other means of communication is what enabled societies to collect and store ever larger amounts of information and thus create the possibility for a higher level of reflexivity than earlier. In other words, we have become able to reflect on ourselves. With an expansion of the level of time–space distanciation, our past, present, and future become visible and are held up in front of us like a mirror. This brings about a situation in which social practice is constantly investigated and changed on the basis of newly acquired information (about this very same social practice). Thought and action are constantly refracted back upon each other. It is not until modern society that history obtains a decisive meaning. History is bound to modernity because modernity means that reflexivity can "use history to create history," and do so far more intensively (consciously or unconsciously) than in the traditional societies. Previously, actions were based exclusively on tradition, and could not be conceived beyond the framework of tradition. Today we reflect on tradition and we act in accordance with it only if it can be legitimated via reflexivity. This can be illustrated by the institution of marriage: previously a man and a woman married because it was a natural part of tradition. Tradition determined that a man and a woman, at an appropriate moment in their lives, entered into marriage, among others with the purpose of sexual and material reproduction. Today we still marry, but we no longer marry because tradition dictates it, and when we do it, it is with a high degree of reflexivity. For example, we all know people who choose not to enter into the traditional marriage. Perhaps they choose to live alone, in a commune, in a homosexual relationship, or together without being married. This knowledge forces us to deal reflexively with our own actions, which we must be able to justify. With the concepts of structuration theory we can say that today we marry on the basis of a discursive rather than a practical consciousness. We can no longer act on the basis of traditions, because tradition in the traditional sense no longer exists.

The increased reflexivity does not automatically lead to more and better knowledge and thereby an ability to control history. This is far from the case. Even though modernity disregards knowledge based on tradition in favor of knowledge based on reason, modern reflexivity entails an undermining of reason insofar as reason is synonymous with obtaining a certain knowledge. Our reflexivity entails a fundamental uncertainty about the truth of the new knowledge, because we cannot be sure that this knowledge will not be revised. The demand for knowledge, therefore, can no longer entail certainty and truth. Scientific discoveries are quickly challenged by new research. One day we have to use lead-free petrol, the next day we read that lead-free petrol causes cancer. This uncertainty has become an existential feature of modern life with consequences for our identity.

After this review of some special features of modernity, I will now go into further detail with the institutional dimensions of modernity, or, in other words, explain what kinds of major societal institutions dominate our era's society.

The Institutional Dimensions of Modernity

An important part of Giddens's analysis of modernity consists in pointing out the institutional dimensions that dominate our society. When Giddens speaks of institutional dimensions, he means the principles of organization that structure society's institutions (see chapters 2 and 3). In his polemic against classical sociology, Giddens emphasizes that the institutions of modern society cannot be characterized according to a single organizational principle, such as capitalism (Marx), industrialism (Durkheim), or rationalism (Weber). This does not mean, however, that the classical sociological heritage should be rejected. Giddens agrees with the classics that their conceptual apparatus can be used if their theories are redefined and adapted to the new context. He believes that all three exponents for the main tendencies of sociology (Marxism, functionalism, and action theory) can enter into an analysis of modernity. Furthermore, Giddens includes structuralism, and especially the poststructualism represented by Foucault. Giddens uses the strongest points from the substantive sociology of these tendencies and combines them in a unique fashion.

Giddens's main thesis is that the institutions of modern society contain four general dimensions: capitalism, industrialism, the capacity for surveillance and control, and military power. These correspond to the dimensions of the nation-state (see chapter 4).

Giddens defines the first dimension, capitalism, as a commodity production system centered on the relations between private ownership of capital on the one hand and the propertyless wage labor on the other. Capitalist enterprises produce for a strongly competitive market, which means constant and continuing technological innovation, in pursuit of profit (1990a, pp. 56–7). Furthermore, the economy and other spheres of society are separated. The separation between economy and politics is conditioned by private property rights which prevent democracy from entering the gates of the factory.

The concept of industrialism elucidates the second aspect of the institutions of modernity. Industrialism entails the use of inanimate sources of material power in the production or the process which affects the circulation of goods. Production is mechanized, and factory production becomes possible. Besides altering labor itself and the workplace, industrialism also changes and reinforces the significance of transport and communication and affects domestic life.

The third dimension, surveillance capacity, explains why it is possible to designate capitalist and industrialized societies as genuine, demarcated entities. At first sight, neither capitalism nor industrialism is confined to state boundaries. That they nevertheless become part of the delimited territorialized societies is because they are embedded in the nation-state. The nation-state cannot be reduced to being a capitalist or industrialized state society and, consequently, it must be analyzed as a separate entity with its own characteristics. A decisive element of the nation-state and the prerequisite for its development is the ability of the state to supervise and control its population. Thus, an independent and strong administrative unit with the capacity to control a specific territory can be developed.

The final institutional dimension, military force, is an extension of the surveillance dimension. The state's development of a fixed territory and the surveillance of the population parallel the development of military power. The state achieves full monopoly over the means of violence, which no other state forms have succeeded in doing. The extended surveillance and the monopoly of the means of violence are crucial aspects of the nation-state itself, and, as mentioned in chapter 4, solely belong to the modern epoch. It should be added that the twentieth century saw an increasing industrialization of the military which has radically changed the conduct of war. War in the twentieth century evolved into total war, culminating with the development of the atomic bomb. This destructive force has undermined Clausewitz's dictum of war as an extension of politics. War is today always potentially present, but as the ultimate war will have horrific consequences for everyone involved, total war has become useless as a political means.

The claim that modernity is synonymous with a fundamental historical break in relation to all traditional societal forms is due, according to Giddens, to a unique interaction between the four institutional dimensions in Western Europe during the 1600s and the subsequent period. The individual dimensions all possess independent logics and their own dynamics, which cannot be reduced to the three others. None of the four conditions determines the other. They are part of a dense network where they mutually affect and reinforce each other (1990a, pp. 59ff). Hence, there is a close connection between surveillance operations of the nation-state and changes in the military. The state's success in obtaining a monopoly of the means of violence is closely connected to the fact that increased surveillance capacity enables the state to develop a new criminal law and a control over 'deviants'. Hence, the army plays only a secondary role in the maintenance of

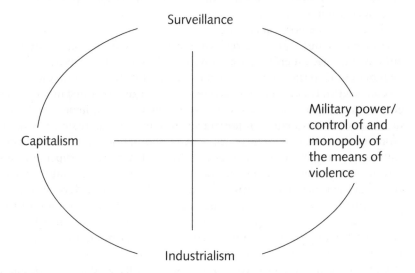

Figure 5.1 The institutional dimensions of modernity (after Giddens, 1990a, p. 59).

internal law and order within the state. Law and order is now managed by the civil authorities, while the army is used against external enemies. Capitalism and industrialism also reinforce each other. They have facilitated the high degree of industrialization of the military and thereby the increased military strength of the nation-state. In other words, the four elements of modernity are all interdependent.

The interrelation between capitalism, industrialism, and the nation-state (surveillance and monopoly of violence) constitutes the very core of the institutions of modernity. These four dimensions and their interaction appear for the first time in Western Europe, but the dynamic of modernity has entailed that modernity has become a more and more global phenomenon.

The Globalization of Modernity

Modernity means that time and space are stretched out. Social relations, which previously took place in a local context, are dissolved and reorganized across time and space. This distanciation process forms part of the globalization which Giddens defines as an intensification of worldwide social relations that connect distant localities in such a way that local relations and occurrences are shaped by events taking place thousands of miles away (1990a, p. 64). Welfare and economic prosperity in Singapore can mean stagnation or collapse in Manchester and Pittsburgh, if the core industries in these cities are not competitive.

If we are to understand modern society and our own conditions of existence at a general societal level, as well as in our own everyday life, it is imperative for sociology to understand these globalization processes. The "local" and thus our everyday life are part of these global processes. Of course, the global dimension affects our lives when unpredictable events occur or when actions with unintended consequences take place, e.g. natural disasters or armed conflicts in other parts of the world. But this is not really new. Globalization in the modern sense also affects our daily routine actions, as local actors and institutions are closely interwoven with external actors and external institutions. Our local banks, supermarkets, and other stores are often units in a larger chain or network. The goods on the shelves are to a great extent the result of a global process in terms of both production and distribution. According to Giddens, the globalization process has four axes or dimensions (see figure 5.2).

Giddens distinguishes between two phases of globalization. The first phase of globalization was governed primarily by the expansion of the four Western institutional dimensions. These institutions originated in the West, and

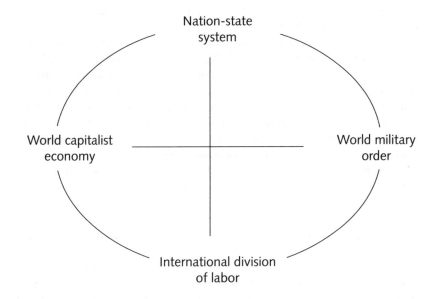

Figure 5.2 The dimensions of globalization (after 1990a: 71).

since the sixteenth century they have gradually developed and spread to the entire globe (Beck et al., 1994, p. 96). The Western world had a pervasive impact on the rest of the world. It tried to shape it in its own image.

The postwar era, and especially the past 20–30 years, has furthered the globalization of the four institutional dimensions of modernity, but this second phase of globalization must be seen in relation to the connection between disembedding consequences and abstract systems that generate decentered processes of a complex and multidimensional nature. This means that globalization in the second phase is not just a continuation of the first phase where modernity, i.e. the four institutional dimensions, was extended to the whole world. An important indicator of the beginning of the second phase is instantaneous electronic communication across the globe. Satellite communication has made it possible to spread the same image to billions of people. These processes of communication penetrate and restructure the experiences of everyday life. Globalization in Giddens's terms is something more than economic globalization. Globalization means transformation of time and space and "actions at distance" (1994a, pp. 4–5).

The globalization process means that we live more and more in one world, in that we are bound together by economic networks, interstate relations, military alliances, and the global division of labor.

When we speak of one world, it is linked to the development of communication technology, which has created a world where the media transmit a stream of news across national borders. The only common denominator is the time of the event. In villages in Ukraine, Sweden, and Bolivia, radio or newspapers confront us with the same news about elections in South Africa, the coffee harvest in Brazil, or the presidential election in the Philippines. Giddens emphasizes that the most important aspect here is not that everyone today has knowledge he or she was previously cut off from, but that this knowledge makes possible a global extension of the institutional dimensions of modernity. The communicated knowledge is a necessary part of our level of reflexivity. Knowledge of the foreign exchange markets in London, New York, and Tokyo is shared by everyone involved in the financial and money markets, so the stock brokers and currency brokers can continue and intensify the global transactions (1990a, pp. 77–8).

Giddens stresses that globalization does not only mean the development of huge economic, political, and cultural systems and networks. Local and personal experiences and activities influence and are influenced by processes of globalization. In other words, globalization does not only take place out there in the big systems, but is also related to the private and most intimate part of our life. Our daily life is increasingly mutually related to activities and events taking place elsewhere in the world. It is really difficult to grasp the depth of this development. Our lifestyles have global consequences. When we buy an item of clothes in Copenhagen – an item designed in Britain but produced in Poland or Taiwan – it has consequences for the international division of labor and the ecosystem of the Earth.

Where the first phase of globalization was a more unitary process going in a single direction from Europe toward the rest of the world, the second phase is a more complex process. "Now there is no obvious 'direction' to globalization at all, as its ramifications are more or less ever-present" (1994b, p. 96). Globalization is a "complex set of changes with mixed and often quite contradictory outcomes" (1994a, p. 81).

These global influences simultaneously fracture, unify, and restructure the social order. These influences create new forms of stratification and often produce different consequences in different areas of the world. A well known example is the industrial development in East Asia, which is linked to the deindustrialization of the old industrial core areas in the West (1994a, p. 81). The new or revitalized nationalistic movements can also be seen in this light. Moreover, on a cultural level, globalization produces cultural diasporas which are interrelated across time and space. Millions of communities unified by taste, customs, or belief exist everywhere, transcending nation-state borders. For example, we find many lifestyles centered on specific clothes, films, music, or religion (e.g. Scientology). A number of these cultural diasporas often have a standardized character, influenced and shaped by cultural commodification, mass media, and advertisement. These processes do not homogenize our culture, because new lifestyles emerge and confront older lifestyles, which often undergo changes. "Globalization leads also to an insistence on diversity, a search to recover lost local traditions, and an emphasis on local cultural identity – seen in a renewal of local nationalisms and ethnicities" (1994a, p. 81).

I have presented Giddens's analyses of the institutional changes in society since the 1700s, when the institutions evolved in Western Europe. The emergence of these new institutions, in conjunction with the pace and intensity of the aforementioned changes, constitutes the uniqueness of modern society, especially at the end of the twentieth century. The transformation processes reinforce and are reinforced by the institutional processes of globalization. Globalization, time–space separation, the disembedding of abstract systems, and the increasing social reflexivity are all changes taking us to a so-called post-traditional social order. The next section elaborates on this notion, which Giddens used more and more during the last part of the 1990s.

The Post-traditional Society

The post-traditional society is still a part of modernity. The radicalizing consequences of modernity have transformed society beyond tradition, but not beyond modernity. Giddens has replaced his notion of late modernity with the post-traditional society.

In order to understand Giddens's idea of the post-traditional society, we need to take a closer look at the concept of tradition (1994a, 1994b, 1996d). Tradition is seen as a way to organize time. It is an orientation to the past which at the same time influences and is a guidance to the future. It is important to understand that tradition always changes, but at the same time involves duration. Tradition contains an integrity and continuity which resists some changes (1994b, p. 62). According to Giddens, tradition has five main characteristics:

1 Tradition is an organizing medium of collective memory. We do not find private traditions and neither do we find private languages. The integrity or authenticity of tradition is not derived from a repetition or persistence of a tradition over time. It is derived from the continuous work of interpretation by a group or a society in order to "identify the strands which bind present to past" (1994b, p. 64).
2 Traditions involve rituals which are practical means to ensure preservation. Rituals manifest traditions in practice. Rituals connect the con-

tinuous reconstruction of the past with concrete activities and enact-
ment.

3   Traditions involve a formulaic truth which attributes causal efficacy to
     ritual. Formulaic truths are often expressed in rituals and cannot be
     disagreed with or contradicted. They are an efficient means of remov-
     ing or preventing dissent.

4   Tradition has guardians who interpret tradition and function as media-
     tors between tradition and its causal powers. Guardians are not experts
     in a modern sense. They have special arcane qualities, and they are the
     only persons with access to the causal powers. This access is not com-
     municable to the outsider. It is status in the traditional society and not
     competence as experts in modern society which characterizes guardians
     and their position.

5   Tradition has a normative or moral content which gives it a binding
     character (1994b, p. 65). Tradition is not only what we do in society,
     but also what we ought to do. An example is marriage, which over a
     very long period has been seen as the only morally correct way to or-
     ganize a family.

In contrast to understanding tradition as something unchangeable, Giddens
stresses that tradition involves a continuous and active work of interpretation from the actors involved. Only active social actors create, through
interpretation and rituals, a solidarity and a guidance for the future.

Despite the fact that the Enlightenment contained an attempt to reject
the yoke of tradition, modernity and tradition coexisted in a special symbiosis for almost two hundred years until the 1960s. We find an example
of a modern tradition in Comte's claim that religion must be replaced by
science as the foundation of society. Science became a kind of tradition –
an authority – which could respond to problems and questions of almost
every kind. Concepts such as folk, nation, and education (*Bildung*) are
other examples of new traditions linked to the emergence of modernity.
These traditions were either invented or rediscovered and became articu-
lated in a new context. Also, new family traditions were constructed
just as the relations between sexes were redefined and resulted in what
we call the traditional pattern of sex roles, a phenomenon belonging to
modernity.

It is crucial to the society of today that tradition has been interrogated,
problematized, and undermined in such a way that no social activities or
actions can be carried out only guided and influenced by tradition in the
traditional sense. If we act with a point of departure in tradition, we are
always at some level conscious that it could be done differently. To act in a
traditional way requires justification, an explanation or a reason. I can claim

that we intend to get married or share the Christian religion because tradition prescribes it. In reality it is a choice (which can be more or less conscious), because we are well aware that we could live together in other ways than the traditional marriage or we know other people who have left Christianity.

Tradition becomes detraditionalized. Detraditionalization involves a form of "setting free" (*Freisetzung*), a thesis argued by Ulrich Beck and Thomas Ziehe. When the tie of tradition is loosened and the compulsiveness of repetition disappears, new opportunities are created for the individuals in society. With an increasing reflexivity and an undermining of tradition, more options are created for each individual, but this implies that more decisions have to be made.

Detraditionalization, however, does not mean that tradition completely disappears. We can find a number of examples where social groups have attempted to revitalize or defend certain traditions of religious, ethnic, or national character. The defense of these traditions often leads to fundamentalism. In other words, fundamentalism, which is a fairly recent phenomenon – the term dates from the beginning of the twentieth century, but was not included in the Oxford English Dictionary until the 1960s – has its origin in the defense of tradition. Tradition is defended in the traditional way – by reference to ritual truth (1999c). The defense of tradition takes place in a world which is global and cosmopolitan and asks for reasons. The problem is, of course, that traditions cannot be justified. They contain their own truth – a truth emphasized and presented in the very rituals. To defend a tradition in a traditional way is very problematic in a cosmopolitan world, because it is a refusal of dialogue in a world whose peace depends on it.

In a globalized and detraditionalized world with an increasing level of social and institutional reflexivity, we get a society with more clever people – not necessarily more intelligent people, but with more information. With this knowledge, all human beings – individually as well as collectively – are confronted with hundreds of options which require decisions to be made; otherwise they are made by others. Such a situation can be seen as a "setting free" of the individual but it is not a process of individualization which Giddens sees as more egocentric, egoistic, and narcissistic. Giddens claims that one characteristic of the post-traditional society is a process of individuation, which implies that individuals now actively have to work for trust in their social relations. Increasingly, social reflexivity involves the interrogation and undermining of tradition, and consequently tradition can no longer provide a firm set of norms and beliefs, which used to create trust. Now we have to negotiate about the conditions of all social relations; we negotiate about the norms and ethics which should form the basis of relations between man and woman, between friends, and between parents and children. The post-traditional society is a society in which social bonds have to be actively created. It is a dangerous and difficult project but also a project which is rewarding and opens up a number of opportunities. In terms of authorities, it is a decentered society. In interpersonal relations an opening up in relation to the other is necessary, and as a consequence new forms of social solidarity can be created. This is not necessarily an individualistic process because it forces individuals as well as social groups to generate trust in relation to the other. Only violence or dialogue are possible outcomes and, Giddens claims, dialogue is not necessarily less likely than confrontation.

The next section takes a closer look at the interaction between the general institutional changes and the individual human being.

Trust, Risk and Ontological Security

Trust

In this presentation of Giddens's modernity project, I have so far emphasized the institutional conditions, i.e. the general social conditions of our everyday life. In accordance with structuration theory (chapter 2), Giddens is aware, however, that modernity and thus the existing society are created and reproduced in social practice, i.e. in a reciprocal interaction between individuals' actions and societal institutions. In Giddens's words, society's institutions and structures are the means and the outcome of the agent's actions. Hence, globalization of institutions is only one aspect of the problematic of modernity. Another side of modernity concerns how our everyday life radically changes character and affects the most personal and intimate sides of the individual, including our self-identity. Giddens characterizes this as a dialectic between extentionality (the global effects) and intentionality (changes caused by our personal dispositions and choices). In other words, the process of change points toward an interaction between external changes, which are beyond our immediate influence, and local changes, which are results of our personal choice of life and lifestyle. Before we examine self-identity more closely, I will briefly describe the concept of trust, which is the concrete link between social structures and systems on the one hand, and the individual, the agent, on the other.

Society is conceived by Giddens as social practices that take place across time and space. The many actions and interactions that constitute social practice are bound together by relations of trust. Giddens distinguishes two types of trust relations: facework commitment and faceless commitments. These types of trust relations create the foundation for a society's maintenance. Facework commitments are trust which can exist when the agents are in the same place and interact directly with each other. Hence, the co-presence of actors is a necessity. This takes place when we eat dinner together, meet strangers in the street, or speak with the clerk at the post office. Faceless commitments are manifested in our relations of trust with society's abstract systems. Here it is a case of trust not in persons but in systems. For Giddens the concept of trust is therefore connected to the trustworthiness and reliability of a person or a system, as one expects a certain reaction or outcome of an action. One has confidence in the person's integrity, reciprocal love, or, in terms of the system, that certain abstract principles will be respected.

Giddens's point is that the character of trust relations has changed in the transition from traditional to modern society. Traditional society possesses small time–space distanciation, which means that much social interaction is face-to-face, and trust is thereby sustained by or expressed in direct contact with other people. Giddens cites kinship, the local community, religion, and tradition as the four elements that contribute to the maintenance of trust among people and make possible the traditional society. Tradition and religion provide the foundation of morality and values which regulate mutual actions among people.

Adherence to certain rules, created by tradition or religion, is the basis of security and therefore of trust among people. The framework for these relations of trust is most often the family and/or the local community. This framework changes radically with the appearance of modern society. Many relations of trust are still direct personal relations in family and community. But the significance of this form of trust has been reduced in favor of trust in abstract systems, as the very essence of modern institutions is connected to mechanisms of trust in relation to expert systems. The basic structure of capitalism, in all its variations, consists of several abstract systems which presuppose trust of the agents in order to operate. In our daily life we interact with hundreds of expert systems which are so anchored in our practical consciousness that we rarely reflect on our degree of trust in them. From the moment I open my eyes in the morning, I use several of these systems with great confidence. My house is constructed by expert systems. When I turn on the light in the bathroom, I also draw on a system constructed by experts. I do not need to know how electric particles move, or how electricity becomes light. I only need to know that the light comes on if I press the switch. If I am tormented by back pain, I come into contact with another expert system, the health service. My trust in this system is not only a blind trust in an abstract system. It also depends on my interaction with certain system representatives, i.e. doctors, nurses, and physical therapists. Such representatives, whom Giddens calls the access points to the systems, can be decisive for my trust in expert systems. If these persons can no longer legitimate the system, I may take matters into my own hands and choose an alternative system (if it is available). In the worst case, it can mean total powerlessness on my part.

In some cases we know that trust in these persons or systems may be risky. Although the appliance repairman repairs my refrigerator, I know it can break down again. I take a risk when I call him, but I am not always aware of the risk. Most people have never regarded industrial culture as a threat to humanity in the form of an ecological disaster. In fact, risk awareness did not exist prior to our modern era, and we may still be without a general recognition of its real significance.

The risk society

The concept of trust is closely connected with the concept of risk, and here Giddens draws upon the work of the German sociologists Niklas Luhmann and Ulrich Beck. To live in modern society involves risks. We have a calculative attitude to our actions in the sense that we constantly assess the extent to which our actions entail elements of risk and evaluate the probability of our actions obtaining the expected outcome. If the result does not correspond to our expectations, it can entail a danger. If, for example, I purchase shares on the stock market, I risk losing my money. If I drink up my salary, my wife may leave me. If the Western industrial countries do not significantly reduce their consumption of energy, we risk ecological disasters of unknown dimensions.

High-modern society is a risk society in which modern systems force us into a permanent state of risk. At the same time, modernity reduces the danger of certain risks compared to traditional societies. Hence, we need no longer die of small pox or starvation after a bad harvest, these risks having been removed by new types of systems which evolved with modernity. What distinguishes the premodern from the modern is not the emergence of risks, for social action has always been connected with risks. Rather, the difference between the two types of societies is a different risk profile. Whereas the earlier societies were primarily subjected to the vagaries of nature in the form of natural disasters, bad harvests, or epidemics, the situation is different in modern society. The problems caused by nature are essentially reduced, and instead conditions made by humanity create the greatest dangers. The risk profile of modernity entails that certain types of risks are globalized and intensified. Hence, the threat of nuclear war and its consequences are not local phenomena. The consequences of such a war are massive and intensive, as no one can avoid them. If changes occur in the international division of labor, they affect people throughout the world. Most risks, therefore, no longer stem from nature, but from human-manufactured environments, such as atomic bombs, nuclear power plants, industrial pollution, and over-consumption. Modern society consists of several institutionalized risk environments, such as the stock market and investment markets, which affect the life chances of millions of people.

The reflexive character of modernity is of such a nature that in several cases we possess a knowledge of the inherent risks. We know the danger of the atomic bomb, but the comfort, security, and trust we used to derive from religion are no longer available. The limitations of expert systems are widely recognized, which implies that we have to live with pragmatic acceptance of the modern systems. In addition, the modern risk profile entails an acknowledgement that an "Other" no longer exists in the sense that many risks do not respect the border between rich and poor, young and old, or power-holder and powerless. Unintended consequences of certain actions have implications for all of humanity. Nuclear war, the greenhouse effect, destruction of rain forests, and radioactive fallout strike randomly, and no one can ensure himself or herself of a privileged position and avoid it.

The consequences of modernity for ontological security

The modern human being lives with the duality where, on the one hand, we respect and trust systems, and, on the other hand, we feel a certain skepticism. We strike a deal with modernity, as it were, because we can neither live without it nor avoid it. Within the framework of modern society, we choose solutions which are, at times, very pragmatic. When we are ill, we cannot just reject the health system if our encounter with a system representative weakens our trust in the system. We seldom give up the entire system, but instead choose a new system representative. If I have back pains and physiotherapy does not help, I try another form of treatment. If the water is polluted, I purchase bottled water in the supermarket.

An important point here is that consciousness of this duality and the great knowledge about many societal risks often leads to a situation where we ignore or suppress this knowledge and avoid action. The list of risks and threatening problems is repeated so often that it appears boring. We are bombarded each day with news of the destruction of the rain forests, greenhouse effects, acid rain, nitrates in our drinking water, and the like. This bombardment of risk information entails a very specific pattern of reaction. Here Giddens cites various adaptive reactions, among them pragmatic acceptance, which entails an attitude that the world around is beyond our control. We suppress it and continue our lives as if nothing had happened. Another mode of reaction is sustained optimism, which implies that faith in the future continues. For example, some people have faith that the new technological advances can save the world (the technological fix). Cynical pessimism also occurs. Here the danger is clearly acknowledged, and cynicism is used to deal with anxiety through black humor, as in the film *Doctor Strangelove*. Cynical pessimism also entails a paralysis of action, in contrast to the radical engagement expressed, for instance, in many social movements, which exhibit a certain degree of optimism. These patterns of action, while certainly understandable, are not appropriate, says Giddens.

The increased reflexivity of modernity contributes to creating a radical doubt which is found at both the institutional and personal-existential level. We are therefore familiar with the dual character of modernity and the many risks. The radical doubt prevents us from having blind trust in all systems, and the existence of certain knowledge has thus disappeared. Instead, knowledge becomes hypotheses which can constantly change. What is seen as correct and fruitful today can be rejected and replaced by something else tomorrow. Today someone recommends a chiropractor for my bad back, tomorrow it is physiotherapy.

This doubt has great significance for our notions of trust and risk. When insecurity and many choices exist, trust in a person or a system is decisive for the choice being made. Relations of trust are therefore absolutely critical for a person's developmental and action potential, and the concept of trust is therefore critical for Giddens.

For Giddens, trust is closely connected to "ontological security." The foundation of ontological security evolves in the infant in relation to the mother and father. The child possesses a strong ontological security system if there are many strong, positive routines in relation to the mother. The trust that evolves between the child and the mother is a kind of vaccine which prevents the child from being exposed to unnecessary dangers and threats. Trust is thus the protective shield of the self, enabling it to handle the many new situations of choice which constantly appear. Consequently, trust becomes a necessary precondition and foundation for interaction with the abstract systems.

Trust in the systems and the risk connected with this trust are critical for ontological security. Ontological security constitutes the foundation of our own identity and confidence in the social and material world which appears before us. Trust in abstract expert systems creates trust in our everyday life, but it cannot replace either the mutuality or the intimacy of personal relations. Trust in impersonal principles and anonymous "others" becomes an unavoidable and necessary part of our existence. It creates a new form of psychological vulnerability.

The Self as a Reflexive Project

In this section I examine more closely the aforementioned "intentionality process," which concerns the personal choices we make in our everyday lives in the attempt to create and reproduce our self-identity. Furthermore, I discuss aspects of self-identity which create and are created by the institutions of modernity and which help to construct trust. Giddens emphasizes that "the self is not a passive entity, determined by external influences; in forging their self-identities . . . individuals contribute to and directly promote social influences that are global in their consequences and implications" (1991a, p. 2).

Our relations of trust, risk profile, and thus our ontological security system have in the past 20–30 years undergone radical changes with serious consequences for our identity. The institutionalized radical doubt, uncertainty, and the many situations of choice we constantly face influence the self and the identity's developmental process, and vice versa.

Ontological security is fundamental to human self-identity. It constitutes a protective cocoon such that the self avoids situations of strong anxiety and fear that might threaten our basic feelings of trust in the environment, and thereby threaten the integrity of the self. A strong ontological security gives us the capacity to develop a self-identity which enables us to recognize the existence and identities of other persons and objects. An agent in Giddens's universe is a person who must possess the ability to intervene in the world, make choices, and make a difference. In order to be able to make decisions, the agent must possess a self-identity. In other words, our self-identity with a high ontological security provides the foundation for our ability to give answers and models for solutions to the innumerable existential questions with which we are confronted in our daily life. Answers and solutions are necessary, for otherwise the self will be exposed to anxiety and chaos.

Yet what does Giddens mean by the concept of self-identity? Self-identity is not a given and constant entity, but a process. Self-identity must be continually produced and reproduced, something that takes place as part of the individual's reflexive, routinized activities and actions. Self-identity is when a person, in relation to his or her biography, views the self as reflexive. "A person with a reasonably stable sense of self-identity has a feeling of biographical continuity which she is able to grasp reflexively and . . . communicate to other people" (1991a, p. 54). The person's identity is not found in behavior and actions or in others' reaction to this behavior. Rather, the identity is found in the ability to maintain a unique narrative about oneself. This narrative, which constitutes the person's biography, cannot be a purely fictive narrative, however. It must constantly incorporate events which take place in the external world and simultaneously filter these, so that they can enter into the continuous narrative of the self. Besides the ability to keep this self-narrative going, a stable self-identity also requires other aspects of ontological security, above all knowledge and recognition of external reality, with objects and persons. The feeling of self-identity is simultaneously fragile and robust. Fragile because the biography with which the individual reflexively is working is only one narrative out of many possible narratives that can be told about the development of the person's self. Robust because it is linked to the strong ability of the self to prevent the conflicts, tensions and changes which the self encounters in the constant change of environments from undermining the feeling of identity.

For Giddens, self-identity must be understood as a reflexive project, in that reflexivity, which is so characteristic for modernity and its institutions, also pervades the very core of the self. In the premodern societies, kinship, gender, and social status meant that identity was largely established at birth. If someone was born into the German peasant class in the 1700s, it did not enter into his or her thoughts that he or she could be anything other than a peasant. External conditions as well as tradition determined one's identity. This changed with high modernity, where self-identity became exclusively a reflexive project for which the individual is responsible. We are not what we are, but what we make ourselves into. Consequently, life becomes a question of choosing and making decisions so that we can continue to maintain a "narrative of the self."

When tradition no longer provides us with a self-identity, the individual is more and more often confronted with the central questions, such as "What should I make of my life?" "How should I act?" "What should I become?" We reflect and answer these questions when we act. It occurs at both the practical and discursive level of consciousness. When I open the refrigerator and take out a bottle of milk, this action operates as a natural part of my practical consciousness. While pouring the milk into the glass, I might decide that in the future I ought only to drink skimmed milk due to its low fat content. The action, and thereby the decisions to change habits, is pushed to a discursive level (see chapter 2). An infinite number of times every single day, we are confronted with such thoughts and choices. And the choices we make become part of the continued narrative of the self, and hence of our self-identity.

It is important to point out that the body is an integrated part of our self-identity and a natural part of the self's reflexive considerations. The body is not viewed as a passive, external object. Giddens speaks of various bodily regimes as special areas where we learn a practice which can control our organic needs. He cites food, clothing, and sexuality as regimes subordinated to various forms of self-control. For example, many of us are constantly on diets. We choose among a myriad of food products each day, and to a great extent we decide how the food should be compounded in relation to our body and its appearance (1991a, pp. 56–63, 77–8). We attempt to control our body so that it fits into the reflexive project of the self. Eating habits and food are the means of creating and maintaining a special self-identity. Anorexia is an expression of an extreme attempt to control a bodily regime as part of an identity process, but it ends tragically when the body itself takes over control.

Choice of Lifestyle as Part of Self-identity

Modernity confronts the individual with an infinite number of choices but offers only limited guidance in how to make them. One consequence of such a situation is that the individual must choose a specific lifestyle. Lifestyle should be understood here in a broader sense than the style of consumption, with which it is often connected in daily conversation. Giddens defines lifestyle as

> a more or less integrated set of practices which an individual embraces, not only because such practices fulfil utilitarian needs, but because they give material form to a particular narrative of self-identity. . . . Lifestyles are routinized practices, the routines are incorporated into habits of dress, eating, modes of acting and favoured milieux for encountering others; but the routines followed are reflexively open to change in light of the mobile nature of self-identity. (1991a, p. 81)

Every single decision a person undertakes in his or her daily life, concerning matters such as habits of eating, clothing, behavior at work, and leisure time interests, contributes to these routines. Giddens does not claim that all possibilities of choice are open to all people. Education, gender, and economic ability influence the individual's possibility to choose. However, regardless of gender, social status, and the like, Giddens claims that in the era of modernity one is forced to choose a lifestyle as part of one's self-identity. Lifestyle contains a special set of practices which create the routines necessary for maintaining ontological security. A person with a given lifestyle finds it easier to choose, as certain options and certain types of choices lie beyond the lifestyle. An unskilled female factory worker does not have the possibility of choosing designer gowns by Karl Lagerfeld, a white Porsche, and a country estate. The chairman of the board of the Bank of America would hardly choose to eat hot dogs and hamburgers every day, even though nothing immediately prevents him from choosing these foods. Whereas material circumstances prevent the factory worker from acquiring expensive cars and the like, it is the chosen lifestyle that prevents the bank director from eating fast food every day.

There are several explanations for the many choices and opportunities offered by modernity. First, Giddens argues that we live in a post-traditional society, which means a society where tradition no longer constitutes the basis for our actions. Since society contains a modern reflexivity, we cannot simply refer to tradition. When tradition, and hence its associated moral code, disappears, society is pluralized.

A second factor, says Giddens, is modernity's time–space distanciation, which makes possible social interaction in many different contexts. In the course of one day we move through various environments of action: for example, the home, the train station, the train, the workplace, the supermarket, the local cafe, and back to the home again. These many contexts increase the number of situations in which we must make decisions.

A third factor which increases society's pluralization is the basic methodological doubt that pervades society. The reflexivity of modernity increases doubt, which again leads to the emergence of authorities. These authorities compete and contest the truth. Giddens cites the therapy market as example. When we seek therapeutic help, we are confronted by an infinite number of competing forms of therapy, all of which claim that they can help.

A final element is the media's transmission of experience. The growth and globalization of media has meant that 24 hours a day we can receive information from the entire globe which influences our choice of lifestyle.

We live in a society with many risks, risks which are created and prevented by abstract systems. When we have chosen and developed a lifestyle, we obtain better guidance for making the many choices. No one in our society can reject the many abstract systems that surround us. They are incorporated and used in the reflexive project of the self, and lifestyle decisions are synonymous with utilizing certain systems over others.

To select a lifestyle means that one acknowledges one's trust in certain abstract systems. But lifestyle choice not only concerns trust in abstract systems. It also involves trust in those persons who form one's closest circle of acquaintances. In the next section we will examine more closely how relations of trust within the area of intimacy have changed.

The Transformation of Intimacy

High modernity and its pervasive, intensive, and rapid changes of society have liberated the self and self-identity. Today's self is not a fixed entity but a reflexive project. In order to create a coherent self-narrative and thereby a self-identity, choices must continually be made, even in the area of intimacy. Here, too, the breakdown of the bonds of tradition has created an opening which means that the individual more actively has to choose his or her intimate relations.

Giddens points out that human relations of trust are being increasingly freed from external bonds, which are found outside these relations. As people increasingly commit themselves to abstract systems, the bonds to the family, home, and local community are weakened. These domains no longer provide the necessary relations of trust of the self. Abstract systems cannot fully replace the ontological security once provided by family and kinship relations. Consequently, the burden lies exclusively on the individual, who must create the intimate relations of trust necessary for the development of the self.

The individual therefore develops part of his or her self-identity in close and intimate relations, in what Giddens calls pure relationships. The emergence of the pure relationship is due precisely to the dissolution of the significance of external factors for the relationship. The term pure relationship refers to a situation "where a social relation is entered into for its own sake, for what can be derived by each person from a sustained association with another; and which is continued only in so far as it is thought by both parties to deliver enough satisfactions for each individual to stay within it" (1992b, p. 58). Close relations of trust with great significance to our ontological security evolve in social contexts in which the pure relationship is the prototype. We enter into several necessary intimate relations: sex, marriage, friendships. Earlier relationships of this character were subordinated to the fixed rules presented by tradition, something which is no longer the case, and consequently the involved parties must continuously and reflexively negotiate about the conditions of the relationship. It is unique in history that intimate relations are in principle subject to renegotiation every day and not bound to fixed normative and value systems. We choose not only a partner, but also the rules for the relationship.

Marriage was formerly subordinated to external conditions. Often it was arranged by the parents and/or entered into for economic reasons. Until the late 1960s the character of marriage was determined largely by external conditions. The division of labor, where the man was responsible for earning the daily bread and the woman took care of the house, constructed the framework for the marriage. These external conditions have disappeared in the Western world, and modern marriage or cohabitation – understood as a pure relationship (having nothing to do with sexual purity!) – has become a contract between two equal persons. If they can no longer achieve the desired satisfaction (emotionally, sexually, and so on), they have the possibility of leaving the relationship and starting over with someone else.

Friendships, like marriage and sexual relations, have also changed character. Friendship is an example of a specific form of pure relationship. In traditional society "friend" was a general term for all non-strangers, and there was therefore no distinction between friends and family members. This changed with modernity, where friendships could now be entered into for friendship's own sake. Friendship is a relation between two persons, both of whom desire to achieve mutual benefit; if this is not achieved, the friendship crumbles. We know from our own lives how several friendships are dissolved after our school or university years because "we no longer have the same interests." The friendship does not continue, as the two parties can no longer contribute to or gain anything from the friendship.

Marriage and friendship are examples of pure relationships. The stability and degree of development of such relations are conditioned by a high degree of mutual trust among the parties. It requires that the involved parties open up and disclose themselves and their intimacy. This process of disclosure can create the foundation for strong, intimate relations of trust. The process, however, is also risky, as the self can be fragile. If one experiences rejection after having disclosed oneself emotionally, this can seriously damage the self.

As the relationship is no longer bound together by external factors, commitment becomes a critical concept because now the parties make commitments to each other. For example, love between two people is conceived as a type of commitment which entails mutual agreement between the two persons involved. Mutual commitment, therefore, is also a key word in connection with pure relationships.

When all close relations now become part of the reflexive project of the self, our intimacy undergoes a transformation. Intimacy is subordinated to a continuing and reflexively organized process. As part of our lifestyle and self-identity, we are able to choose both what type of relationship and which person can become part of the development of our intimacy and/or sexuality. Sexuality, too, is now part of the reflexive project of the self. Plastic sexuality, freed from the reproductive demand and purpose, enables us to form and use sexuality in the development of our self-identity process. Sexuality in itself becomes an important part of our self-realization process, and thereby our identity development. Consequently, it can also become an important factor in the choice of partner.

With the concept of plastic sexuality, Giddens also points out that an individual's sexuality is no longer fixed once and for all. Giddens cites various studies, among them the Kinsey report, which reveal that many supposedly heterosexual men and women are not 100 percent heterosexual (1992b, p. 13). Sexuality is far more fluid than we usually think, and transcending sexual norms has opened a sea of possibilities for testing sexual limits. Again, the individual faces several choices.

To make it easier to choose, expert systems are constantly incorporated into our process of reflection. Each day, we may read about our intimate relations in newspapers, books, and magazines, and we evaluate commentaries by relationship experts, therapists, sexologists, psychologists, etc. The results of their surveys are incorporated into our practical and discursive consciousness and used whenever we reflect on certain situations or face difficult choices. When we have read in an article that one out of two marriages ends in divorce, we take this knowledge with us into our own marriage. Even though we have decided to live with our partner till death do us part, the awareness of divorce as a possibility and as a probability exists. By using this knowledge developed by expert systems, we are able to control a part of our everyday life, and we therefore become reskilled. However, the expert systems also deskill us. The great knowledge about production of goods, services, and the like, formerly possessed by the individual peasant or artisan, has now been taken over by specialized abstract systems which deprive us of the ability to control our work day.

The above should illustrate how modernity is synonymous with fundamental changes for both institutions and individuals. In light of these processes of transformation, individuals must create their own identities and lives. As a part of everyday life, people consequently attempt to affect and place demands on life and on the institutions that influence everyday life. The final sections look more closely at these political aspects of Giddens's analysis. A closer examination of Giddens's political project can be found in chapter 6.

Emancipatory Politics and Life Politics

The increasing institutional reflexivity, the development of more abstract systems, and the restructuring of social relations – elements that contribute to a strong interplay between local and global processes – are all key aspects in the transformation of modern society. What are the implications of these changes for the political agenda? Giddens attempts to comprehend these implications with the concepts of emancipatory politics and life politics.

Since the Enlightenment and the appearance of modern institutions, the struggle for human emancipation has been high on the agenda. Modernity meant primarily a break with the constraints and moral pressure of religion and tradition on the individual. Emancipatory politics is an attempt to remove the bonds of the past, which will enable a transformation and a future emergence of freedom. The general goal is to remove exploitation, inequality, and oppression, as justice, equality, and participation must be achieved in order to realize freedom. Emancipatory politics is therefore a struggle against the barriers to individual autonomy. Autonomy, the fundamental pillar of freedom, can only be achieved by the development of new abstract systems that guarantee an extended degree of freedom and justice (Cassell, 1993, p. 33). The basis of such a system, according to Giddens, is modern representative democracy.

Life politics requires a certain level of emancipation, i.e. equality, freedom, and justice. The fixed character of tradition and the unequal distribution of power in premodern societies must be destroyed before we can think in life-political terms. Life politics is about making choices, and it does not focus on the conditions under which we make choices – this belongs to the emancipatory political sphere. Life politics is politics about lifestyle and life decisions. Hence, it is about the politics of those decisions that concern the development of the self-identity.

The self is constantly confronted with existential questions where choices have to be made. As Giddens has pointed out, all fields are open for life political decisions, since all conditions of life are incorporated as a part of the reflexive project of the self. Even the question of our sexual identity has become an area of life politics. Today, we are not even limited by anatomy: we can choose our gender identity and shape and reshape body, gender, and sexuality according to individual taste. We can have sex without worrying about reproduction, and we can have children without having sex. This opens new options, but it also raises moral and political questions which become important for life politics. The issue of abortion is one example, because it raises fundamental questions about life, death, and the ownership of the body. What rights does the unborn child have? What ethical principles will control developments in gene technology?

Ecological problems constitute another area of life politics. The main reason for our era's focus on ecology is not our intensified intervention in and subordination of nature. Primarily, our attitude toward nature has changed. We know that nature is continuously being destroyed, and that only a change of lifestyle can save nature and the earth from an ecological disaster. Therefore, the individual's choice of lifestyle has global implications, as can the individual's choice whether or not to have children. The decision has consequences for the reproduction of all of humanity, since reproduction is no longer a necessary part of nature. The human species reproduces itself only if it decides to do so. This is a radical departure from the circumstances of premodern societies.

Giddens claims that life politics raises moral questions of the aforementioned character. Such ethical problems have been suppressed for years, especially because of the blind trust in several abstract systems. Life politics therefore becomes a question of developing new kinds of expert systems which can move the limits for the existing abstract systems that control and alienate us. But we must not simply develop new expert systems which maintain control over the everyday lives of normal people. Health is an example of how the individual has lost his or her body, which is today controlled by experts. Therefore, the goal must be to organize the health system in such a way that the alienating elements are reduced. Lay persons must use experts' knowledge to reskill themselves, so that they are able to take care of themselves and at the same time continuously and constructively cooperate with the experts.

The Juggernaut and Utopian Realism

There is a need for both emancipatory politics and life politics. The enormous dynamics created by modern abstract systems contains the potential to produce an apocalypse. At the same time, however, their power and energy contain many possibilities for resistance and reconstruction of social relations and of society. The process is further complicated by the disappearance of the ultimate forms of authority. The radical doubt is inherent in modernity, and we therefore find ourselves in a world without guarantees of any kind.

Inspired by Hinduism, Giddens uses the figure of the juggernaut to illustrate the developmental features of modernity. The juggernaut is

> a runaway engine of enormous power which, collectively as human beings, we can drive to some extent but which also threatens to rush out of our control and which could rend itself asunder. The juggernaut crushes those who resist it, and while it sometimes seems to have a steady path, there are times when it veers away erratically in directions we cannot foresee. (1990a, p. 139)

Giddens says the juggernaut's journey is not exclusively unpleasant and unrewarding. One often feels exhilarated and hopeful, as when the walls fall between West and East. However, the euphoria quickly disappears because the continued existence of the institutions of modernity means that the path and speed of the journey cannot be controlled. The numerous civil wars and ethnic conflicts now taking place are obvious examples. The terrain we cross is uneven and involves great risks. Modernity possesses an inherent ambivalence in which the feelings of ontological security and existential anxiety always coexist.

We must live with the duality, but should we try to steer the juggernaut? "Yes," says Giddens, but we must find new ways. It demands a special form of utopian realism, where we do not maintain the rigid division between realism and utopia. We must renounce the idea of historical subjects which create freedom equivalent to the role Marx assigned to the proletariat. History has no end point. The way to desired social changes demands connections to the "institutionally immanent possibilities" (1990a, p. 155). By this, Giddens means that institutions and systems always contain contradictions which can be exploited so as to achieve a more progressive development. Whenever power evolves in an institution, it simultaneously reproduces a counter-power (see the concept of the dialectics of control, in chapter 2). When, for example, the state increases its surveillance and control of the population, certain groups of people begin to exert pressure to increase influence in the form of rights. Increased military rearmament often leads to stronger resistance to the military and large-scale peace movements. These inherent contradictions create the possibilities for social change. If these conditions of resistance and change are to be understood and implemented, it demands a new type of critical theory, which must:

- Be sociologically sensitive and thereby sensitive to the hidden contradictions in the institutions of modern society that can be used to promote progressive forces on the path to a better world.
- Be politically and geopolitically tactical. By this, Giddens understands that moral convictions and "good faith" alone will not lead to the desired changes. On the contrary, it can be dangerous in a world of high risk. Hence, it can be naive and risky to carry out unilateral disarmament.
- Be model-creating for the "good society," which must be conceived not in a nation-state framework but globally and across institutions. If we are to promote greater equality among the earth's population, we must think in terms of societal models that transcend the narrow nation-state framework. The resolution of fundamental environmental problems cannot occur in the nation-state framework. The problems are global, and they demand a global solution.
- Recognize the fact that emancipatory politics must be linked to life politics. It is not enough to present emancipatory political demands for the removal of inequality and exploitation. These demands must be accompanied by demands for self-actualization via life political choices.

Various probable scenarios can be presented about the future, but Giddens maintains that it is important for our utopias to be made open. Otherwise there are no models to determine future development. Utopia can also mean a partial freezing of the openness of modernity, and this may help us to steer the juggernaut toward a goal, at least for a period.

In order to see how Giddens develops his own utopian realism into a political program we have to turn to chapter 6, which focuses on Giddens's recent shift into politics and political theory.

6

Giddens and Politics: toward Positive Welfare, Generative Politics, and the Radical Center

In recent years, Giddens has moved into the domain of politics. With a number of articles, mainly in the *New Statesman* (1994c, d, e, f, g, 1995b, 1996b, c, 1997, 1998c, 1999a), and the two books *Beyond Left and Right* (1994a) and *The Third Way – A Renewal of Social Democracy* (1998a), he has increasingly become much more concerned with political issues, including party-political matters. It seems that he – at least for a while – has left sociology and social theory behind in order to concentrate on politics.

Giddens has never operated with a clear-cut distinction between sociology and politics. Thus, he has worked with the sociological as well as the more political parts of the works of Marx, Weber, and Durkheim. Especially with regard to the two latter figures, he has paid attention to the political aspect of their works (1972a, 1986a). Moreover, his social theory has far from neglected the political dimension of social life. Thus, *The Nation-State and Violence* (1985a) stresses the role of the political and military aspects of social life in the development of the modern nation-state in Europe and later when this became a globalized form of political organization. He has, however, until recently, abstained from a more normative political discussion (apart from his contribution to a normative theory of violence in the final chapter of *The Nation-State and Violence*).

His more recent work on politics has some continuities and discontinuities with his previous works. On the one hand, there is clearly a shift from being interested in meta-sociological issues, including the dualism between actor and structure, rethinking the classics, and analyzing modernity and the post-traditional order, to his more recent involvement with normative political theory, his manifesto of third way politics, and his attempt to redefine social democracy. On the other hand, we see a continuity from his analysis of modernity, detraditionalization, globalization, and social reflexivity to his analysis of the welfare state and current politics and his attempt to provide a policy framework for modern social democracy. His sociological diagnosis works as a backdrop to his political thinking. The analysis of a post-traditional society with accelerating processes of globalization, detraditionalization, and social reflexivity is the point of departure for his contribution to politics.

I shall not repeat his analysis in this context (see chapter 5). This chapter first presents some of the challenges and dilemmas confronting the welfare state and the current political agenda. Today, the welfare state meets changes of a different kind compared to the first decade or two after the Second World War. Later in the chapter we shall take a closer look at Giddens's conception of democracy, and his ideas of generative politics and positive welfare. We continue with a focus on the third way project and his more explicit ideas of a renewal of social democracy. We conclude the chapter with a focus on Giddens's position versus dominant political theory, such as conservatism in different versions, neoliberalism, and socialism.

New Challenges to the Welfare State: the Alteration of Work, Solidarity, and Risk Management

Often, the welfare state is seen as a socialist project only. Giddens, however, points out that it has heterogeneous sources of origin going back to the late seventeenth century. The foundation of the welfare state mainly took place in the nineteenth century, when state and industry realized that it would be advantageous for all to support and protect the poor and the unemployed. The social insurance system in Bismarck's Germany was created to remove the threat from socialism. The mobilization of the workers' movement was also influential, but to a lesser extent than usually argued by most welfare theorists. Consequently, the skeleton of the welfare state was in place well before the Second World War, although the very term "welfare state" was first used years after the war.

The Second World War had a strong impact on the welfare state. The war itself involved a shift from income-specific to universalistic welfare programmes. During the war, people realized that they were all in the same boat. Bombs fell everywhere and everyone was at risk. Thus, after the war, a majority found it sensible to share risks among every member of society. The postwar years also brought the social democrats to power, or in some countries their power was strengthened. Consequently, the postwar years became dominated by a welfare state based upon two key socialist principles: centralized direction of economic life and the pursuit of greater equality. Giddens here points to the fact that the social democrats inherited a welfare state which was not entirely their own creation.

To characterize the fundamental principles of the welfare state Giddens emphasizes three important dimensions: work, solidarity, and risk management. When the welfare state emerged in the nineteenth century, work understood as labor in industry had a defining role in society. Work was, moreover, thought of as permanent full-time jobs occupied by the male population. Women's fate was domesticity. It is fairly obvious that work in this respect has changed and, therefore, it has challenged the originally designed welfare model. Now women participate in the labor force and pursue their own careers. The work itself has changed character. The number of full-time permanent jobs in industry has declined considerably. The industrial working class has been replaced by a middle class as the largest class. Even work itself as an important societal value is now questioned by many people, which symbolizes the emergence of post-materialistic values.

The second key dimension is the alteration of solidarity. The development of the welfare state was related to the consolidation of the nation-state. Welfare programs were used as a means to promote national social solidarity. At a time when globalization, according to Giddens, undermines the nation-state as a self-contained sovereign entity and also threatens industrial jobs because of global competition, national and social solidarity are under considerable strain. The processes of economic globalization threaten not only the economic basis of the welfare state, but also "the commitment of its citizenry to the equation of wealth with national wealth" (1994a, p. 140). Solidarity is, however, also under pressure from another side: the increasingly critical voice of the middle class. A critique has been formulated by the new right, stressing the problem of welfare dependency and welfare bureaucracies, and the "culture of contentment" thesis has been brought forward by J. K. Galbraith (1992). Galbraith asserts that the middle classes, who have benefited most from the welfare state, have now become resistant to it. A taxpayer revolt is looming. Giddens rejects both explanations of why the middle classes have started questioning the welfare state. According to Giddens, processes of detraditionalization and social reflexivity have led to a situation where the middle class feels constrained by the few choices provided by the welfare state. It is a uniform system with uniform provisions and very few opportunities to influence the provisions you want or need to use. Thus, the critique against the welfare state raised by the middle class is not necessarily an indicator of weakened social solidarity. Rather, it reflects fundamental social changes which require a redefinition of the concept of solidarity. This point is strengthened by the general changes in the class structure of post-traditional societies. The strong connection between class and collective social engagement has weakened with the expansion of reflexive modernization. Class used to be connected to a communal experience, but this has broken down. Traditional working-class communities have broken down. Class still exists, but has more become an individualized experience. Class is experienced less and less as a collective fate, and is more and more expressed through the individual's "biography" (1994a, p. 143). Class is no longer just defined by the relation to the means of production. The consumption dimension is as least as important, and consumption is a marker of social differentiation.

Another problem with regard to the solidarity dimension concerns the relation between promoting economic efficiency and redistribution. One of the failures of the welfare state has been the incapability to redistribute wealth and income to an extent where the gap between the well off and the less well off closed. A gap remains, and the problem has only temporarily been solved by an overall increase in wealth.

There is a close connection between simple modernization, the emergence of the welfare state in the nation-state context, and external risks (see chapter 5). Consequently, a society penetrated by manufactured uncertainty, detraditionalization, and globalizing forces undermines the national welfare state as a system of social insurance, with the aim of protecting against external risks. A society based upon a high level of reflexivity and manufactured risks necessarily leads to a society which is much more difficult to control. Risk management has to be redefined. Manufactured risks escape or confound insurance: "high-consequence risks . . . are risks the damage associated with which cannot be compensated for – because their long-term consequences are unknown and cannot be properly evaluated. They express 'a causality and a temporality that is no wide diffuse and extended' that they escape orthodox modes of attribution" (1994a, p. 152). Giddens argues that the welfare state is not mainly in trouble due to fiscal problems. Rather, the crisis of the welfare state should be linked to the problem of risk management. The risk management issue is further illustrated in the next section where we discuss the problem of ecology.

We now turn to some of the other problems and dilemmas the welfare state has to face today in order to survive the crisis which we have seen develop since the mid-1970s.

Five Dilemmas

Contemporary society and current politics are facing problems and dilemmas to which traditional political theory cannot respond. In the following, I outline some of these challenges as they are presented in *The Third Way*.

First, globalization is restated as a dilemma. Giddens carefully explains that globalization is not only an economic process. Globalization is about the transformation of time and space. The key problem of globalization concerns the implications for the nation-state. Has the nation-state become a fiction? No, Giddens says, but it has been transformed. Globalization removes the conditions of the Keynesian welfare state. It is no longer possible to use Keynesian economic management (1998a, p. 31). Globalization also pushes down problems. A number of local identities are emerging or re-emerging, with Quebec, Scotland, and Catalonia as recent examples. Moreover, globalization creates new economic and cultural regions across nation-state borders. Thus, Barcelona is a part of the southern French economy.

These processes affect the position and power of the state. Sovereignty is no longer a zero-sum game. Nation-states do not disappear because sovereignty is changing. In some respects the framework of the national government is expanding rather than diminishing while globalization proceeds. The nation-state retains considerable economic and cultural power externally, as well as over its citizens. But this power can only be retained by active cooperation with others – with its own localities, other states, regions, transnational groups, and associations. Giddens argues that we have to move from government to governance: "'Government' hence becomes less identified with 'the' government – national government – and more wide-ranging. 'Governance' becomes a more relevant concept to refer to some forms of administrative or regulatory capacities. Agencies which either are not part of any government – non-governmental organizations – or are transnational in character contribute to governance" (1998a, pp. 32–3).

Giddens is very much aware that globalization is not a force of nature. On the contrary, states, companies, and other actors have actively contributed to these processes. States actively took part in the development of satellites and the Internet; the financial world market is an unintended consequence of state action, since states needed money to finance their economies and the means was issuing bonds. Furthermore, privatization and deregulation were launched by the state. In other words, the state has never been a passive observer of these globalization processes, but it has been and still is an active player in this game.

The second dilemma is related to individualism. In recent years, it has often been argued that social solidarity is under threat from the rising individualism. A post-traditional order, with a pluralization of lifestyles, cultures, and values, involves societal changes with a new individualism. The key question is, however, how we can characterize the new individualism. To what extent is it related to the expanding role of the market? Are we witnessing a "me generation"? The questions have been approached from both left and right, and both sides are concerned about the development of a "me generation." The left explains it by market forces and Thatcherism and Reaganism, while the right claims that these problems are caused by the youth and student movements of the 1960s. Neither explanation is satisfactory to Giddens. He argues that the term "me generation" is a misleading description of the new individualism. The new individualism or, more precisely, individuation – a term Giddens uses elsewhere – must not be conflated with moral decay. Recent surveys show that the younger generations are more oriented toward moral issues. Younger people do not relate these value and moral issues to tradition. They do not accept traditional forms of authority as deciding lifestyle issues. These new moral values have a post-materialist character. The new individualism is closely connected to the welfare state. The welfare state has institutionalized a certain individualism by providing a set of individual rights, including the right to have an education and pursue a career. A society with a large number of people with higher education leads to a liberation from old patterns and tradition. Today, Giddens asserts, we are living in a period of moral transition, not moral decay. Thus, this individualism is not egoism and not immediately a threat to solidarity, but it implies that we must produce solidarity by other means. Being forced to make more active decisions concerning our lifestyles, we are also forced to be more responsible for ourselves and the consequences of our choices and decisions. Here there is a difference from the old social democratism, where collective provision was a dominant feature. The new individualism challenges the dichotomy between individual and collective responsibilities. A new balance must be found.

Third, the left–right dilemma is emphasized. The dichotomy between left and right in politics has always been and still is contested. The left–right distinction will continue to be relevant to an understanding of politics in the future but, according to Giddens, there are strong arguments for sustaining a claim that the importance and the character of the distinction between left and right has clearly changed in recent years. The left, in particular, has been transformed since the collapse of the communist countries. Earlier, a major difference between the two sides was the problem of the state–market relation. Now it is difficult to spot an alternative to capitalism. This is a severe blow to the marked difference. Of course, we will still have a discussion about the extent to which capitalism can be regulated, but even here the tension is smaller than just a few years ago. With the impact of globalization, a classical Keynesian interventionist policy cannot be on the agenda.

Another important dimension has changed the left–right dichotomy. Traditional emancipatory politics has not disappeared, but it has been supplemented with life-political issues, which are taking up more and more space on the political agenda. Value and moral questions, ecology, the importance of work in relation to life quality, and the changing nature of the family, including the choice to have children or not, are problems we all are facing and, as a starting point, none of these issues can adequately be conceived in relation to the right–left dichotomy. Moreover, none of the parties on the two wings can formulate policies which can be seen as related to right or left political ideologies. These issues simply break down the left–right distinction. The implications of technology and science, the European Union (EU), and devolution issues are also challenging the left–right distinction. Consequently, Giddens concludes that renewed social democratic thinking needs to approach these new problems in an innovative way, and this cannot be done from the old social democratic position on the left. Only a political thinking taking its point of departure from the radical center or active middle can encompass these issues and be capable of formulating a convincing and coherent response to these challenges.

> Nearly all the questions of life politics mentioned above require radical solutions or suggest radical policies, on different levels of government. All are potentially divisive, but the conditions and alliances required to cope with them don't necessarily follow those based upon division of economic interest. . . . Bottom-up alliances can be built, and can provide a basis for radical policies. Tackling ecological problems, for instance, certainly often demands a radical outlook, but that radicalism can in principle command widespread consensus. From responding to globalization to family policy the same applies. (1998a, p. 45)

The term radical mainly refers to the importance of implementing a comprehensive solution to problems common for the left and right, including the development of the welfare state, e.g. life-political issues, the question of an aging population and how to deal with it, and changing patterns of health and disease. The center does not mean an empty place, but a place where alliances can be built between various lifestyles.

Although Giddens argues for a move toward the radical center, he has recently sustained a center-left position (1998a). He argues that the problems of social justice, equality, and emancipatory politics in general will remain at the core of social democratic politics. The social democrats need to reform the welfare state in order to meet criteria of social justice. At the same time, it is important to "recognize and incorporate active lifestyle choices, be integrated with ecological strategies and respond to new risk scenarios" (1998a, pp. 45–6).

When a coherent political program has been developed, the perennial problem concerns the question of agency. This is the fourth dilemma. Who are the political actors? Who can implement the program? Who can govern? We often hear that politics has ended and globalization has led to an undermining of state and governmental power. Giddens rejects this claim, although, as already indicated, he accepts that changes have taken place in the political sphere. Giddens argues that state and government still have many tasks – in some areas even more than ever. Thus, a number of task can be listed:

- government is still an important means for representation and reconciliation of various interests;
- the state can regulate the market in the public interest and also promote market competition when monopolies threaten;
- by controlling the means of violence and providing a police force, the state can secure social peace;
- the state is the only organization to sustain a system of law;
- government has a direct economic role to play as employer, it provides an infrastructure, and intervenes in the micro and macroeconomic structures;
- the state possesses civilizing aims – "Government reflects widely held norms and values, but can also help shape them, in the educational system and elsewhere" (1998a, 48) – Giddens admits that this is a controversial point;
- the state can contribute to create regional and transnational alliances and pursue global aims.

Some of these tasks overlap with those of non-state agencies. The number of problems listed clearly demonstrates that state and government have not disappeared and are unlikely do so in the near future.

Giddens agrees with the German sociologist Ulrich Beck that societal changes, not least globalization and detraditionalization, have created a new sphere of politics: "the emergence of sub-politics." Politics and political activism have spread from the formal political sphere to other levels of society, not least single issue groups, NGOs, etc. While Giddens agrees with Beck that sub-politics has become more important, he emphasizes that single-issue movements and other sub-political actors have not replaced government and political parties. Governments have been forced to cooperate with them and will do so in the future, but state and government are still the prime political actors.

The ecological question is the fifth dilemma to confront modern social democratic parties. Much of the political innovation since the 1980s, in Germany in particular, has come from the green movements, and taking part in a process of ecological modernization is absolutely vital for modern politics and, therefore, for the renewal of social democracy. With reference to ecological modernization, Giddens (1998a, p. 57) refers to the ideas formulated by Maarten Hajer. We find: sustainable development in place of unlimited growth; prophylactics rather than cure; pollution equated with inefficiency; and environmental regulation and economic growth seen as mutually beneficial. These issues are closely related to modern social democratic policies, as these dimensions of politics can only be developed when government, business, and industry cooperate.

There are some conflicts inherent in this idea of ecological modernization which have to be faced: the tension between economy and ecology; the problem with proposing environmental solutions within the framework of the nation-state when the problems are global in nature. No one can pretend to have solutions to these problems, but the idea of ecological modernization has to come to terms with the conflicts.

The ecological problems in general raise two fundamental issues: our relationship to science and technology, and how we respond to risk. Scientific intervention in the body has transformed our conception of nature. Much can now be humanly achieved which previously was given by nature. Scientific and technological changes affect the whole population, and often we can observe major resistance to new advances or innovations. At a sub-political level, people respond to these changes because many have realized that we cannot leave all decisions to the scientific world itself. We have to interrogate and question science. Science cannot decide what is the good life for us, and we cannot be sure that science provides the truth. "They should be called upon to justify their conclusions and policies in the face of public scrutiny."

The risk problem has already been discussed (see chapter 5). In this context, it is important to stress that our society is exposed to a new set of risks which cannot be calculated or predicted in any sense. Even the existence of these risks is contested. The old social democratic parties developed a welfare state with a basic set of institutions which could cope with simple risks, such as unemployment or illnesses. The welfare state provided security for its members, but a rethinking of the welfare state must relate to the new sets of risks. The BSE crisis in the UK illustrates the problem. How can we develop institutions which can respond to these new types of risks? Is it possible at all?

Giddens attempts to meet the risk problem by taking an offensive approach. While admitting that we all are exposed to risks, he stresses the need for an active exploration of risk environments. Some risks have to be reduced as much as possible, while others, such as those related to investment decisions, are positive and inevitable risks if we want to change society in a better direction. "We all need protection against risk, but also the capability to confront and take risks in a productive fashion" (1998a, p. 64).

The challenges and dilemmas of the welfare state have to be met by contemporary politics. Giddens attempts to go beyond left and right. This step, however, requires a rethinking of democracy, which is an absolute precondition of a more coherent third way position. In the following, we shall see how Giddens defines democracy.

Democracy: Deliberative and Dialogic Democracies

Giddens's conception of democracy contains many features, but first and foremost it is related to the possibility of developing a new social solidarity and responsibility. As a foundation, he outlines a general and abstract understanding of democracy which is not bound to just one specific level of authority (supranational, national, regional, local) or to one specific political form of organization (e.g. the classical nation-state).

His reflections on democracy take their point of departure in the concept of the *deliberative democracy* (1994a, pp. 113–17). It is not representation versus participation but procedures which Giddens sees as the key to democracy. The central aspect concerns transparency in phases of discussion and decision-making. The most important thing is not procedures that ensure the correct and most appropriate solution to political questions, but procedures that ensure that discussions carried out before decisions are made are transparent and, in themselves, can legitimate the result.

Most important is democracy as a principle of deliberation and debate. The level or form of organization within which it takes place is not crucial. According to Giddens, a deliberative democratization can lead to more transparency not only in the formal political sphere, but also in the day-to-day life of the individual and in large global systems.

The concept of deliberative democracy is supplemented with dialogic democracy. With increasing individuation and globalization, individuals as well as groups are forced into new relations in which it is important to work actively for the development of mutual trust and confidence. Many social relations are sustained by dialogue – a dialogue which does not necessarily involve consensus, but which is sustained by common interest, since the alternative can be fundamentalism and violence.

Giddens sees dialogic democracy emerging in a number of areas outside the formal political sphere (1994a, pp. 117ff):

1   The personal arena and intimate personal relationships. Sexual relation-
    ships, marriages, friendships, and parent–child relationships are all
    relations which are undergoing tremendous changes. These relation-
    ships are moving toward the "pure relationship" where those involved
    enter into and sustain the relation for its own sake and only as long
    as it brings rewards (see chapter 5). The relationship in itself must
    be sustainable because it is not sustained by external conditions, e.g.
    economic conditions or external coercion. Consequently, the pure
    relationship is dependent on both persons opening up. This process
    is important for trust generation and mutual commitment. Intimate
    relations today therefore require a different responsibility and a
    mutual engagement, which requires dialogue and a moral of negoti-
    ating. Some of these preconditions for the development of a good and
    well functioning marriage or friendship are also preconditions for a
    well functioning political democracy. Consequently, Giddens sees a
    close connection between democratic dialogue at the personal and
    societal levels.
2   With the spread of social movements and self-help groups, there is a
    potential increase in dialogic democracy in society. These movements
    and groups open spaces for public dialogue and, as can be seen with the
    women's movement, they become agenda-setting in society. Self-help
    groups can potentially contribute to increasing the autonomy and com-
    mitment of the members of society. Giddens points out that a number
    of self-help groups are capable of reskilling their members by "wresting
    power from experts" (1994a, p. 121). Consequently, they can reclaim
    some of the power lost to experts during the past 30 and 40 years.
3   Within the area of organizations and corporations, many processes of
    democratization are taking place, and in this context better conditions
    for dialogic democracy have developed. The more general processes of
    individuation of society are now reflected in corporations and organi-
    zations. Organizations and companies must, therefore, to a much higher
    degree, create conditions for dialogic democracy if they want a good
    working environment and efficient production. Giddens calls this form
    of organization the post-bureaucratic organization. It possesses a higher
    degree of social reflexivity, and therefore it is better able to respond to
    a world characterized by manufactured uncertainty than the traditional
    top-down bureaucracies. The new forms of organizations are based upon
    active trust and mutual responsibility, and this extends the dialogic space.
4   The larger global order is also a domain in which dialogic democratiza-
    tion is on the agenda. Many global relations do not flow through the
    nation-states, but bypass them. For example, today we find a vast number

of global and international organizations and social movements, such as Greenpeace, Red Cross, and Amnesty International, which interact with states and non-state actors and organizations. Consequently, they contribute to developing a space for dialogue and a higher degree of democratization.

The creation of social solidarity is essential for a positive development of society. In this context, social solidarity is a process in the making, partly interrelated with the development of dialogic democracy, but also as a consequence of processes of individuation and detraditionalization. We are forced into solidarity with others because active trust, faith in and commitment to the other, combined with mutual responsibility, are necessary aspects of the development of modern self-identity. Giddens emphasizes that trust in personal relationship is connected to the acceptance of the integrity of the other. To know the other, to trust him or her, we must use the difference between us and him or her as a means to develop a positive emotional and active trust in communication. Trust in the other creates solidarity across time and space.

Where citizenship in Giddens's universe can imply affiliation and loyalty to several levels and various types of organization (nation-state, family, European Union), then trust, responsibility, and solidarity are the core of the concept of citizenship. In *Beyond Left and Right* Giddens does not focus on rights in relation to citizenship. Rights specify the autonomy of the citizen (and therefore belong to the domain of emancipatory politics), but rights do not define obligations – and obligations are central to post-traditional cosmopolitan citizenship. Obligations, however, are not to be conceived as the codified obligation of the citizen, such as conscription or tax. Giddens's conception of obligation is more abstract, and responsibility and commitment are more appropriate terms. At first, this focus on responsibility gives connotations of some form of communitarianism. However, this does not entirely seem to be the case, because Giddens is not suggesting a common set of values which could form the basis of solidarity in society. Values and responsibility are conditioned by processes which are continuously negotiated between all actors involved, individuals as well as organizations.

The dialogic space, in which these rules and values are negotiated, and the creation of social solidarity in intimate relations do not solve the problems of society as a whole. Today we can, however, observe processes of democratization at various levels which indicate that Giddens is not being entirely utopian when he argues for dialogic democracy. These tendencies toward democratization are seen mainly within the area of life politics.

Generative Politics, Life Politics, and Positive Welfare

At the time when new political issues – life-political issues concerning lifestyle choices – emerge on the political agenda, not least as a result of increasing manufactured uncertainty and the "end of nature and tradition," the traditional welfare institutions become constrained. The welfare state was originally designed as a repair mechanism when things went wrong. Today, a new type of risk management is needed which accepts that solutions and measures cannot always be implemented from the top, and welfare measures need to be more preventive, rather than just repairing when the damage has been done. Giddens advocates generative political programs which involve a more reflexive engagement with expert systems. Generative politics is about the development of relations of trust – trust between individuals and between individuals and expert systems. In a world of manufactured uncertainty, it is absolutely vital to generate trust. Trust is no longer inherited from tradition. With the end of tradition and nature as external trust-generating frameworks, trust has to be actively generated. Generative politics implies going beyond the traditional left–right understanding of politics. Generative politics involves a number of changes:

- generative political programs must provide some conditions which enable political ends to be achieved, without these ends and intended results being formulated and decided from above in the political system;
- conditions need to be provided which enable development and maintenance of active trust in relation to the government and other institutions;
- an extended degree of autonomy needs to be developed for those who depend on various welfare provisions;
- it is important to create mental and material resources which contribute to an increase in the autonomy of individuals;
- generative politics means a decentralization of political power, and decentralization and devolution are preconditions for an efficient political system, because "bottom-up" information and recognition of autonomy are fundamental conditions for efficiency.

Giddens mentions several areas in which generative political programs could be advantageous for all. Health is an obvious example. The problem of cancer is well known, and to combat cancer in a generative way we cannot only rely on treatment, but we have to prevent it actively at source. This involves us in life politics, where our choice of lifestyle is relevant for our health. To avoid smoking or certain types of pollution is important. Thus health care is not only our right, but also our own responsibility. Generative politics mixes educational, regulative, and material components, and therefore close cooperation is needed between governmental agencies, other organizations, and individuals.

A major problem to be approached is poverty, and this requires innovative solutions. The poverty issue does not only concern the welfare state and the discussions of the new underclass and new poverty. It is truly a global problem. Whether we focus on poverty in the First World or in the Third World, we need to reconstruct the problem along the lines of the idea of positive welfare. Poverty cannot be combated by welfare provision or international aid alone. Much more emphasis is needed on "mobilizing life-political measures, aimed once more at connecting autonomy with personal and collective responsibilities" (1994a, p. 18). By life-political measures, Giddens means, among other things, a shift of focus from a purely material conception of poverty and welfare to a redefined notion of a positive lifestyle with a focus on inner happiness and the relief of dependency. Concerning Third World poverty, an alternative development needs to draw upon existing experiences among local groups and movements in the Third World. Local attempts to reconstruct a sustainable economy and political autonomy, with a respect for local tradition and cultural heritage, are important starting points to improve life conditions. A basic concern in this development is damage limitation. Local cultures and the environment must be respected and to some extent preserved. Other key words are self-reliance and integrity, which means a reconstruction of local solidarities and a local support system. A better health care system based upon autonomy from Western health models is needed. Aspects of the Western scientific medical system need to be incorporated, but with an attempt to avoid its counterproductive tendencies (1994a, p. 161). Self-care and one's own responsibility need to be stressed. A policy relying on local experience and traditions must be combined with cooperation between states, businesses, and international organizations. Interventions from these actors need to be "generative in nature, sensitive to local demands and protective of local interests" (1994a, pp. 162–3).

Many of these ideas can be transferred to the problem of poverty in welfare states. Poverty and inequality do not enhance happiness. Consequently, we need to combat it, but we need to do so in new ways. Positive welfare means rethinking welfare beyond the idea of a passive repair mechanism. Positive welfare means preventive measures in the short as well as the long term. Also, the idea contains a redefinition of welfare. The very idea of welfare has to be connected to the Aristotelian problematic of pursuing the "good life." The good life and happiness do not necessarily mean material wealth, although a certain level is normally seen as a precondition.

Happiness is best "promoted by security (of mind and body), self-respect and the opportunity for self-realization plus the ability to love." Happiness in this sense is not necessarily entirely dependent on external material conditions. The traditional left focused on improving material conditions in order to achieve happiness but, according to Giddens, we need to focus on the inner experience, the inner dialogue, as well. Happiness is also, to some extent, dependent on how we *interpret* our life and life conditions (1994a, p. 181). Giddens is not suggesting that a better distribution of wealth is not important to happiness at all, but it is not the only aspect. He argues that happiness needs to be included in a redefined notion of welfare, and positive welfare as such is not necessarily connected to wealth. Positive welfare aims at creating conditions for the development of the so-called *autotelic self.*

> The autotelic self is one with an inner confidence which comes from self-respect, and one where a sense of ontological security, originating in basic trust, allows for the positive appreciation of social difference. It refers to a person able to translate potential threats into rewarding challenges, someone who is able to turn entropy into a consistent flow of experience. The autotelic self does not seek to neutralize risk or to suppose that "someone else will take care of the problem"; risk is confronted as the active challenge which generates self-actualization. (1994a, p. 192)

Central to happiness is the relief of dependency (psychologically as well as materially). To remove dependency is an overall aim in a society based upon positive welfare. However, Giddens sustains that this cannot be done without combating structural inequalities, which must still be one of the primary goals of positive welfare programs. But it is not only a matter of redistributing wealth from the wealthy to the poor, although it might in some cases be necessary. More important is a lifestyle shift among the affluent as well as the less affluent. So emancipatory politics and life politics must go hand in hand in a redefined program of positive welfare.

The Third Way

According to Giddens, most of the political theory we have inherited from the Enlightenment – conservatism in several versions, neoliberalism, and socialism – is unable to form the basis of a theory which can respond to the challenges of a post-traditional society (1994a, pp. 22–77). So far, we have mentioned some of the problems which the future welfare state has to

meet: a new conception of work, solidarity and risk management, economic polarization, ecological threats, denial of democracy, globalization,
and individualization. We proceeded with a presentation of Giddens's conception of democracy and new concepts such as generative politics, life
politics and positive welfare. These ideas provide the foundation for the
notion of third way politics. In the remainder of this chapter, I concentrate
on the contents of third way politics – conceived as a renewal of social
democracy.

The idea of a third way to a better society is far from new. It has been
used to label Mussolini's idea in Italy in the 1920s and 1930s, various
socialist strategies in Eastern Europe to oppose Stalinism and Western capitalism, and many other attempts to go beyond the state versus market problem in modern politics. Consequently, it is a term with many different
connotations, and in *Beyond Left and Right* Giddens actually distances himself from using it (1994a, pp. 68–9). Why did Giddens change his mind
and adopt the term in 1998? Because it has been widely used to designate
the Clinton–Blair policies, and one of Giddens main purposes with the
book *The Third Way* is exactly to provide substance to the British New
Labour Party's political ideas and perhaps even to push them in a certain
direction. One possible strategy is to accept the current political discourse
and then, from within, gradually reformulate whatever is possible and necessary. Consequently, it is not the term itself which is in focus in this chapter, but an attempt to grasp the substance of the ideas Giddens suggests. It
is worth noting that throughout *The Third Way* (1998a) he writes about a
renewal of social democracy. This is his real project.

Third way values

In a period of radical change and the exhaustion of traditional political
ideologies, we need radical politics. To move to the radical center means
developing a political program based upon a set of "third way values" and
combining aspects of philosophical conservatism, modernization, and the
critical part of socialism. Such a program is needed to guide citizens through
these changes, including globalization, and transformations in personal life
and our relationship to nature (1998a, p. 64). Giddens finds useful elements in the string of conservatism called philosophical conservatism because preservation is here a key notion. Preservation of nature and some
traditions are important in a rapidly changing world. Giddens wants to save
the preservation aspect from conservatism. He detaches the notion from its
original context embedded in conservatism, where preservation is based upon
tradition, authority, and allegiance. From socialism, Giddens emphasizes

that the persistent critical approach to society and dominant ideologies is a valuable asset which needs to be included in a third way project.

The third way program is based upon values such as equality, protection of the vulnerable, freedom as autonomy, no rights without responsibilities, no authority without democracy, and cosmopolitan pluralism (1998a, p. 66). The foundation is the apparently contradictory terms "philosophical conservatism" and "modernization." We need to modernize at the same time as we need to preserve. We need to respect local cultures, traditions, and history, and adopt a preserving attitude to environmental problems. We need to modernize in terms of democracy, government, citizenship; but the relationship between freedom and equality in traditional social democratic thinking also needs to be redefined.

There is a slight change in this set of values presented in *The Third Way* from the previous work *Beyond Left and Right*. Whereas Giddens is more unclear about the equality issue in his former work, he is unequivocal in his latest. Inequality is a problem because it reduces the level of freedom, although he admits there can be a conflict between individual freedom and equality. He stresses that social democratic thought cannot and shall not accept that high levels of inequality are functional for economic prosperity, but at the same time social democrats "should move away from what has sometimes been in the past an obsession with inequality, as well as rethink what equality is. Equality must contribute to diversity, not stand in its way" (1998a, p. 100).

A key notion in the new politics is "no rights without responsibilities." The state has a responsibility for its citizens, but whereas the old social democracy transferred rights to individuals as unconditional, Giddens emphasizes the necessity of claiming an extension of obligations. The increasing individualism which processes of social reflexivity and detraditionalization have generated requires a stronger responsibility. Thus Giddens mentions that, for example, the right to unemployment benefit must carry the obligation to look actively for work, and the government must ensure that this happens. In this context, it is important to stress that "no rights without responsibilities" as a principle applies to everyone in society – not only the poor and less affluent (1998a, p. 68).

Another ethical principle brought forward by Giddens is the idea of no authority without democracy. In a post-traditional society, authority can only be established and sustained via democracy. Tradition does not work as a means of legitimizing authority.

The third way political programs

What does a renewal of social democracy actually mean? With these third way values as a backdrop, Giddens develops an outline of a political program. He lists a number of key issues which must be incorporated in future social democratic politics (1998a, p. 70):

- the radical center;
- the new democratic state;
- an active civil society;
- the democratic family;
- the new mixed economy;
- equality as inclusion;
- positive welfare;
- the social investment state;
- the cosmopolitan nation;
- cosmopolitan democracy.

Giddens stresses that this framework is only a preliminary one which needs to be elaborated. Giddens accepts from the start some of the criticisms against the welfare state raised by the right. Thus, the welfare state is not democratic enough, since most welfare provisions are distributed top-down without any influence from the receiver. The welfare institutions are often too bureaucratic, alienating, and inefficient. It is stressed that welfare benefits too often produce perverse effects. Where the right sees these problems as the reason for dismantling the welfare state, Giddens sees them as a reason for reconstructing the welfare state.

Central to his reconstruction ideas are democratization, the democratic state, and the state–civil society relation. Giddens does not equate *democratization* with *democracy*. Processes of democratization go deeper and are overtaking democracy. Democracy is simply not democratic enough, and this is the source of the crisis of democracy. It is under pressure from processes of democratization which are taking place in close connection with the declining influence of tradition and the end of nature. Today, democratization is widespread in most areas of social life, including intimate relations, family, and work. What is needed is a reformulation of the role of state, democracy, and government.

How can democracy become democratized? How do we develop a *democratic state*? Globalization forces the state to decentralize power downwards to the regional and local levels as well as upwards to the international and global levels. This step does not necessarily lead to a decline in the sovereignty and power of the nation-state. On the contrary, it can strengthen the state because it becomes more responsive to processes which could otherwise outflank it (1998a, p. 72).

Another important necessary change concerns the fight against sleaze and corruption. State and government must extend the public sphere, which involves constitutional changes that create more transparency and openness. Consequently, in many countries, and not only the UK, it will require constitutional changes.

This leads to another problem concerning the present structure in many welfare states – the problem of inefficiency and mistrust. The state does not need downsizing, as the right is claiming, but a restructuring which improves services. Without arguing for privatization, Giddens is pointing to businesses as a source of inspiration.

How the state tackles the risk problem is, of course, important to Giddens. Giddens argues that crucial to the legitimacy of the state is the capacity for risk management. During most of history, the legitimacy of the state was based upon its ability to defend its domain of sovereignty in war. Since 1945, and especially since the collapse of the communist regimes in Eastern Europe and the USSR, this has changed. The state no longer has enemies, but dangers which need to be handled with close cooperation between government, experts, and lay people. Thus, the problem of risks cannot be left to the experts alone. Government must also deal with the ethical issues which arise from various risk problems, including many scientific and technological innovations.

A cosmopolitan outlook by the state is needed, which involves pressure for democratization at a global level. The downward direction of the process of democratization presumes a *renewal of civil society*. Here we see a change from Giddens's previous thinking about future politics. In *Beyond Left and Right* (1994a, pp. 124–5) he quite categorically rejects civil society as an answer to the problems of democracy. Now, he argues for the need for a renewal of civil society, not least because he has been convinced that a real decline in civic culture is taking place, involving a weakening sense of solidarity, more crime, and break-ups of marriages and families. However, these problems cannot be solved by civil society itself. A change to the better can only take place if government and civil society work together in partnership (1998a, pp. 79–80). "State and civil society should act in partnership, each to facilitate, but also to act as a control upon, the other." There are no permanent barriers between state and civil society. A highly reflexive society provides the basis for a high level of self-organization in civil society. Recent research gives evidence of such a development in the USA and the UK (1998a, pp. 80–1). Giddens stresses the importance of linking policies of community renewal to an open public sphere to avoid a separation of civil society groups from the wider society. An open public sphere is also very important at a local level, and it is the only way to develop and consolidate a process of democratization. Public includes physical space, because the disappearance of safe public spaces is undermining the opportunity to renew local communities. To walk around feeling safe is a precondition for generating the trust necessary to rebuild civic culture.

Moreover, it is stressed that a healthy civil society protects individuals from state power. On the other hand, the state must protect individuals from conflicts of interest in civil society. This is a logical consequence of Giddens's understanding of civil society as an entity conditioned by the state and not the reverse (1985a, 1998a). Civil society is not a spontaneous harmonious order.

The formulation of a positive family policy is important. The family is a highly sensitive area, and many of the current changes – with an increasing number of divorces, more single-parent families, and more children born outside of marriage – reflect new conditions of the family. It is neither possible nor desirable to recapture the traditional family (which in reality only existed to some extent in the 1950s), but it is important to recognize that we need to respond to many of these changes. In the detraditionalized family it is important to secure a balance of autonomy and responsibility. Giddens sees the break-up of families as a problem which is difficult to solve. However, it is important to enhance the ability to sustain relations through change, including divorces, and both parents need to take part in the responsibility for child care. Besides co-parenting, Giddens suggests life-long parental contracts where parents commit themselves to a shared responsibility regardless of a divorce. A precondition for a better family is a democratization which involves emotional and sexual equality and mutual rights and responsibility in the relationship.

The Social Investment State

A key player in the third way political program is the state, redefined as a social investment state. Throughout *The Third Way*, Giddens stresses the importance of creating a society in which we see a redistribution of possibilities in order to create a more inclusive society. Equality is put on the same footing as inclusion. The mechanism of exclusion must be limited, and we need to be more concerned about inclusion. Wealth creation and a dynamic society are necessary to avoid exclusion, and the state as a social investor is the most important means.

The state needs to invest in human resources and infrastructure. It has a role to play in a new mixed economy in which the public and private sectors are brought closer together within certain areas. Society can use market dynamics as long as the public interest is always kept in mind. We need to move toward a society of risk-takers in the spheres of government, business, and labor markets.

The new mixed economy does not refer primarily to a balance between state-owned and private industries. It refers to a balance between regulation and deregulation; and between the economic and the non-economic in the life of the society.

Giddens sees a part of the exclusion problem as linked to the erosion of the public realm. This needs to be rebuilt, but this can only be done by a strengthening of civic liberalism. Public space can be recaptured by the fostering of a more cosmopolitan nation, which implies a notion and feeling of membership of this community. Such a membership feeling increases the possibility of feeling commitment to others and thus increasing social solidarity. Moreover, social solidarity depends upon preventing the new corporate rich and the professional middle class from voluntary exclusion: society cannot bear a class pulling away from public space into a privately insured world. The social investment state must incorporate this part of the population into wider society and must target it by offering welfare to this class as well. It is important that welfare is not only linked to the poor and excluded, because that gives the idea of welfare a negative connotation. "Only a welfare system that benefits most of the population will generate a common morality of citizenship" (1998a, p. 108). Policy areas which, re-defined, can have an improved effect on inclusion include: improvement of public education and health care, reduction of environmental pollution, and strategies to reduce poverty.

In particular, education is emphasized by New Labour as the key to securing inclusion. Giddens accepts that education is important, but he is well aware that education in itself does not solve all problems. It reflects wider economic inequalities and education alone cannot create jobs. The latter is seen by Giddens as the answer to the problem of involuntary inclusion. A job gives access to an income, stability, direction in life, and it generates wealth to society as a whole. However, work alone does not provide inclusion. "An inclusive society must provide for the basic needs of those who can't work, and must recognize the wider diversity of goals life has to offer" (1998a, p. 110). Here Giddens argues that a society too focused on work and merely built upon a work ethic is not very attractive. A wider set of values is needed, and civil and political rights alone cannot create inclusion; basic social rights are also needed.

There is a hidden dilemma, and only with some difficulty does Giddens come up with a response to a situation in which people are either marginalized or close to total exclusion, receiving social benefits, but being pushed into changed behavior while unemployed. This change in behavior leads to dependency. On the one hand, Giddens argues for a change in the benefit system to enhance the pressure on the unemployed in order to force them into any job or into education, but, on the other hand, he argues the necessity of extended social rights, including the right to unemployment benefits.

Giddens advocates a strategy which provides members of society with resources. Only this step can promote a more risk-taking attitude. Each individual must possess resources enough to challenge himself or herself to give up benefits and go for work in another area. To supply people with these resources, the state needs to take an active part in investment in human capital.

The state cannot easily provide jobs; nor can a model continue which leaves people on benefits, because this just excludes them from the larger society. The state as a social investor must change strategy from conventional poverty programs to more community-focused approaches. The state here supports already established local networks and seeks to promote self-help and the generation of social capital, which, again, can help to create economic renewal, including jobs in local areas.

Giddens does not see deregulation as the answer to job creation, but welfare expenditure need to be invested in human capital. To reduce the level of unemployment and create better and more secure jobs, the state, business, and other organizations have to cooperate. Stronger and more partnership-oriented action needs to be taken by combining the focus of government and businesses to develop public projects where private enterprises are invited to play a larger role than used to be the case.

Giddens mentions old age provisions as another key area in which the social investor state has to be more active than previously. First, the government has to raise a debate about the tacit consensus that a certain age, 65 or 67, gives the right to a pension. Why are you old at 65? According to Giddens, this is just another typical welfare state constructed category which leads to dependency and loss of self-esteem for many resourceful people. Giddens suggests abolishing the fixed age of retirement, because many older people are a very strong resource, and they still want to contribute to the active labor force. Pensions should be more flexible and seen as a life-long investment from state, individuals, and other organizations, such as employer organizations. The money invested by all contributors can be used to finance education and old age pensions or to reduce work hours while bringing up children. By making it a personal decision to leave or stay in the labor market, Giddens argues, society will have a stronger, more flexible, and larger labor force and also more happy retired people.

To sum up, it can be said that the radical center argues for a reformed welfare state – a social investment state with a positive welfare society. This implies a state working in partnership with other agencies and businesses, but also a state responsible for generating and distributing positive welfare. A welfare society is not just a national society, but stretches beyond any border. A key feature of the positive welfare society concerns the shift toward more autonomy and the development of the self as a medium to strengthen individual responsibility.

Global and World Politics

Welfare state reforms are not an isolated Western phenomenon. These reforms are interrelated with global processes. Despite these processes, Giddens maintains the argument that the nation-state remains important and will not wither away. A strong nation-state, however, is no longer a state with strictly defined borders and the ability to defend itself by military means. Increasingly, we see a tendency for borders to become more fuzzy. For example, within the European Union we see strong regional economic cooperation between areas belonging to different nation-states, such as North Germany and South Jutland, or Catalonia and Southern France. Moreover, war as the extension of politics has disappeared in the Western context. Consequently, a strong state today is a state with the self-confidence to accept these new limits to sovereignty. Also, the modern nation must be prepared to respond to a changing world, including a new conception of nation and national identity.

Giddens maintains that national identity is still important, even if the world has become more multiethnic and multicultural. National identity is important as a source of personal identity. Only by belonging to a national community can an individual obtain an identity and ontological security which enables him or her to take a more cosmopolitan attitude to the surrounding world. Giddens argues for a cosmopolitan nation which is a more open and reflexive construction of national identity than the nation-building projects of previous generations. Nations in the past were propelled to unity through antagonism toward others, whereas today national identities "need to be sustained in a more open and discursive way, in cognisance not only of their own complexities but of the other loyalties with which they overlap. Implied is a more reflexive construction of national identity, a modernising project par excellence" (1998b, p. 20). Only a truly cosmopolitan nation can be multicultural. Multicultural politics can only take place with support from the broad national community. Only an open national community with a feeling of justice reaching beyond the local and specific groups, such as ethnic or religious communities, can provide a framework for multiculturalism.

Quoting David Miller, Giddens emphazises the necessary interdependence between an open national identity and multiculturalism: "Much more rests on the majority's sense of fairness than multiculturalists appreciate, and that sense of fairness is liable to be contracted if groups issuing demands reject the identity by which they belong in the same community as the majority" (Miller, *On Nationalism*, quoted in Giddens, 1998a, p. 133).

A key issue for the new cosmopolitan nationalism and multiculturalism concerns the problem of immigration, which is looming large in most European countries these days. Immigration forces the Western countries to reflect in a new way upon questions such as: "Who are we? What is it to be German?" A cosmopolitan nationalism is the only position that can contribute to dialogue between different national, regional, ethnic, and religious groups, and prevent fundamentalism and violent clashes.

The notion of a cosmopolitan nation opens up space for a reconceptualization of the political order, in which the previous sharp division between internal and external political issues is abandoned. It opens the way for a connection between national and global governance. Central to this development is the disappearance of large-scale warfare, fixed borders, and a weakening in the importance of territories, but also a globalization of the economy.

An indicator of the development of a global political order is the growth of cooperative organizations – the emergence of a global civil society. This, again, is a sign of democratization which needs to be strengthened because globalization also means transferral of power from nations into a previously depoliticized space. Thus, globalization has, to some extent, undermined national sovereignty and transferred power to the market. Here, we find a highly unregulated area in which many social actors are without fundamental rights and obligations. Only more concrete attempts to introduce global governance can contribute to a more stable and democratic development. Consequently, Giddens proposes further cooperation, stretching beyond regional cooperation, such as the European Union, NAFTA, or ASEAN. Giddens finds some inspiration in the regional models, the EU in particular, to promote a stronger global governance. At a global level he would like to see a representative body (parliament), an administration (similar to the EU Commission), an intergovernmental association (similar to the EU Council of Ministers), and a federal court of law (such as The European Court of Justice) (1998a, p. 144). In this context, he sees a possibility of incorporating and reforming the International Monetary Fund, World Bank, World Trade Organization, United Nations, and Organisation for Economic Co-operation and Development. The establishment of an International Criminal Court in 1998 gives him some optimism about the development of a global court with a cosmopolitan law.

It is important to note that cosmopolitan democracy is not only directed toward global governance. It also implies diffusion of democratization downwards to the EU and other regional organizations and then again at national and local levels, as mentioned above. The EU, for example, is an institution which provides governance above the nation-state level and at the same time reaches down to the individual. The EU is responsible for 75 percent of economic legislation and 50 percent of all domestic legislation across all member states (1998a, p. 142). This development seems to create a democratic problem, because the system contains little transparency and accountability. However, seen in a larger context, the EU is breaking barriers as a new model of global governance. Concerning the democratic deficit problem within the EU, Giddens suggests a strengthening of the European Parliament, but the enlargement process might also apply pressure for more democratic structures.

A further development of the EU model into a model of global governance is necessary. Without global governance and regulation of environmental policies and the world economy, Giddens foresees big problems. Let us leave aside the prospect of the great meltdown, either ecologically or economically, and just focus on the volatile finance system. Deregulation of the world economy and in particular the finance system has generated a system with inherent and recursive crises and volatility, with severe consequences for millions of people. Thus, the crisis in Indonesia created an army of beggars from one day to the next. Giddens rejects the neoliberal argument that these crises are just problem-solving devices which bring back the economy to an equilibrium. These crises are the result of untamed market fundamentalism. How do we regulate the financial market, where investors and speculators are seeking fast gains? The central aspect is creating a stable exchange rate and, in agreement with other scholars, Giddens proposes the introduction of the so-called Tobin tax. The idea is to tax currency exchange for pure financial speculation. Long-term investors, governments, financial institutions, and businesses will all benefit from such a move. Moreover, Giddens suggests an Economic Security Council in the United Nations system. These proposals are not too utopian; according to Giddens, it is a matter of political will.

The attempt to draw attention to the need for global governance is important. The problems of inequality and risk-sharing, which are high on the agenda of a renewed social democracy, need to be tackled both at a nation-state level and at a global level. We cannot continue to live in a world where a large share of states and people are excluded because of poverty. This is not only a problem concerning social injustice, but also an environmental problem: poor people (for good reasons) tend to ignore environmental problems more than people in the richer countries, because in their struggle to survive they cannot afford to be too conscious about the environment and future generations.

From Left and Right to the Radical Center: Beyond Enlightenment Thinking, a Conclusion

In his attempt to go beyond left and right, Giddens draws upon certain elements from traditional Enlightenment thinking, conservatism, liberalism, and socialism. He is, however, very critical because he finds these political ideologies exhausted and without a useful content for an adequate response to the challenges of contemporary society.

Giddens accepts some of the principles in liberalism and in the social liberal tradition, among other things the market, representative democracy, and civil and political rights of the individual, but he rejects market fundamentalism, moral individualism, and moral rearmament, which are found in neoliberalism in particular. Also, he finds several inconsistencies in neoliberalism which lead to an erosion of this political ideology. Thus, neoliberalism advocates a congruence between capitalism, the free market, and the nation-state. Stress on the free market is not compatible with a defense of the maintenance by a strong state of its sovereignty by military means. Capitalism is a dynamic force transcending all borders and it cannot be contained within national boundaries. Maintaining a strong defense capability is not to do with capitalism and markets, but with the international system of states and their positions within this system.

The strongest contradiction in neoliberalism, Giddens argues, concerns the encouragement of free market on the one hand, and the defense of traditional family values on the other hand. Capitalism and a radical free market philosophy cannot go together with a critique of the decline of morals in families and other institutions. Capitalism in the unregulated and unconstrained form is the strongest force undermining family traditions and values. When parents have to work on night shifts and weekends in an increasingly commodified world, it is difficult to see how traditional family values can be re-established.

Since neoliberalism is a political theory with strong inherent and insoluble contradictions, the solution could be to move to conservatism. Giddens rejects such a step, since most of these contradictions are also found in various strands of conservatism (1994a, pp. 22–50). The only variant of conservatism which attracts Giddens's interest is the so-called philosophical conservatism. The political philosopher John Gray has formulated a response within this framework. He argues that civil society is not merely a spontaneous order relying on the pursuit of individuals' interests, but depends on a "common culture" and "it is only by strengthening the resources of a common culture . . . that we can hope to renew the institutions of civil society across generations. To assume that we can rely on a regime of abstract rules is the merest folly" (quoted in Giddens, 1994a, p. 43). Moreover, he argues that an unlimited market will destroy the much needed common culture, and therefore the market has some limitations. Market principles are still important, but they should be separated from the unconditional endorsement of capitalism. An important point of Gray's version of philosophical conservatism concerns its relationship with the ecological movement and green thinking. Both intend to preserve and, therefore, a bridge can be built between the two positions when it comes to nature and environmental issues. Conservative thought and the green movement have both come to the conclusion that a world with continuous growth cannot be sustained.

Can this rethinking of conservatism form the basis for future politics? Giddens says no. Not even philosophical conservatism solves the inherent problem of conservative thinking, and neither can it work as a strong response to contemporary challenges. Giddens's critique of all sorts of conservatism is related to his sociological analysis of our society – the post-traditional order. As previously described, Giddens argues that the transformation of traditions is one of the most significant and important changes in the postwar period. The change in tradition in contemporary society is crucial to an understanding of why conservatism cannot be a successful response to the challenges our society is facing now and in the future. The failure of conservatism to understand how traditions are no longer traditions in the traditional sense is interrelated with the various concepts of tradition which predominate conservative thought. Here tradition is often conceived as continuity or inheritance.

Giddens's concept of tradition stresses that it contains an idea of rituals or revealed truth. To practice a tradition through rituals gives rise to authority. The role of tradition in a post-traditional society is constantly changing. It is no longer possible to legitimize authority just by referring to tradition and the ritual truth. Reflexive modernity, with increasing social reflexivity, interrogates tradition continuously. The transformation of tradition and the disappearance of nature indicate that tradition and nature no longer work as external frameworks for human activity. Today we have to decide about nature and tradition. We have to provide reasons for all social activities. Consequently, a conservative position is difficult to sustain, since here the fundamental principle is an unconditional defense of tradition. To defend tradition in a traditional way means to assert its ritual truth. This is an impossible position in a cosmopolitan society in which tradition is questioned and needs to be justified. A clear defense of tradition can have severe implications. Ultimately, it can lead to fundamentalism and violence.

Giddens concludes that the various types of conservatism cannot provide a foundation for modern politics. They have collapsed precisely because they have not been able to respond to the transformation of tradition and nature. Moreover, they have become self-contradictory. However, Giddens accepts that some traditions need to be saved or recovered in so far as they can be justified and provide "generalizable sources of solidarity" (1994a, p. 48). Social change no longer only means progress. Clearly, the preservation and renewal of some traditions and nature (environmental resources) are needed. Consequently, Giddens wants to save this preservation aspect from conservative thought, but stressing that the usefulness of these ideas depends on a detachment from their original context in conservatism.

As demonstrated, Giddens also has a critical stance to socialism. In *Beyond Left and Right*, he claims that the useful part of the socialist heritage is the inherent critical approach embedded in socialist thought. One of the major problems, however, concerns the belief in the control and coordination of economic activities – the problem of the so-called cybernetic model (1994a, pp. 66–9). When tradition and a low level of reflexivity dominated, it was possible to practice some sort of economic planning, which we saw with some success in the Soviet Union for a number of years, in most countries during the Second World War, and also in the Keynesian welfare states in the Western world for most of the postwar years. Some kind of cybernetic model proved to be successful in the phase of simple modernization. With the gradual disappearance of simple modernization, large-scale economic planning no longer worked. Social life, penetrated by globalization, detraditionalization, reflexivity, and many different lifestyles, is more changeable, and it is very difficult to predict and control demands and needs. Under certain conditions the cybernetic model did work, but when reflexive modernity gradually became a reality, the model broke down.

Giddens demonstrates a close tie between modernity and conservatism, liberalism, and socialism. This leads to the conclusion that with the emergence of a radicalized modernity – a post-traditional order – these political doctrines have been exhausted. They cannot provide the foundation for modern politics. Consequently, it has paved the way for going beyond left and right – the way to the establishment of the radical center (see above).

This chapter has presented the core ideas of Giddens's political thinking. *Beyond Left and Right*, articles in *New Statesman*, and *The Third Way – A Renewal of Social Democracy* are not only the first pieces of work from Giddens's hand with a political normative dimension, but also a direct intervention in the current political debate. This intervention addresses key issues and problems in the New Labour movement, but more generally he identifies challenges to the whole political system.

Giddens is pointing to important problems of the welfare model – a model constructed for a very different society. He is not arguing for a demolition of the welfare state, but for a reconstruction in order to modernize and respond to contemporary challenges. A new model of risk management has to be developed. Moreover, he is aware that a shift from government to governance is necessary to bring the local, national, regional, and global levels into closer agreement with each other. This is badly needed to govern and regulate the local and global systems. A volatile world economy and transnational environmental problems require a new model of governance.

Giddens demonstrates that classical and contemporary political theory has little to offer when it comes to an understanding of the contemporary world, and new ideas have to be developed. Giddens has contributed to such a new political program, but more substance and content are needed in terms of a more coherent political theory and more clearly developed policies (for a critical assessment of his political dimension, see chapter 8). Time will tell if and how his political project will be further developed.

7

The Post-traditional Society and Radical Politics: an Interview with Anthony Giddens

This chapter consists of an edited version of two interviews conducted with Giddens.[1] The purpose has been primarily to elucidate certain current issues as viewed through Giddens's sociological lenses. In this connection, parts of the main ideas of Giddens's book *Beyond Left and Right* (1994a) are presented.

The Post-traditional Society

LBK: In many respects your work can be seen within the context of the questions posed by the classical sociological tradition, concerning the problem of defining the modern social order and conceptualizing the transition from traditional to modern society. Like Marx, Weber, and Durkheim, you attempt a diagnosis of contemporary society, and in this connection you often use the term post-traditional society. Here you distinguish yourself not only from "the founding fathers," but also from contemporary sociologists who characterize our society as postindustrial or postmodern.

AG: There are several reasons why I use this terminology. Primarily I attempt to distance myself from concepts such as postmodernity and the postmodern. The postmodernists view our world as fragmented, which in my opinion is not the case. The development of society is to a great degree characterized by a duality between fragmentation and unification, between disintegration and integration. Today we can observe the dissolution of states, families, and friendships, but at the same time we see being recreated new units and relations which cut across the former bonds. For example, new surveys from the United States show that divorced families in some contexts develop both new and more social bonds compared with the classical nuclear family. The surveys also show that family members have more frequent contact with each other than earlier. So the post-modernists' talk of societal disintegration is not an unequivocal fact.

The very concept of post-traditional refers to a societal form where something special happens to tradition. For me, tradition has nothing to do with time. Tradition is when one claims that there can be found a truth in certain forms of ritual practice, as in getting married or allowing oneself to be confirmed in the church. For example, heterosexual marriage has until recently been an act which was carried out on the basis of tradition. This is no longer possible, as the tradition itself has changed character. We now know that most practices were formerly carried out with their point of departure in traditions, and we also know that there exist an infinite number of ways of acting. Therefore, all practice involves reflection and justification. We cannot immediately refer to tradition. Our society has become a reflexive entity.

LBK: Yes, you speak often of modern society's reflexive character. What does this mean?

AG: With the expansive development of means of communication and transportation over the past 200 years, a world has been created where knowledge and information are diffused with the speed of light. It has also strengthened what I call the reflexivity of modernity, which is a key concept for understanding our post-traditional society. The level of reflexivity in society has increased along with our ability to store and assemble information. Knowledge, which is diffused with great speed and to a global extent, is transforming traditions in the traditional sense. When women in the furthest reaches of China marry, this now occurs with a very different knowledge and awareness than it did just a generation ago. Marriage as ritual practice, and thus as an unambiguous truth, no longer exists. The Chinese women are to a large extent familiar with the concepts of divorce, cohabitation, and homosexual couples from other parts of the world, and they even bring this knowledge with them into their marriages. They are therefore forced to reflect over and justify their actions, which is different from a traditional act carried out precisely for traditional reasons and which thus needs no justification. This being said, it cannot be concluded that the increased options have made them more free or even emancipated. Rather, the cosmopolitan world, with its information which runs back and forth between different parts of the world, helps to confront us with other ways of thinking and acting. Over the long term, this can allow for openings, breakthroughs, and perhaps more authentic options.

Such a development has taken place at the political level, where the increased global reflexivity has meant that the European model of democracy in its various manifestations is now being diffused throughout the entire world.

Reflections on the Conditions of War in Europe

LBK: You have reflected somewhat over the importance of violence and war for social change. You have especially pointed out how the outcome of several wars created the Europe which we know today. How do you see the conditions for war today? You mentioned that the existence of the atomic bomb and the possibility of total war removes the conditions for large-scale war.

AG: Nuclear weapons and other large-scale weapons are double-faced: on the one hand, they are potentially more powerful than earlier weapons. On the other hand, they make weapons into something profoundly obsolete. Take Bosnia, for example. Large-scale weapons are not good for fighting small-scale wars. Conversely, the large-scale wars are too destructive to be fought anyway. These weapons have this baroque form, as Mary Kaldor pointed out. But along with this development we can observe an intensified globalization. Globalization produces new forms of fragmentation which do not necessarily coagulate around the lines of nation-states. To some extent they go forward, and to some extent they go backwards, so you find some of the old lines of fractures are rediscovered. For example, the old imperial patterns arise again, whereby we again see a fracture between Ottoman and Christian empires in Europe. These lines of conflict cut across Yugoslavia, which is an example of a place where these old fault lines of battle are rediscovered and again allowed to play themselves out. These things are closely bound up with globalization, in which fundamental changes arise in international relations which again change the nature of violence and war. This happens everywhere. But at the same time there exists the hope that we will achieve a world where most boundaries and territories are in fact agreed upon peacefully. But here we also have a tension, as we now observe that a main reason for the many years of peace in the Western world is due to the fact that one prepares oneself for war in relation to an external enemy. If one has clear-cut enemies, it creates the internal order, it creates citizenship! To prepare oneself for war without enemies is something positive, but it is also disturbing and difficult.

LBK: If we examine European developments, a part of this process seems to be marked by the formation of the image of the enemy. Some European intellectuals speak more about our common European identity. We stand on the one hand with a common Christian-Jewish-Greek background, and on the other hand we have the Muslims. Are we starting to develop new enemy images?

AG: I think the situation is far more complex. The European integration process is, rather, a symptom of globalization. The European Union is not a superstate or a national state. Nor is it a confederation, but something completely different. It is an entirely new political order where there exists a recognition of a new connection between globalization, locality, and political organization. There exists some evidence that it is a new political order which I believe could become a positive thing for the world. If, on the other hand, it turns round to the other side of the coin that the European Union simply contributes to rediscovering the old imperial divisions of conflict, which could be moralized in such a way that the emerging powerful right-wing groups could make use of them, it would then be extremely dangerous, and it would be used for the construction of an enemy image.

Personally, I don't think it is very likely, in any case not as a large-scale phenomenon. It will more probably influence specific groups or create tensions in certain areas. If you take Bosnia, for example, there has constantly been presented a criticism of the West's (lack of) effort. On the other hand, I think that despite the horrors of the war, it is important to emphasize that the civil war has not evolved into a wider war, nor have any of the larger nations desired such a war. This is very different from preceding events in the region, which led to the two world wars. And it gives good hope for the future because even though the world cannot function as a policeman in local conflicts, it is a fundamental step forward that the world now has the will to consider them as local conflicts.

Of course, we cannot say anything about the extent to which the old Holy Alliance will re-emerge, or whether Russia, Germany, or Japan will become aggressive states in the future. This kind of thing is possible. Germany and Japan certainly today possess the two largest plutonium stockpiles, precisely the two countries which on the face of things have turned their back on war. Most of these processes are double-edged, so I think that we should refrain from speaking of optimism or pessimism. Instead, we should speak in terms of risk, and understand risk as infecting all of our lives. Furthermore, we must realize that many important forms of risk cannot be calculated, they cannot be subjected to a technical table like in the way you can calculate the flood on the Chang Jiang river. I believe that all of us, not only in the academic world, are forced to think in this way.

For certain fundamental reasons, it is impossible not to think in terms of risk. It is linked to our society's detraditionalization. The more you have to make your life in relation to other possibilities, the more you are forced to think in terms of various kinds of possible futures and therefore in terms of risk scenarios. This is precisely what happens when you consider whether to live together with someone, marry, or simply have a sexual relationship. Your knowledge that the relationship can fall apart or the awareness about AIDS automatically leads to risk calculations.

Fundamentalism

LBK: A life with several risks must produce various reactions. But is it not true that most people cannot constantly live a life where they consciously attempt to face all the risks head on?

AG: No, of course not. Therefore, various life strategies develop where some people relate pragmatically to their life. Others are uncritically optimistic, with a modernizing ethos with an endorsement of progress, while others again relate skeptically or nearly cynically ironical to life, as, for example, some of the youth cultures or the Generation-X culture. These reactions are necessary because in a risk society there occurs a recognition that "everything is not just going to become better and better," or "that I can't be sure that things will work themselves out." In a society without ultimate authorities, there is no one who can make the decision for us. This is why neo-religious movements and New Age philosophies are coming on so strong today. And why fundamentalism can be so appealing in this context. I have been doing a good deal of research on fundamentalism in recent years.

By fundamentalism I mean tradition which is defended in a traditional way in a cosmopolitan world, where traditions are forced into contact with each other. If one is part of a certain religious tradition, tradition affecting the nation or gender, defending tradition in a traditional way means asserting the existence of a certain ritual truth. If you defend the tradition with traditional means in a world where you are constantly in contact with other traditions, then there arises a new risk of violence. This we observe chiefly in local violent conflicts in Bosnia. Therefore, I argue that fundamentalism can be found in any area which has been evacuated by local traditions, and where people in one way or another attempt to reinvent or cling to tradition.

Tradition should not be connected with something which has existed for a long time. Tradition is not about sedimentation in time. Rather, tradition involves viewing something as given, as a truth. Tradition contains certain views of truth and certain views of rituals and how these are protected. In my most recent work, I have tried to argue that traditions have guardians, while the modern secularized world has experts, and experts are something completely different than the guardians of tradition. To live in a world of expertise is entirely different than living in the world of tradition. And when the two clash, various possible fault lines appear.

Since the world today is of such a character that tradition is no longer isolated and protected but is constantly exposed to pressure from either other traditions or the expert society, this leads to many conflicts. The recent flowering of fundamentalism around issues of, for example, family values, abortion, religion, or ethnic affiliation is an expression of a post-traditional social order. Our society is characterized by a condition of tension between communication, fundamentalism and violence. When tradition is evacuated, then it often leads to fundamentalism, which means a defense of tradition in a traditional way. This entails that you do not listen to others, and it easily leads to violence, which we see in the American abortion debate, in Bosnia, and in Iran. Groups of people attempt to maintain and recreate traditions in a world which is not positively disposed towards these. The reaction therefore becomes a purification of traditions. The ethnic cleansing in Bosnia is one example. Globalization affects local traditions and the attempt to give these a new and pure form is certainly a part of ethnic purity or a renewal of the idea of ethnic purity.

Tradition versus Modernity

LBK: The concept of tradition comes to be of great importance for your analysis of modernity.

AG: Yes, I am very interested in this problem. When I began to study this aspect more closely, I became surprised that there is no literature in this area. Everybody talks of traditional societies, and anthropologists take for granted that tradition is something which has existed for a long time. In my opinion, this view is not very reasonable, especially because we seldom have records to verify when and how long a certain traditional practice has existed. For me, all traditions are something invented. They are invented because special groups in the population could use these traditions to create and maintain power. There is some sort of dialectics between tradition and inventedness.

For example, as Ulrich Beck says, in the early years of industrialization you get a reinvention of tradition. A reformulation of gender traditions arose which implied an invention of a particularly desirable family form (the nuclear family), the persistence of some forms of masculinity, and certain relations between men and women. These traditions were especially important for the stabilization of early industrial society. Now, however, these traditions are breaking down because of the women's movement, because of women's entry into the labor market and for other reasons. The traditions are being strongly interrogated, and a great deal of what today takes place in society is bound with such changes, which are of a global character. When women throughout the entire world attempt to break with traditional forms of marriage in order to change their lives, we may speak of a global revolution. This is connected to the transformation of nature. In the traditional sense, nature is often linked to the external landscape. The external given nature no longer exists, as it is organized and formed socially and technologically. Nature's disappearance occurs together with the disappearance of tradition, and in my discussion of reproduction and reproductive technologies you find a mixture of the two factors. One observes processes of detraditionalization coupled to a process whereby relationships which used to be natural now have to be decided about by somebody. For example, having a child today does not necessarily have anything directly to do with sexuality. There is no longer the need for any kind of sexual contact to occur between two persons in order to have children, and having children no longer has any necessary direct connection to the nuclear family.

The Global and the Local

LBK: The global changes and thereby the subversion of traditions also affect other aspects of our everyday life.

AG: The increased reflexivity creates fundamental doubts in our daily life. Earlier, science functioned on an equal footing with tradition as an authority we could trust. Today we construct our relationship to science on a widespread skepticism, as we know that researchers are in disagreement and are always finding new results which contradict the previous ones. When we are confronted with a serious illness, we are seldom content with the doctor's diagnosis. Perhaps we seek a second opinion, seek out an acupuncturist or another alternative form of treatment. We find ourselves in a more questioning and interrogative relationship to science. We have realized that our lives are too short to wait for the results of science. This means that the individual is constantly confronted with choices. We ourselves must choose whether to eat butter or margarine, quit smoking, drink coffee, and so on.

LBK: So globalization and reflexivity have an influence on our self-identity and body?

AG: To a great degree. We are pushed out into a world which creates new forms of anxiety. Just think of the entire complex of problems centered around eating disorders, anorexia, and bulimia. These phenomena hardly existed just 20–30 years ago, only as a quasi-religious phenomenon in the nineteenth century. Technological developments have entailed that food production, processing, and distribution no longer take place in a coherent process in a local community. With container transport, the emergence of deep freezes and supermarket chains, food production and consumption have also become a global process whereby the entire world, in any case the western part, now are on a diet. We receive goods from all over, and we are constantly forced into a situation with a great number of choices about how we shall eat in relation to our appearance and lifestyle. This in turn creates an enormous pressure on the individual, who has sole responsibility for creating his identity, his lifestyle, his appearance, and his status. This can lead to eating disorders in many people.

It is important to maintain, however, that this development is not only anxiety-creating and fragmenting. Fragmentation interacts with the possibility for achieving much more autonomy in your life than anyone ever had before. The interesting thing, however, is the connection between the possibility for autonomy on the one hand and addiction and compulsion on the other. Addiction and compulsion as phenomena started to be recognized in the late nineteenth century. You get the term addict emerging about the same time as Foucault's term homosexual and notions like that emerge. First of all, it is mainly alcohol and drug addiction, but now there is this tremendous everyday literature on ordinary addictions. One can be addicted to work, coffee, nicotine, going on holiday, exercise, sex, or food. As mentioned, it is food addiction which is especially hazardous, and it can obtain fatal consequences. Anorexia is a kind of addiction, as it entails an attempt to control the body and the self.

One can discuss why addiction is so widespread today, but I believe that it is bound up with these changes affecting the self and tradition. Addiction and compulsion are traditions without tradition, which is to say that the past has a kind of emotional hold on you. It is not rationalized into a larger social and ritual order. The rituals have become personal rituals. It is a secular form of disintegrated tradition.

I find sexual compulsion or sexual addiction especially interesting, because it is linked to violence. I have been trying to develop the idea that men are more violent towards women today than earlier, in any case in everyday life. This is because there was once a traditional control system over women, which largely operated through men's violence against other men. The patriarchate used to depend upon the fact that if you as a man did not follow the norms of the sexual system, other men would punish you. If, for example, you had relations with a women with whom you were not allowed, and perhaps even made her pregnant, then her kin group would probably punish you. Today men can no longer exert sanctions in this way. The patriarchate no longer functions according to principles. I therefore believe that we are now experiencing more violence directed specifically against women in an attempt to control them. This is difficult to document, even though some research indicates that rape or domestic violence, for example, have presumably become more frequent today than earlier.

The Transformation of Intimacy

LBK: In one of your most recent books you speak of the change in intimacy. How do we characterize these changes?

AG: It is clear that the processes of global reflexivity also apply to the individual person in relation to his most intimate love and friendship relations. With the transformation of tradition, the kin group obtaining less importance and we ourselves creating our self-identity, our choice of partner and friends also becomes a part of a reflexive process which enters into the creation of our identity. We therefore attempt to live in the pure relationship. The pure relationship as an idealtype means that a person enters only into a relation for its own sake, and the relationship lasts only so long as the parties achieve sufficient satisfaction of needs. The two involved parties negotiate the form and content of the relationship, and the relationship is in principle always subject to renegotiation. Most couples and friendship relations operate this way today. Earlier, these relations between people were often founded upon external social and economic relations. This applied especially to marriage, which was a contract determined by economic considerations.

Modern friendships also exhibit these characteristics. Friendships today are entered into because both parties wish to get something out of the friendship. Perhaps work or leisure-time interests stimulate the initiation of the friendship, but it lasts only as long as the relationship to the other is positive for its own sake.

The pure relationship is a reflexive relationship which is constantly evaluated and negotiated. Only as long as it can operate as something positive for our self-identity is it possible to remain in the relationship. It therefore has a very open character, which enables relationships to dissolve more easily, but as mentioned, also allows such relationships to be re-established with new partners.

LBK: What significance does plastic sexuality have in this connection?

AG: Beyond the reflexive, open character of the pure relationship, the emergence of what I call plastic sexuality has great significance for the liberation which has taken place in intimate and friendship relations. Plastic sexuality entails that sexuality is disengaged from the purpose of reproduction. Sexuality becomes manipulable and can be molded into our personality. It becomes an important part of our identity formation and suddenly becomes especially important to many intimate relationships. The degree of sexual satisfaction can constitute an important element of the pure relationship. If mutual satisfaction is not obtained, it can easily lead to the dissolution of the relationship.

LBK: In several places you claim that it is especially men who have been having problems with the pure relationship. Why is it the case?

AG: Yes, because as I mentioned before, masculinity is subjected to pressure. Until recently, men could find self-identity in work and status, but have forgotten that identity also contains an emotional dimension. Men have sought their emotions in women and have made themselves dependent on women to maintain their masculinity. But with the liberation of women and the greater autonomy which the pure relationship entails for the woman, the man's emotional dependence on the woman is breaking down. Hereby the man loses control over his own emotional safety net.

We are then back to the problem of traditions which are subjected to change. The traditional masculine role no longer exists really. Nevertheless, there are attempts to revive it, and in extreme situations it is defended by violence. We see today an increasing tendency to domestic violence and men's violence against women, which are indications that men are losing control over their sexuality and over their own emotional basis.

LBK: Nevertheless, you believe that the pure relationship contains potential?

AG: Yes, absolutely. With the emergence of the pure relationship, there lies a potential for a democratization of private life, which over the long term cannot avoid affecting other areas of life. The pure relationship foreshadows great possibilities not only in sexual relations, but also between parents and children and other forms of kin and friendship relations.

The democratic aspect in the pure relationship lies in the very conditions of the relationship. When a relationship is initiated, the involved parties enter consciously into certain conditions for the relationship's content and form. In principle, a kind of constitution is established. Via our reflexivity, these conditions are considered during the continuation or dissolution of the relationship. The prerequisite for this process being able to take place is not only respect for the other, but also an opening up of the self. An intimate and emotional disclosure is therefore a necessity if the pure relationship is to be developed and maintained. In this intimacy and mutual respect for each other and our mutual autonomy lies the democratic potential.

Radical Politics: Beyond the Political Right–Left Problematic

LBK: In your latest book, *Beyond Left and Right*, you discuss the possibility of developing a radical political program which would transcend the endless discussions between right and left wing in the political debate. How do you see the radical politics of the future?

AG: Since the beginning of modernity and the Enlightenment, we have had a clear idea of the social development of the future, and which politics had to be carried out in order to achieve what we wanted most. We have based this politics on the clear view that the more we knew, the more we could control. But these ideals of the Enlightenment do not correspond to the world of today. We live in a cosmopolitan, post-traditional social order in a runaway world. It is a world with many inherent elements of insecurity and risk. And these elements cannot simply be removed by more modernity, progress and knowledge. We live in a manufactured uncertainty; that is, an uncertainty which does not derive from nature, but which is inherent in the humanly created world. Our world today is globalized. Globalization entails a closer connection and a greater reciprocal effect between the local and the global. It also means profound changes of time and space, everyday life, as well as a diffusion of the social and institutional reflexivity. Precisely this reflexivity process is the main cause of inherent manufactured uncertainty of society.

This globalization and the connected change process undermine the conditions for the dominant ideologies, especially socialism, liberalism, and conservatism. It is often claimed that it is primarily the left wing which is in crisis. This is not correct. Conservatism is also in crisis. It stands in a dilemma where on the one hand it desires to maintain certain values, but on the other hand supports the free unfolding of the market forces. It is a contradiction, as there can hardly be found a single mechanism which breaks down traditional family values, for example, more than the market forces.

Instead we must formulate a political program which directs itself towards local, national, and global conditions. The program should have four axes. First, we must explore the interesting connection between certain parts of conservatism and the ideological basis of the green political movements. Conservative thinking, as far as I can see, is manifested in three forms. There is the New Right, which attempts to defend traditional values with traditional means. This ends up in a fundamentalism, even frequently in neo-fascism. The second manifestation is the classical conservative thinking which I also label philosophical conservatism, with a focus on preserving and which perhaps has a more skeptical attitude towards the free market forces. Finally, we have neo-liberalism, which with its uncritical praise of free market forces destroys all forms of tradition. All three forms contain several contradictions, but philosophical conservatism is interesting because it discusses several of the societal problems which today are very relevant and central; problems such as how we develop social solidarity, and problems centered around the family, children, and relationships between generations are raised in this conservative tradition. No satisfactory answer is given, but several of our society's most pressing problems are in fact subjects which have been raised primarily by the right. The conservatives thereby bring important elements onto the political agenda, but do not facilitate the necessary models for solving them. However, it is interesting that the philosophical conservatism has several themes in common with the green movement of recent years. Both are interested in conserving, and both understand that continued modernization is not necessarily progress or good. The conservatives place emphasis on the family, on bonds between generations, and on preserving nature. The greens operate with the same themes, and precisely here one can build a common bridge which can form the basis for a part of the themes which must dominate the radical political agenda of the future. The destruction of nature and the destruction of solidarity must be halted. We must be concerned with solidarity and the preservation of nature, but not in a traditional way nor by traditional means.

Second, we must develop a more positive critique of the welfare state. There can be no doubt that the society which constituted the basis for the construction of the welfare model no longer exists. The welfare state, as mentioned, did not develop within a cosmopolitan, post-traditional world. It is therefore not adequate as a societal model. However, the recent years' strong attack from the right and the corresponding attempts at defense by the left have not been useful. The critique and the defense have been negative. All too often, the problems of the welfare state have been represented as a fiscal crisis. The right claims that we are paying too much, and that we instead ought to allow the market to govern, while the left says that the welfare state model can be saved if we just pay more. This is simply not the way forward. It is not a tax question but, rather, a question of the welfare institutions which are no longer in keeping with the times. These institutions were developed for a society with a fixed order, fixed lifestyle, fixed habits, with reasonably fixed relations between the sexes, a specific family form, etc. The state was a kind of repair mechanism, which intervened when problems arose. The welfare state's crisis is connected with the lack of possibilities for controlling a risk society.

In our times, the institutions must instead be adapted to a far more reflexively organized society. They must no longer be based primarily upon intervening and picking up the pieces when the damage is done. Rather, the institutions must to a greater degree be oriented towards people ordering their own lives by their own efforts and own involvement. A problem with the welfare state is dependency. This applies to the unemployed, the elderly, and other groups. The elderly are a good example. After Bismarck invented the welfare state, the elderly were viewed as a problem for society. When they turned 65, they were to go on pension, and thereafter became dependent on the state. This is a form of disqualification. Today, people between 65 and 80 possess many resources which are totally lost when they are maintained in a state of passivity. They must instead be considered as a resource which can be used. This is what I mean by a positive critique of the welfare state. The goal is to develop institutions which can contribute to creating happiness, which in many ways is more important than equality. Happiness means that you must evolve a reasonable life for yourself, such that you come to terms with some of the more existential parts of your own life.

The third program point concerns a further development of the democratic dialogue. The potential for democratic dialogue is found in intimate relations, couple relations, and global relations. The main goal must be to develop some institutions which can enable this dialogue to take place between all the levels.

The final point is the problem of violence in society. As mentioned several times, the problem of violence is considerable, both globally and locally. Therefore, the radical politics of the future must contain a normative political theory dealing with violence.

Note

1   The two interviews were conducted in Aarhus and Copenhagen in September 1993 and June 1994. I am grateful to Giddens for his willingness to undertake four hours of conversation. This version has been translated from the Danish edition.

8

Giddens's Social and Political Theory: Some Critical Viewpoints

Giddens's sociology and social theory, a wide-ranging project developed over a 30-year period of research, contains theoretical development and critique, a contribution to a theory of the state, and an analysis of modernity. Most recently he has added a more explicitly political dimension to his project. Over the past decade and more, various aspects of Giddens's project have been subjected to debate and critique (see, for example, Kiessling, 1988a; Cohen, 1989; Held and Thompson, 1989; Clark et al., 1990; Bryant and Jary, 1991a; Craib, 1992a). This chapter summarizes some of the key points which have been raised, and these are supplemented with some of my own critical viewpoints (Kaspersen, 1991, 1992a, b, 1993). In particular, I examine seven aspects of Giddens's social theory, sociology, and political theory: (a) the critique of classical and modern sociology and social theory; (b) Giddens's position within philosophy and the theory of science; (c) the theory of structuration; (d) the critique of historical materialism; (e) the state project; (f) his analysis of modernity; and (g) his contribution to politics. Finally, this chapter places Giddens in a context of the history of social theory and discusses his significance for the development of social theory.

Giddens's Critique of Classical and Modern Sociology and Social Theory

Giddens utilizes his critical theoretical reading to create a platform for his work. He reviews the four general theoretical schools (action theory, structuralism, Marxism, and functionalism) and points out their specific features. He then applies these special characteristics to construct idealtypes[1] which reflect the key figures in the various theories. The choice of the core components of these idealtypes, however, is determined by Giddens's problem, and not by the theories' own problematic and basic structure. Hence, his method implies some kind of arbitrariness, and he does not attempt to understand a theory on its own premises. Since he ignores what is essential or non-essential to a theory as seen from the theory's own perspective, he also has difficulty capturing its main nuances. Including these aspects in his considerations would have improved his discussion of the attempts by the various theories to reconcile the structure and actor perspectives. One is left with the feeling that Giddens's reading and interpretation is often very literal and somewhat simplistic. Giddens makes grand generalizations which are all too often problematic. In discussing structuralism, for example, he compares Saussure, Barthes, Althusser, Foucault, Lacan, Piaget, Lévi-Strauss, Derrida, and Kristeva. I find this untenable, as there are marked differences in their views of the concept of "structure." Moreover, the aforementioned theorists are also embedded in different positions within the theory of science.

One example of Giddens's somewhat unsophisticated interpretations of these theorists is his treatment of Louis Althusser and Talcott Parsons. He repeatedly maintains that Althusser neglects human action and considers people as determined, passive automata or "cultural dopes," and here compares him with Parsons. Giddens commits a serious error on this point. Althusser and Parsons do not regard human agents as automata. Rather, as Paul Hirst points out,

> they ask how it is possible for men to function as agents. Agency is not a mere given. The answers both give may be less than satisfactory, but they do ask pertinent questions. If human agents were wholly determined by the structure of a mode of production, then the questions Althusser asks in his paper on "Ideological State Apparatuses" – how is the subject constituted as an agent? how is its conduct patterned although not pre-determined? – would make no sense whatever. (Hirst, 1982, p. 82)

There can be no doubt that Giddens's version of structuration theory is an eclectic project, with bits and pieces selected at his whim from the entire spectrum of sociological and philosophical theories. I nevertheless believe that by working within a Wright Mills sociological imagination, Giddens makes this eclecticism reasonable and fruitful in many contexts. It is strongly doubtful, however, whether this method can entail any theoretical innovation.

Giddens's Position within the Theory of Science and Philosophy

What of the conditions under which social systems undergo change? How is social change handled in structuration theory? One thing to make clear is that it does not offer a theory of social change. No generalized account of social change (such as that offered by historical materialism) is possible in the social sciences, because of the erratic element introduced into history by human knowledge of history – or more accurately, by the reflexive appropriation of conditions of social action. (Giddens, 1990e, p. 303)

As indicated from this quotation, Giddens rejects analyses of social processes which explain development or change by invoking a single cause. However, he does not deny that social science must contribute with causal explanations. He praises only those explanatory models which incorporate several factors (multicausal explanatory models) and which always base the explanation in a specific historical context.

Why does Giddens claim that social sciences cannot and must not produce laws of general character, and why does he consider contextual multicausal explanations so essential? This question brings us back to the classical discussion within the philosophy of science between positivism and hermeneutics. The point of controversy between these philosophies of science lies in the relation between the natural and the cultural/social sciences. Positivism asserts that there is no difference between the physical and social order, and both worlds are causally determined. Both worlds thus contain a law-determined development. Therefore, similar methods can be applied to the study of laws in both the physical and the human world. Hermeneutics agrees with positivism with reference to nature. The great difference can be localized in the view of the cultural sciences, as human beings constitute a quite different object than the physical world. In nature there exist physical laws, whereas society consists of people who act on the basis of values and intentions which at any time are unique. Moreover, human beings can reflect upon their values, intentions, and actions and they can change behavior. This prevents us from deducing universally valid laws. This uniqueness therefore entails a special method, hermeneutics, the art of interpretation. Giddens anchors himself in such a hermeneutic philosophy of science. As he points out in structuration theory, humans are knowledgeable and reflexive, and can therefore always change their behavior. Since human beings are unique, and since actions and the consequences of actions, both intended and unintended, can be unpredictable, it requires contextual analyses, i.e. analyses that are always placed in a

specific social and historical context. Such a hermeneutic point of departure has some general implications for structuration theory itself. The problem is of a philosophical character. Giddens is well aware of the difficulty of
establishing a sociological theory on an epistemology which avoids subjectivism or objectivism. This is an unsolved, perhaps unsolvable, problem of
philosophical character. His "solution," therefore, is to push epistemological questions into the background and allow the ontology to come out into
the light (1984a, p. xx).

Directly against Giddens's intentions, this type of strategy creates an epistemological problem instead of solving it. With his ontology, Giddens
attempts to legitimate the validity of structuration theory with a postulate.
Structuration theory starts from the premise that reality is constituted by
social practice, "human being" and "human doing." A more fundamental
discussion of the character of ontology and reality is excluded. How do we
know that this is reality? Derek Layder emphasizes that "the question of
what we take to be the basic features of social reality is inseparable from
questions relating to the procedures we adopt in coming to know this reality" (Layder, 1987, p. 30). Thus, ontological and epistemological questions are inextricably linked. Such an ontology calls for an epistemological
explanation. Giddens claims that social reality consists of social practice.
Giddens makes this assumption with support in hermeneutic philosophy.
In this way, however, we have returned to one of the problems that Giddens
has explicitly attempted to avoid: the dominance of philosophical and epistemological problems over sociology (1984a, p. xx).

Giddens runs into another problem by separating epistemological and
ontological questions. The moment that ontology, and thereby reality, has
become demarcated as such from knowledge of this reality (epistemology)
and thereby from thought, one is automatically placed in a new subject–
object position. If it becomes a postulate that the existence of an already
given social world is of a given character, then the (epistemological) object
becomes separated from the knowing subject. Being is thereby conceived
as a given entity which exists independently of our thinking. The process of
generating human knowledge (the knowing subject) thereby takes place
only on the precondition that something exists, the object, prior to our
thought. It does not seem to help Giddens very much to assert that the
production of knowledge takes place via a double hermeneutic circle, which
runs in and out between sociology and the lay person. The separation between the real object and the knowing subject (the researcher) has already
occurred at the very moment when the researcher, in this case Giddens,
bases his sociology on an ontology. As the objective of Giddens's
structuration project is precisely the transcendence of this dualism between
subject and object, the project must in this respect be said to have failed.

The Theory of Structuration: Some Critical Remarks

Most critics agree that the dualism between actor and structure is a fundamental problem for all of social science. Most of them, therefore, praise Giddens's project and his efforts to find new paths. Several observers, however, have also offered various criticisms. One group of critics, including Thompson (1984a, 1989), Archer (1982, 1990), Layder (1985), and Livesay (1989), point out that Giddens places too much emphasis on the actor aspect and gives too much leeway to the agent's possibilities for action at the cost of the action-constraining aspect, the structural framework.

The problem of structure

J. B. Thompson (1989) is of the opinion that Giddens's point of departure in the agent, and his definition of structure as certain rules which the agent utilizes in his or her practice, gives the theory a bias and underemphasizes the constraining aspects of structure.

Thompson argues that the definition of structure as rules (and resources) creates confusion rather than clarification. It blurs important questions and gives the concept of structure a loose, abstract character. Society contains various kinds of rules, but the study of rules is different from (and at another level than) the study of social structures. Thompson further notes that if Giddens sought to more precisely point out what rules are relevant for concrete social structure – capitalist society, for example – it would entail a "criterion of importance." Some rules are more important and some more constraining than others. The criterion of importance cannot be derived from the rules themselves; hence, an analysis is needed which is separate from the study of the rules.

Thompson concretizes the problem by pointing out that Giddens lacks a concept of structural differentiation. As an example, he mentions that access to higher education is socially differentiated. Access to higher education differs for different groups of people. In order to investigate this differentiation, the population can be placed into certain categories based upon assumptions about the social structure. For example, it is assumed that the social structure contains individuals with various backgrounds in terms of sex, income, status, region, or ethnicity. This categorization, determined by the social structure, can contribute to an understanding of the structural differentiation in relation to education. The differentiation cannot be grasped solely through a concept of structure, which is based mainly upon the notion of rules.

According to Thompson, the problem arises because Giddens's concept of structure has evolved via a comparison between language (*langue*) and speech (*parole*). The very definition of the concept of structure as rules and resources can be traced back to this source. The inclusion of rules in the definition is – as shown above – the core of the problem. Instead of considering structure and action as complementary entities, as does Giddens, Thompson proposes that we see them as antagonistic poles in a relationship of tension.

Morphogenesis versus structuration theory

Margaret S. Archer (1990) agrees with Thompson. She is an exponent of a "morphogenetic approach," which considers the processes which evolve or change the form, structure, or state of a given system. Furthermore, the goal of her theory is to examine the specific structural elaborations more closely. Archer claims that elaborated structures, although created by practice, have properties which cannot be reduced to practice alone.

Giddens's structuration theory fails to discuss fixity, durability, or a fixed point in a development as consequences of practice. Structuration is always a process, never a product, because of the dynamic interaction between the two constitutive elements in the theory.

Archer instead emphasizes the difference between the first and initial interaction processes and their final product, the social system: "Action is ceaseless and essential both for the continuation and further elaboration of the system, but subsequent interaction will be different from earlier action because conditioned by the structural consequences of that prior action" (Archer, 1990, p. 76). In order to distinguish between actions in their origin and the finished structural form – the product – an analytical dualism is maintained when the structure–actor problem is discussed. The morphogenetic perspective is not only dualistic but also sequential; it analyzes social processes as a number of endless cycles of structural conditioning moving to social interaction moving to structural elaboration. Consequently, the dualism is maintained, and the objective is to expound and clarify the interaction between structure and actor. By contrast, structuration theory makes structure, action, and system into coherent, inseparable entities which enable us to conceive both aspects, but the theory never produces a concrete analytical instrument with which to grasp the problem. The theory, according to Archer, becomes sidetracked as it cannot specify when more voluntarism than determinism is likely, or vice versa. The problem is analogous to that raised by Thompson.

It is important to emphasize that Giddens has difficulty answering the "when" question. When can actors be transformative and alter the given frameworks? It requires a specification of the degree of freedom. When are they "imprisoned" in routinized activities? If such questions are to be answered, a clarification of the constraining character of structural properties is necessary. Giddens states that structures are both enabling and constraining. Archer, however, insists that one of the tasks of sociology must be to investigate which aspects of a social organization determine the connection between the enabling and constraining dimensions. Giddens does not do this.

Giddens aspires to construct a theory of society. He is not interested in answering questions of who and when. Precisely this problem has led to criticism from, among others, Thrift (1983, 1985), Bertilsson (1984), and Gregson (1986, 1987, 1989), all of whom claim that although structuration theory is interesting and perhaps transcends some dualistic problems at a theoretical level, it is inapplicable in empirical research. The theory's abstract level, obscure concepts, and neologisms weaken its fruitfulness.

Giddens and the Concept of Culture

Despite Giddens's enormous production, he never provides a concept of culture. In an interview he touches on the problem:

> In *Central Problems* [*in Social Theory*, 1979a] I tried to argue that the theory of culture would involve a theory of signification and coding systems in relation to a duality of structure notion in respect of everyday social practices, and that's where I'd see an analysis of culture lying. Basically, I just don't think that I tried to produce one. (Bleicher and Featherstone, 1982, p. 68)

Giddens elaborates on this point in "Structuralism, poststructuralism and the production of culture" (1987a, b), but he is unable to develop an actual concept of culture. Instead, he attempts to link his concept of signification with cultural production, and these concepts are combined with theoretical aspects from structuralism and post-structuralism.

It is important to emphasize the lack of a concept of culture, because it has consequences for sociological analysis. Giddens's theory emphasizes how the agent's day-to-day life has the character of repetition and routine, and it explains how the agent draws upon structures consisting of rules and resources. He does not explain, however, why people act differently, why rules and resources utilized in action are not the same for all, or why the agents have very different practices. Here a culture concept would have provided the possibility of examining people's various forms of everyday life, and how this life manifests itself in concrete terms.

Structuration theory allows no possibility of analyzing cultural differences. As an illustration, we may take a seamstress, a lawyer, a retired policeman, and a shopkeeper. Their day-to-day lives are quite varied, their daily activities are differently structured, and they have entirely unequal possibilities for action. Neither can Giddens's theory account for the differences in the actions, as he does not oppose the value and norm systems of the various agents (and cultures). The same problem applies to the time–space aspect. The time–space perspective is interesting, but it appears as a universal, generalized concept without any specific meaning. It is evident that action must be considered contextually. Action is located in time and space, but time and space are not the same for all people. The constitution of time and space is determined by cultural dimensions.

Giddens's Critique of Historical Materialism

Giddens's polemic with historical materialism is his jumping-off point for the development of a non-evolutionist, non-determinist social theory. It is therefore important to examine the degree to which Giddens's critique of historical materialism is justified. Historical materialism exists in many variants, but in Giddens's version it often appears in a vulgar or an orthodox Marxist variant. This can be partially explained by the emphasis he places on certain parts of Marx's production. When he criticizes Marx, he frequently cites *The German Ideology*, parts of the *Grundrisse*, and the Preface to *A Contribution to the Critique of Political Economy*. His reading is fragmentary and selective, and does not possess the sensitivity which seems both reasonable and necessary when the aim of one's critique is historical materialism as a whole.

Another problem is the neglect of nearly all Marxist theoretical traditions which have evolved since Marx, and which in fact deal with some of the problems Giddens points out. Hence, Giddens ignores the Leninist tradition, Althusserian Marxism, the Frankfurt School, and neo-Gramscianism, to name just a few of these schools.

Several theorists (e.g. Appelbaum, 1988; Sayer, 1990) praise Giddens's work, but point out that Giddens misses the point in his critique of parts of historical materialism, as Marx can be read entirely in the spirit of structuration theory. Hence, Sayer mentions that there is a very close correspondence between Marx's and Giddens's methods.

As mentioned, Giddens claims that there are no universal laws in the social world, and consequently no basis for theories based upon explanatory propositions of a generalizing type. For Giddens, generalizations are possible only within a specific spatio-temporal context, and only if the agents share some form of consciousness and understanding. Sayer claims that Marx would agree with Giddens on this point. As an example, he notes that Marx used the concept of law only in a historically specific context. He refers to *Das Kapital*, where Marx analyzed specific economic forms, among them the commodity, money, and profit. Here he emphasizes the historical circumstances under which these can be applied. The circumstances are always social and historical. Marx emphasizes the limits and the validity of applying concepts and theories. For example, it is not possible to generalize the concept of value, for value is not a universal characteristic of products of labor. Value is specifically linked to the commodity form which exists in connection with private property and thereby the capitalist mode of production.

The point here is not whether Marx's theories are valid. Rather, it is to show how he takes a given phenomenon and demonstrates its dependence on a unique configuration of social relations. Hence, Marx does not end up developing laws of a universal character (Sayer, 1990, pp. 236–8). The purpose of this example is not to demonstrate which interpretation of Marx is most reasonable, but simply to point out that various readings of Marx are possible, and they always depend on the criteria upon which they are based. Giddens never touches on this question. Giddens's critique of the evolutionistic element in Marxism is also problematic. There exist various orthodox, vulgar Marxist interpretations of Marx which are evolutionist, but I find it doubtful whether this critique can be directed toward all forms of historical materialism. This theme has been taken up by several scholars, among them Erik Olin Wright (1983, 1989) and Paul Bagguley (1984). Bagguley demonstrates that Giddens's alternative to historical materialism can also be read as an eclectic combination of evolutionist elements. However, Bagguley expands and revises a part of Giddens's definition of evolution, which of course makes it easier to reject Bagguley's critique. I still believe that the critique has some validity, as the definition in large part incorporates Giddens's own. Bagguley claims that the central core in an evolutionary theory should consist of

> a social entity, which shall be the unit of analysis, [and which] moves through a series of stages by virtue of its own immanent forces of adaptation. The environment in which the social entity adapts may be social and/or material in form. The knowledgeability or the agency of human subjects play no active role within the analysis. The adaptation of the social entity is a structural process and not the product of intentional human agency in any straightforward sense. (Bagguley, 1984, p. 20)

Bagguley emphasizes that the unit of analysis can be both an individual society and a group of societies. Giddens's approach entails two units of analysis. One is the individual society, the other an intersocietal system (the state system), where the latter seems to be dominant. This can be seen, for example, in Giddens's exposition of the development of European state forms, in which he emphasizes the relationship between the individual societies or states within the *intersocietal system* or *state system* as the most important. Here Bagguley emphasizes that the immanent forces, i.e. the evolutionary adaptive logic, consist of the existing 'time–space edges' between the various societies with different levels of time–space distanciation. It was shown that Giddens's typology of societal and state systems has a tendency for societies with a higher level of time–space distanciation to absorb societies with a lower level; see, for example, the extermination of tribal and class-divided societies. Thus, Bagguley clearly sees that Giddens's theory also contains a mechanism of adaptation, such that the "lower societies" (lower in terms of time–space distanciation) adapt to those state systems which are "more developed" (Bagguley, 1984, p. 21). Bagguley thus turns the evolutionism problem against Giddens. So does E. Olin Wright, who, unlike Bagguley, defends a modified evolutionary version of Marxism, but devoid of any teleology, i.e. without an idea that history has an endpoint, such as the communist world (Wright, 1989, p. 90–101). I will not deal with this problem in any detail, but simply conclude that Giddens, like Marx, can be read in an evolutionistic way. Furthermore, it should be emphasized that Marxist theory can be developed so as to avoid teleology and evolutionism (e.g. Hirst and Hindess, 1975; Højrup, 1983, 1995). In sum, Giddens's critique of historical materialism can be said to be unjustified and imprecise. Several of Giddens's critical points have been rejected by recent Marxist research, but his critique is still relevant to the concept of the state. Marxist theoretical development has maintained a concept of the state understood as a direct extension of civil society, a superstructure, a concept which has colored our conception of social change. It has led to a neglect of the importance of the state system, the external relations between states, and particularly the problem of warfare.

The State Project

In his exposition of the emergence of the modern state, Giddens is aware that the development of the state is a result of a structuration process, where external conditions (the state's external relations) and internal conditions (in the state apparatus and in the state's relation to its civil society) closely interact.

However, with its incorporation of both exogenous and endogenous factors, this structuration process does not appear from the generalized definition of the state as "a political organization whose rule is territorially ordered and which is able to mobilize the means of violence to sustain that rule" (1985a, p. 20). This Weberian definition creates a problem for Giddens. Since Weber ignores the external state system, it does not enter into Giddens's general definition of the state either. This seems odd, in as much as Giddens claims that all state forms since the first traditional states have always existed within larger state systems. His theoretical definition of a state, therefore, does not correspond to the empirical analyses of state formations in which he demonstrates his awareness of the state system's significance for the development of all state forms generally. Only in his definition of the nation-state does Giddens mention that the state form exists in a system of other states.

There exists another discrepancy between Giddens's empirical analyses of the state's development and his theoretical work. According to structuration theory, every historical analysis must take its point of departure in the interaction among four structural levels. These four structural levels are the precondition for every action, and include ideological (symbolic order/modes of discourse), political, economic, and legal (modes of sanction) structures. In his analyses, Giddens fails to account for this interaction, as he often emphasizes only one or two of the four structures. In particular, ideology (the modes of discourse), primarily religion, is underemphasized in his analyses of the nation-state and the emergence of capitalism. One does not need to point to Weber to emphasize the importance of religion. The fact that the Reformation takes place with the disintegration of feudalism and incipient absolutism ought to lead to a more fundamental analysis of the phenomenon. Giddens fails to see how the entire Reformation process contains two important elements of the nation-state: (a) the church's estates and property are nationalized, and the state derives from this considerable economic benefit; (b) the entire pan-European communication system, with the Papal chair at its center, collapses. Communication and ideology are nationalized, such that the once so strong church, with its close bonds to Rome, is reduced or disappears in the Protestant countries. In explaining the emergence, consolidation, and decline of various state forms, Giddens makes no clear connection between the four institutions. Generally, Giddens ascribes to the political institutions the decisive dynamic of change. The factor which in the last instance seems to be the driving force for the political level is war. Emphasis on politics and war is a common feature in the analysis of all state forms. However, this contradicts Giddens's claim that none of the four levels can obtain dominance at the expense of others, or that a complex historical development can be reduced to a single axis, which in this case is war and politics. In relation to the theory of structuration, which seeks to develop up-to-date concepts for analysis of processes of social change, it is thought-provoking that these concepts are not applied to a greater extent in the concrete analyses. Admittedly, the demonstrated features of change specified in *The Nation-State and Violence* are pointed out with these concepts in mind, but, for example, concepts such as "episode" and "time–space edges" are never applied in the concrete analysis. This leaves the impression that many of the sophisticated concepts in structuration theory are redundant, and that empirical work does not necessarily have to be embedded in a theory of structuration in order to provide an adequate and interesting analysis.

It is also pertinent to call into question the various types of societies. Several critics have pointed out that these types contain internal contradictions. Smith (1982) points out that the character of so-called class-divided societies is very variable. Smith notes that Giddens's focus on the town as the power container overlooks the great land-owning aristocracy, which in some states – even under absolutism – became an autonomous power container in the state. This in turn led to a long period with an inherent conflict between the landowners and the king concerning the distribution of surplus product (to either feudal rent or royal taxes). Smith therefore rejects the idea that the town–countryside conflict under absolutism constitutes a situation where the town had dominance over the countryside. Rather, he finds an ongoing conflict between the king and the landed aristocracy, who are constantly fighting for dominance of the political space (Smith, 1982, p. 96).

Giddens demands contextual explanations, but how do we define context? When he describes European state development from 1500 to 1920, the development is perhaps contextual in time and space, but what about the obvious differences in, for example, French and English state development? France became the first absolutist state with a strong army, whereas England became a constitutional monarchy and the leading economic power, not least because of its navy. Hence, a comparison between the individual European states must certainly be more historically specific than that carried out by Giddens. The question remains: which criteria are to be applied to specify the contextual?

The Analysis of Modernity

A fundamental problem in Giddens's sociology concerns the consistency and coherence between, on the one hand, his more substantial sociological theoretical works, which led to the development of the theory of structuration in the 1980s, and, on the other hand, his work in the 1990s, focusing on modernity, self-identity, globalization, and politics. The purpose of structuration theory has been to transcend the dualism between actor and structure. In his analysis of modernity it has been an underlying intention to base this analysis on the theory of structuration in order to provide a more adequate diagnosis of modernity without falling into the actor or structure gap. This ambition is not fulfilled. His analysis of self-identity, life-political choices, and the transformation of intimacy does not specify the constraining aspect of the structures. According to Giddens we create ourselves – the process of identity is a project in which we actively take part and are reflexive about. Our sexuality, eating habits, clothes, choice of education, and career are all means in this process of creating ourselves. Giddens's analysis has, however, a voluntaristic list because the actors seem to create and generate the structures by making decisions. In other words, Giddens needs to specify and be more precise about the constraining side of the concept of structure. It is fairly obvious that not all actors have the same number of choices or can make the same decisions. Giddens's focus is on the very processes, but he is silent when it comes to specifying the conditions for how the processes take place. Some actors might have more resources, with more opportunities as a consequence. The well educated doctor can, better than a single mother with three kids, choose to live a healthy life. By possessing a higher level of cultural and economic capital, the doctor has easier access to high-quality organic food, a healthy house, a better job, etc.

Another problem in this context concerns Giddens's many sweeping generalizations. Often he paints a picture of a world undergoing the same changes at high pace and depth all over the world at the same time. After reading his analysis you are left breathless and with the impression that many social changes, such as a shift toward life politics, women's liberation, processes of democratization overtaking democracy, globalization, and an increasingly social reflexivity, can be found all over the world. Obviously, this is not the case. Social changes are happening at different speeds and depths and with a variety of outcomes, depending on the context. Life-political issues might have become a more widespread phenomenon, and not only related to the Western states, but they do not play the same role among women in sub-Saharan Africa and Canada. Also, there is a difference between poor people on welfare and middle-class people employed within the media area. The majority of the Earth's population probably find emancipatory politics, including the struggle for more equality, the improvement of material conditions, and justice, more pertinent to their lives than animal rights and the ethical questions raised by the development of genetic technologies.

These problems show that Giddens does not sufficiently succeed in combining the level of agency with the institutional dimension of society. A political sociological analysis of modernity only becomes fruitful when we begin to understand the interrelations between, on the one hand, social actors, their actions, and the norms, values, and ideologies connected to these actions and, on the other hand, social structures of political-legal, military, economic, and ideological character. Pierre Bourdieu has made such an attempt by introducing the concept of "habitus." Bourdieu argues that human beings possess different types of habitus which enable and constrain people in their social activities. The concept of habitus designates a system of durable dispositions through which we perceive, judge, and act in the world. Being brought up in a specific context involves a habitus with certain embodied dispositions which enables us to act in a specific way. At the same time, habitus expresses different types and levels of social, cultural, and economic capital. An analysis of habitus-related dispositions and the embodied capital embedded in the habitus of different people and social classes provides an understanding of the differences in opportunities among people. Also, by analyzing people's different habitus we begin to understand why people make different choices and decisions. In his understanding of "late modernity" or the "post-traditional" society Giddens often emphasizes, inspired by the German sociologist Ulrich Beck, that human beings today to a large extent are sharing many of the same opportunities as well as problems. We are all confronting the same risks and in that respect "high modernity" has no "other" or "others." Rich or poor, black or white, man or woman – everyone experiences the same problems, such as overpopulation, pollution, new diseases, or changes in climate. We become a mass who experience the same reality mediated by the mass media. Thus Giddens universalizes the framework of experiences of modernity.

This has implications for the theory. First and foremost, this aspect of the globalization process in Giddens's theory is conceived as a result of experiences mediated by the mass media. The mediation of the media generates a common experience of the world as one place and one world – an experience and understanding of the world which seems to be problematic. Therefore, Giddens's concept of globalization is closely related to a common "global awareness." He states that modernity creates one world and a "unitary framework of experience" through the experiences which are mediated by the media (1991a). When he can sustain this claim it has to do with his very simplistic and somewhat outdated understanding of the media, the transmission and mediation of the media, and the reception of the content of the media. Media research has demonstrated theoretically as well as empirically that the users of the media are not a (passive) mass who interpret and psychologically receive the message in the same way (Gurevitch et al., 1982; Tomlinson, 1994; Thompson, 1995). Habitus, capital, ethnicity, gender, nationality, age, and a number of other categories can be used to understand how and why a person receives, perceives, interprets, psychologically incorporates, and acts influenced by the content of the media.

As a consequence of his position, Giddens argues that the self is created under conditions where many of our experiences are mediated by the media. This produces a tendency to homogenization and the development of a common framework of experience. This has some negative implications in Giddens's tendency to ignore other aspects which are crucial in order to understand the development of identity. By stressing the mediated character of our experiences through the mass media, he almost completely neglects our relationship to the other (Hay et al., 1993–4, pp. 61–5). In my opinion, the relation to the "other," the "others," the "different" is crucial to the development of identity and self-identity. The self is not constituted by mass media which communicate common experiences about a "unitary world." Identity is created in the meeting with the "other." The "other" is a central concept for understanding the development of different sociocultural identities. The historical identity of the Western world has been created in the meeting between the West and "foreign cultures." The meeting with the strangers brought about a discourse in the West about the identity of the Western world being modern, enlightened, progressive, civilized, and emancipated. At the individual level as well, the meeting with the "other" is crucial. Gender, sexuality, ethnicity, class, life-mode, habitus, nationality, etc. are created and "constructed" in the meeting with the "others." Consequently, the genealogical basis of self-identity is fundamentally permeated by struggle, suppression, separation, and active as well as passive resistance in the meeting with the "other." Thus self-identity and the creation of identity are not only a result of processes which are present in the routinized day-to-day life of the individual. Identity is also dependent on the absent – the "other," the "others," the "different."

Another problem in Giddens's analysis of modernity concerns his concept of reflexivity. Reflexivity is an important factor in the undermining of tradition and the development of modernity and postmodernity. Nonetheless, the concept of reflexivity is far from a clearly defined concept in Giddens's thinking. First, it seems to me that social reflexivity is an irreversible process, and accelerating. Consequently, here too we see some form of evolutionism emerging despite the fact that one of Giddens's main purposes in structuration theory was to remove evolutionism from social theory (1984a). Moreover, we would still like a clarification of who is reflexive. Which actors are or can become reflexive? Individuals, organizations, states? What is the 'motor' of reflexivity (Beck et al., 1994)? Is reflexivity merely a reflection (i.e. knowledge and recognition)? Or is it something else?

Reflexivity has become fashionable in modern sociology, but Giddens's use of the concept is filled with ambiguity. He does not succeed in elaborating a more clearly defined concept which could have increased its applicability.

Some commentators, including Turner (1992a, pp. 141–6), have observed that there are many similarities between Giddens and Max Weber. Turner seeks to demonstrate that Weber is less defective than Giddens claims. Turner reminds us that Giddens sets out in *Capitalism and Modern Social Theory* (1971a) to prove that Weber and the other classics are defective and that modern social theory needs a revision of the classical heritage in order to become an adequate analytical instrument for understanding modernity. Turner argues that many of Giddens's ideas can already be found in Weber's work, and the critique Giddens raises against classical sociology cannot be directed against Weber (Turner, 1992a, pp. 144–5). Giddens's critique of monocausal explanations and his persistent attempt to use a multidimensional view of complex causal processes can also be found in Weber's work. It was one of Weber's main points of criticism against Marx.

I agree with Turner and I think his argument can be further extended. Giddens's thesis of the post-traditional society is essentially a Weberian configuration. The undermining of traditions by processes of reflexivity, abstract systems including expert systems, and globalization corresponds in many ways to Weber's ideas of an emergent modernity, with processes of rationalization, capitalism, and a disenchantment which subverts tradition and traditional norms and values. Weber's analysis of the development of science and its increasing rationalization in the Western world is very similar to Giddens's expert systems. Moreover, Giddens argues that, with tradition withering away, people today have to be responsible for their own actions. This aspect can also be found in Weber's sociology. Weber argues that the disenchantment of the world, the undermining of tradition, and the increasing rationalization create a situation in which people must take responsibility for the predictable consequences of their actions. They can no longer act as in the traditional world in the belief that they as good Christians acted in the right way and the consequences could be handed over to God. Weber was very interested in the problem of the "uniqueness of the West" and how the Western world became globally hegemonic. This corresponds to Giddens's first phase of globalization, and his analysis is not more comprehensive than Weber's. Both thinkers stress the complexity of the development and the multicausal factors driving the process forward.

Giddens defines modernity primarily as the interaction among four institutional dimensions: capitalism, industrialism, the nation-state, and industrialized war. An important part of Giddens's analysis of modernity describes the globalization of these four institutional elements, which takes us to my next point of criticism: Giddens's thesis of globalization.

First, his very definition of globalization contains certain problems. He defines globalization as a process where there occurs an "intensification of world-wide social relations which link distant localities in such a way that local happenings are shaped by events occurring many miles away and vice versa" (1990a, p. 64). It is summarized in his more recent works as "actions at distance" (1994a, 1998a). The definition contains three elements: first, an intensification of certain social relations; second, worldwide social relations; third, the definition asserts that events in one context can influence situations and events in another context, which geographically can be found far away.

The first element seems plausible, but it contains several problems. When we speak of intensification, we must ask: intensification in relation to what? Giddens claims that the capitalist world economy, for example, has become intensified. Yet it is unclear whether he means that it is the capitalist mode of production which has expanded so extensively over a large geographic area, or whether it is the commodity market and the expansion of the circulation of commodities which have become global. Furthermore, Giddens is unclear as to what an intensification of the world economy implies. Concerning the geographical dispersion of the commodity markets, research indicates that some economic activities were in certain respects at least as global in the period before the First World War as at present. If one examines most Western countries' foreign trade in relation to gross national product and foreign direct investment in relation to world output, these figures are not much higher in the 1990s than between 1905 and 1914 (Hirst and Thompson, 1999). Furthermore, most of the trade and foreign direct investment take place within the three great economic blocs or among them (the EU, NAFTA and Japan/Southeast Asia). This indicates that Giddens must produce a stronger argument for the thesis of a globalization of the economy. If, however, we are speaking of an intensification, is it of a quantitative or qualitative character? And what is the real implications of this intensification? Giddens fails to raise these questions as well.

The second aspect in Giddens's definition of globalization concerns the worldwide character of social relations. What kind of social relations are today more worldwide than earlier? Trade and exchange of goods have taken place among states for millennia, and we now have innumerable examples of trade with far-away regions. Hence, despite a quantitative change, today's globalization cannot be said to be more worldwide in this sense.

The final point of Giddens's globalization definition emphasizes that events in Rwanda can have consequences for Bangladesh because we redirect our foreign aid. This thesis, while certainly plausible, requires clarification. Events in one area have always had (often unintended) consequences for other areas, but because of poor communication, we may not have known about it. Hunger, war, or population growth in one place have created massive movements of people, with serious consequences for people in other places. As indicated, the important aspect of the globalization problem is not the mutual effect among various geographic localities, but the knowledge of it. The development from printing to electronic mail and satellite transmission has significantly increased our level of information about other parts of the world. In some of his others works, Giddens stresses the electronic means of communications as a key to globalization. From the early 1960s and onwards, we have had a global satellite system which makes instantaneous communication possible. This changes not only the economic structures but also people's everyday lives (1999b). The marriage of the communications revolution with computerization creates a new world, with instantaneous information and an intensifying globalization. His emphasis on instantaneous information and an increasing 'awareness' among people that we are living in the same world is interesting, because this aspect is not included in his definition of globalization, as we saw above. Thus we find inconsistency between his definition ("action at distance") and his more elaborated reflections on globalization, where the awareness aspect is more salient.

Another problem in his definition and analysis concerns the question of the cultural and ideological dimension of globalization. Giddens's four-dimensional model does not include the cultural and ideological globalization which for many seems to be the most visible dimension of globalization and which Giddens stresses in some of his analyses. He mentions how the film *Basic Instinct* was shown on video in a remote areas in Central Africa (1999c). Giddens may claim, of course, that each institutional dimension (capitalism, industrialism, the nation-state, and the industrialization of war) contains an ideological dimension. Nevertheless, he tends to underrate ideology and culture as independent and important parts of globalization. Moreover, it should be emphasized that ideology ought to be included as an independent dimension if there is to be a connection between Giddens's model for the analysis of social change (see chapter 3) and the globalization model (chapter 5). Giddens stresses that the economic, political, juridical, and ideological factors must be incorporated in a general institutional analysis of social systems, and thereby society. Nevertheless, the ideological/cultural aspects are left out of the concrete analysis of the globalization of modernity. This makes his analysis of globalization unconvincing. Giddens's thesis of the globalization of capitalism also contains problems. In two of his books (1981a, 1985a), Giddens analyzes the development and transformation of various types of states and societies. In reviewing his analysis of social change (chapter 3), I showed how Giddens, with his types of societies, has attempted to demonstrate how history has evolved without having been driven by any single mechanism of change and without being directed towards any specific end (*telos*). In other words, he attempts to break with the many evolutionary and teleological theories which have dominated sociology. His analysis of the globalization of capitalism therefore seems paradoxical. He asserts that with capitalism there appears a dynamic force which to an increasing degree of intensity subordinates the entire globe. Apparently, this is an irreversible process, which irrevocably gives some strong evolutionary associations. A similar critique could be raised concerning Giddens's work on industrialism and the nation-state. His globalization thesis therefore leads – although unintentionally – down into the evolutionary pitfall which he has otherwise attempted to avoid.

A critique needs to be raised in relation to his claim that we are living in a world in which the military dimension has increasingly become globalized. This claim is to be questioned because as long as we experience US hegemony at the military level it seems to be difficult for a truly global military world order to develop. This leads to a final criticism concerning the concept of globalization in general. Globalization seems to be the overall catching frame in Giddens's analysis of society and politics. Globalization is seen as causing fundamental social change in recent history, but at the same time globalization is seen as the effect of structural social changes. He is far from convincing when he claims that modern instantaneous communication changes our everyday life in a fundamental sense. He does not specify the implications of this innovation. We need to know what specific difference it makes to people in Central Africa that they watch *Basic Instinct* on video. What are the implications for their ideology? Does it in a structural sense change the economic and political structures in their local area or the relationship between Central Africa and the West? If these structures change, is it caused by globalization? What kind of globalization? Or are the changes a product of globalization? We are still waiting for the answers, and these answers are important because this is a test of globalization theory. Most scholars and lay people agree that changes have taken place over the past two or three decades, but whether the globalization concept is the key to understanding these changes is an open question. In this context it is also pertinent to raise the question of the uniqueness of the present period of globalization. Christianity as an ideological force seems to have had a much stronger impact on Europe, the Americas, and parts of Africa and Asia than the principles of "McDonaldization" or "Americanization" on the world in general. The spread and impact of the Indo-European languages are also relevant comparisons.

Giddens and Politics: Some Critical Remarks

In recent years, Giddens has moved into politics. He has been involved in several areas of the political field. He has published several articles and books to generate ideas for New Labour, and he has provided some intellectual legitimacy for Prime Minister Tony Blair's politics (Boynton, 1997; Lloyd, 1997). He takes part in the work of various think tanks, such as the Institute for Public Policy Research, and since being appointed director of the London School of Economics he has attempted to turn it into a "powerhouse for a different kind of politics, addressing the crisis in conservatism and socialism" (1997, p. 18). This section takes a closer look at his political move. First, I summarize some of the main points of criticism which have been raised in the wake of the publication of *Beyond Left and Right* and *The Third Way*. Second, I discuss a few aspects of Giddens's position more closely and compare his to other "third way" projects.

The Enlightenment heritage: idealism and etho-politics

Several critics repeatedly point out tensions and contradictions in his political project. Perry Anderson has pointed out that the Enlightenment was a more complex process than Giddens claims. It was not only a belief in progress, science, and the increasing ability to control the future (Anderson, 1994). Thus Giddens exaggerates the confidence the Enlightenment tradition had in the cognitive mastery of the world as the key to beneficent progress. Anderson mentions Montesquieu as an example of an Enlightenment thinker who saw progress as a more complex problem than Giddens attributes to the Enlightenment tradition (Anderson, 1994, p. 40).

Giddens is, however, very much in line with Enlightenment thinking when he argues that people in general face an increasing social reflexivity and an increasing number of situations where they have to make conscious decisions. These decisions have to be made between alternatives and based upon new forms of knowledge. Previously these situations were decided by custom. No Enlightenment philosophers would disagree here. In contrast to Giddens, Anderson argues that knowledge enables control, but not centralized control. For example, contraception enables families and women to control birth but it does not enhance state control of birth. The problem is, according to Anderson, that it is less the increase in knowledge itself that spreads uncertainty than the multiplication of knowers. This pushes Giddens into the arms of neo-liberalism because his argument is similar to Hayek's critique of social constructivism: "that which forecast the worldwide sway of the market, as a spontaneous economic order generated by a multitude of rational maximizers, acting without coordination" (Anderson, 1994, pp. 40–1). As we have seen, Giddens rejects neo-liberalism by arguing that it is an inconsistent and self-contradictory ideology. Anderson argues, however, that although this criticism is right and acute, it is rather limited. First, he points out, self-contradictory elements do not prevent a set of ideas and values from developing into a powerful ideology. Second, neo-liberalism is today at its zenith. It has never been more successful. To challenge neo-liberalism requires other arguments, which include an attack on its strongest expressions (Anderson, 1994, p. 41).

The second point of criticism raised by Anderson concerns the dialogue–conflict relation. Giddens suggests dialogue as the appropriate conception for pursuing and solving contemporary problems of democracy, welfare, work, and peace. Giddens is here embedded in a Habermasian tradition based upon a theory of communication modeled on dialogue. Anderson regards this model as problematic when it comes to an understanding of politics. Although Western democracies exclude violence as a means of persuasion, they do not lead to a system of entrenched dialogue.

> Politics remains eminently strategic: not an exchange of opinion, but a contest for power . . . the danger of conceiving democratic life as dialogue is that we may forget that its primary reality remains strife. All the issues Giddens rightly poses for a radical agenda divide, since they call on material resources that are limited and over which adversary forces maintain a privileged hold. (Anderson, 1994, p. 43)

In other words, Anderson is not convinced that Giddens's notion of dialogic democracy is the means of addressing the key problems of society.

Although Anderson's critique of the notion of dialogic democracy contains some truth, it also bears witness to a very narrow conception of the political. The processes of democratization taking place within many domains in smaller and medium-sized companies, in civil society, and among men and women in marriages are genuinely democratic. The extent to which these processes will influence politics at a national or global scale is an open question, and Giddens might very well be naive and too optimistic in this case, but I agree with Giddens that such processes must be included in an adequate concept of the political. This concept of the political does not replace the strategic understanding of politics, but supplements it.

Other scholars, such as Fuller (1996), also argue that Giddens is still very much embedded in traditional Enlightenment thinking, although he claims the exhaustion of Enlightenment thinking. In his sociological analysis, on the one hand, he shows that tradition and nature are dead as external frameworks guiding our lives. Today norms, values, and traditions are not constants which we just inherit from our parents, but contested variables which always require reflection and decision. On the other hand, he is arguing for some kind of universal values embedded in the Enlightenment tradition (Fuller, 1996, p. 173). Thus, Giddens states:

> An ethics of a globalizing post-traditional society implies recognition of the sanctity of human life and the universal right to happiness and self-actualiza-tion – coupled to the obligation to promote cosmopolitan solidarity and an attitude of respect towards nonhuman agencies and beings, present and fu-ture. Far from seeing the disappearance of universal values, this is perhaps the first time in humanity's history when such values have real purchase. (1994a, p. 253)

Fuller argues that this dilemma in Giddens's thinking might reveal that he has a quest for transcendence. In Giddens's writings his seeking of univer-sal values can be seen as an unanswered question about the anxiety of mean-ing (Fuller, 1996, p. 174). He seems to think that we have lost something by processes of detraditionalization, globalization, and reflexive moderni-zation. However, he cannot say what this something is because it might be something which could force us to defend it with all means. In other words, he would end up with a type of fundamentalism – the worst possible situa-tion for Giddens.

Various commentators criticize New Labour and the third way project in general. Rustin emphasizes that Giddens provides the Labour Party with a "rationalization for the shift from a materialist, economistic and class-based conception of socialism" (Rustin, 1995, p. 21). Moreover, "the space Giddens accords to reflexivity, and its ensuing preference for dialogue and process over plans and outcomes, gives a theoretical legitimacy to New Labour's ethical and idealist discourse. . . . The fact that New Labour is reluctant to outline specific policy objectives . . . now maps on to this theoretical indeterminacy, in a worrying way" (Rustin, 1995, p. 21). Ac-cording to Rustin, Giddens's focus on post-materialistic values in *Beyond Left and Right* pushes him toward "idealistic solutions to the problems of inequality and polarization" (Rustin, 1995, p. 23).

In a review of *The Third Way*, Rose (1999) elaborates on the problem of idealistic solutions. He argues that the idealism inherent in Giddens's and third way thinking is based upon the idea of governing individuals through ethics. Human beings are now considered to be ethical creatures, and we are living in a society where problems are increasingly conceived as ethical problems. Rose claims that the third way is etho-politics, i.e. the senti-ments, morals, and guiding beliefs of persons and groups. Third way politics becomes an attempt to use sentiments, values, and beliefs as a medium "within which the self-government of the autonomous individual can be connected up with the imperatives of good government" (Rose, 1999, p. 12). Politics is a matter of influencing the forces that shape these values, beliefs, and moralities that determine the daily choices we have to make to live our lives. By influencing values and beliefs, the government seeks to influence our conduct in a more subtle way. Etho-politics is about shaping self-techniques "necessary for self-government and the relations between one's obligation to oneself and one's obligations to others" (Rose, 1999, p. 12).

I agree with Rustin and Rose that there is an idealistic dimension in New Labour's project and also in Giddens's political thinking, but some of the idealistic elements are interesting and necessary. Giddens claims that welfare is not only a matter of distributing risks and material resources to reduce poverty, but also a question of redefining welfare, the good life, and happiness. It might sound like an argument for supporting the new right, accepting poverty, and demolishing the welfare state, but this is far from the case. Since Aristotle we have known that to realize the good life does not necessarily mean more material wealth. To bring the definition of happiness and the good life back onto the political agenda might seem problematic and not a very good strategy. On the other hand, it seems to me to be necessary if we seriously want to discuss what constitutes the good society.

The communitarian problem

Rose connects this aspect of the third way program to a more general critique of communitarianism. The new ways of governing behavior through ethics gives the third way a communitarian dimension. A new relation between ethical citizenship and responsible community must be developed, and the aim is to "govern citizens through community." Community replaces society as the most important category. Community is

> the new territorialization of political thought, the new way in which conduct is collectivised. Increasingly, it is the language of community that is used to identify a territory between the authority of the state, the free and amoral exchange of the market and the liberty of the autonomous, "rights-bearing" individual subjects. The space of community appears as a kind of natural, extra-political zone of human relations . . . community is identified as a crucial element in particular styles of political government, for it is on its properties and on activities within it that the success of such political aspirations and

programmes depends. Hence community must become the object and target for the exercise of political power whilst remaining, somehow, external to politics and a counterweight to it. Community, that is to say, names a "transactional" reality. (Rose, 1999, p. 10)

This emphasis on community is related to a reconceptualization of the state. The state is no longer the welfare state or the social state. Now the focus is on the facilitating state or the enabling state. Politics is now a matter of citizens governing themselves by the means of individual morality and community responsibility (Rose, 1999, p. 11).

Although Giddens is vulnerable to such a critique, I do think Rose exaggerates the communitarian dimension in Giddens's position. Communitarianism is in this context understood as an attempt to conceive a society through the idea of a community based upon a common set of values which generate social integration and social cohesion. Rose puts Giddens, Tony Blair, the *Observer* Editor Will Hutton, and other stakeholder thinkers in the same place as Etzioni and other communitarians. A reading of Blair's third way manifesto (Blair, 1998) reveals a much stronger communitarian string in his thinking compared to Giddens. Giddens's works are much more ambiguous, and here we find a tension between, on the one hand, some form of communitarianism and, on the other hand, a strong liberal dimension. His sociological diagnosis of the post-traditional society demonstrates that individuals are less constrained by tradition and do not possess a firm set of values and beliefs which never change. Detraditionalization, increasing social reflexivity, and globalization, with a more and more individuated and pluralistic society, make it impossible to generate a common set of values and norms as guidance for people. Giddens's discussion of democracy illustrates this problem. Giddens advocates a deliberative and dialogic democracy – a notion of democracy that requires only a minimum consensus on certain norms of procedures. Another example is Giddens's critique of Blair before the British general election of 1997. Blair suggested a Christian set of values as a basis for the New Labour political program. Giddens advised against it, because in a post-traditional order, with multiculturalism and with multiethnic populations, such a proposal can lead to fundamentalism. Giddens has also persistently argued that any propensity for moral absolutism must be rejected. Giddens intervened in the public political debate in fall 1996 when Blair on several occasions expressed opinions with a touch of moral absolutism; for example, that only strong families bring about a more cohesive society. This was denied by Giddens, who claimed that only more egalitarian and communicative families could provide social cohesion. Moreover, it has not been moral relativism but moral fundamentalism which has been a danger to social cohesion (1996b,

p. 19). Again, these examples show us that Giddens has a liberal side coexisting with the communitarian strand.

Is this tension the key to the notion of the radical center? Is the radical center innovative because it combines these elements? This is hard to answer. In the New Labour project, both the liberal and the communitarian sides are conspicuous, but the pendulum seems to oscillate toward a communitarian and conservative side. Giddens also contains both elements, but during most of the 1990s he stressed the liberal aspect. This corresponds to his endorsement of the market (although not as an unconstrained entity) and the free-floating self with choices to make in high modernity. Giddens's third way project combines liberal, communitarian, philosophical conservatism, and neo-liberal pieces, but in *The Third Way* he tends to accept more conservative and communitarian thinking, e.g. by emphasizing the state as a moral regulator.

This tension in Giddens's position can be seen as an attempt to reconcile two contradictory positions: to please Blair, while he at the same time attempts to sustain his own integrity. Another explanation could be that he accepts a part of the agenda brought forward by Blair, Peter Mandelson, and others, but at the same time tries to push it in a slightly different direction. A third explanation could be that he actually has changed his mind in a more communitarian direction, but that is hard to believe. It does not correspond to his sociological analysis at all.

Giddens's political move

During the 1990s Giddens produced a number of publications which have tried to make an impact on contemporary politics, in Britain in particular, but also in other places. How can we assess and interpret this political move? Why has he left agency–structure debates and the analysis of the pure relationship and, then, focused on politics? This is difficult to answer, but a guess could be that his sociological analysis, combined with the changing political conditions which generated more space for new ideas, pushed him in that direction. Undoubtedly, Giddens has seen his chance to influence the political agenda, and apparently with some success. It is, however, difficult to determine his impact on politics. Did his ideas push the New Labour agenda forward? His analysis of modernity, and some of the dilemmas stated in *The Third Way*, have probably influenced the agenda, but his answers to the dilemmas and problems faced by contemporary politics have not loomed large in any political program, including New Labour's. This probably has to do with the content of his project, where Giddens's analysis of the conditions confronting politics is more convincing than his policy proposals.

I shall not pursue this point here, only state that Giddens's ideas certainly have fused with some of the main points of the New Labour agenda. There are some similarities between Giddens and Blair, but there seems to be more substance to Giddens's work than to Blair's ideas. Giddens's writings in *New Statesman* and the *Observer*, followed by *Beyond Left and Right*, have definitely been influential at some level, since they framed the debate in many contexts and countries, but, again, more as issue-raising than as policy-proposing and problem-solving. His most recent publication, *The Third Way*, can be seen as an attempt to provide further substance to Blair's project, or perhaps to influence it in a certain direction. This book is a political manifesto for renewing social democracy (Hirst, 1998b), but also a direct intervention trying to push New Labour more toward a wider concept of governance and to avoid a communitarianism with an aspect of moral absolutism. Moreover, the book is an attempt to steer between various positions and avoid a total turn to the market philosophy of the right. He accepts, even endorses, the market, but not as an unconstrained entity. He emphasizes the necessity of tackling problems of social inequality – a claim which has been repeated in several contexts, including very recently (1999a, p. 26). Political measures need to be taken, and this requires a new type of governance, including regulation of the market.

How can we assess the inventiveness and originality of Giddens's ideas? Did he simply pick up certain ideas already formulated in the inner circle of the Labour Party and various think-tanks around the party, and then elaborate on these? Did he just jump on the bandwagon? Is Rose right when he claims that most of Giddens's ideas were already formulated by Ulrich Beck in a German context (Rose, 1999)? Or was he one of the first to actually formulate certain ideas about the radical center which were picked up by Tony Blair, Gordon Brown (the Chancellor of the Exchequer), and others? This is impossible to say and perhaps not even important or interesting. One can always speculate as to why and how ideas suddenly become influential – everything from friendship, personal relations, the right timing in terms of the political and economic mood in the country, international conditions, the *Zeitgeist*, simple contingency, or a combination can be suggested. Consequently, I do not seek the origins of Giddens's ideas in this context. It is, however, worth stressing the affinities between various elements of Giddens's thinking and that of other "third way thinkers." I shall not go into any comparative analysis of these ideas, just point to a few interesting aspects.

Giddens and the middle ground

Giddens's ambition to develop a third way with the radical center as a point of departure is not the only attempt at a political theory which transcends traditional dichotomies, including state–market, collectivism–individualism, communitarianism–liberalism, and state-regulated/centralized control–decentralized individualism. This ambition is, of course, not at all new, but it is remarkable that we see a convergence between various contemporary scholars on these issues. Thinkers such as Jürgen Habermas, Ulrich Beck, David Held, Paul Hirst, David Marquand, and Will Hutton all contributed to a "third way agenda" during the 1990s. In many respects they are concentrated around the political middle, but they do not offer the same analysis or have the same perspectives and ideas. There are many similarities between Giddens's project and those of some of these thinkers. Habermas's theory of communicative action, the "ideal speech" situation, and the dialogue in the center of politics is one example of a thinker who shares some fundamental ideas with Giddens. Giddens never mentions Habermas as a source of inspiration. Instead, he has on several occasions criticized and distanced his ideas from those of Habermas (e.g. 1979c, 1982a, 1987a, 1994a).

It is striking, however, that he rarely makes any reference to these thinkers (with Held as an exception) or tries to link up to these theories in order to develop common ground for a broader basis for political action. Instead, he tries to push them off the middle ground. This can most clearly be seen in his rejection of the critique of the globalization thesis which Paul Hirst and Grahame Thompson have developed in their work *Globalization in Question* (Hirst and Thompson, 1999; Giddens, 1999a, p. 26 – see also *The Director's Lectures*). Giddens stereotypes them as globalization skeptics who have not realized that changes have taken place leading toward a more global world. They are categorized as belonging to the old left, arguing that nothing has changed and that, consequently, we can still have Keynesian state intervention and cybernetic control. This critique is far from convincing. Hirst and Thompson do not deny that the world economy today is different from the economy of previous periods. What they claim, however, is that the economy is never a stable and closed entity. Over – let us say – the past 120 years we have observed many changes and fluctuations. The world economy is sometimes more open than at other times and what we now experience in terms of openness is not unique. Moreover, they argue that the world economy is more an open international economy than a globalized economy. The world economy today is dominated by a triad (Japan/East Asia, North America and the European

Union). Trade, the flow of finance capital, and foreign direct investment mainly take place between and within these three blocs. In that respect the economy is not truly global. They also claim that governance of the economy is possible, but it depends on the will of political actors, in particular the G-7 countries. Giddens's own position is in fact much closer to that of Hirst and Thompson than he is willing to admit. He argues in line with Hirst and Thompson that changes in the economy have not undermined the sovereignty of the state. Giddens, like Hirst and Thompson, argues that the state is the most important political actor and possesses a huge capacity to regulate and govern the economy. Both of them suggest that the Tobin tax could be a way to regulate the flow of finance capital.

Moreover, Giddens claims that Hirst and Thompson are old left representatives, since they argue for the continuous importance of the state at a national level. But this is precisely what Giddens himself suggests as a part of the third way project. Giddens's idea of the state as a social investor and his long list of tasks for the state (1998a, pp. 47–8) is quite similar to some of the ideas brought forward by Hirst and Thompson (1999; Hirst, 1998a). A redefinition of the role of the state toward a less omnipotent but now more facilitating entity, the move from government to governance at different levels, closer cooperation between state and civil society, the creation and strengthening of civil society and voluntary associations – these aspects are a common denominator between Giddens, and Hirst and Thompson (1995; Hirst, 1994, 1998a, b).

Giddens and the problem of political theory

A criticism which has been raised in this section concerns the contradictory and self-contradictory elements in Giddens's third way position. I argue that this inherent contradiction reveals that Giddens's radical center and third way ideas are not embedded in a more consistent political theory. Giddens lacks coherence and consistency in his political thinking. A fruitful political theory needs to analyze and specify the problems inherent in present political institutions and structures, and furthermore point to necessary changes and how we can achieve these. Such an analysis requires a more explicitly developed and formulated political theory which contains clearer ideas of state, sovereignty, state–civil society relations, interstate relations, etc. Giddens obviously has some ideas on these problems, but he lacks coherence and substance. His sociological analysis seems to be his strength, whereas his political theory lacks strong grounding. Compared to other "third way thinkers," such as Paul Hirst, David Marquand, David Held, and Jürgen Habermas, his argument comes over as fairly weak. As already mentioned, it is striking that within certain areas there are many similarities between Giddens and Hirst. It is clear, however, from a reading of Hirst (and Thompson) that his position is much more carefully thought through and therefore more consistent. Hirst's position is deeply embedded in an elaborated political theory drawing upon German, French, and British theory from the nineteenth and early twentieth centuries, with thinkers such as Otto von Gierke, Leon Duguit, Émile Durkheim, and perhaps most importantly F. W. Maitland, John Neville Figgis, Harold Laski, and G. D. H. Cole prominent. Hirst's careful reading of these thinkers and his development of their ideas have created a very elaborated political theory with a clear conception of key concepts such as state, civil society, sovereignty, law, democracy, and their mutual relations. This theory enables Hirst to develop among other things a clear understanding of governance, the extension of competence between different levels (local, state, regional, and global), and the need for the development of a *rechtsstaat*.

Where Hirst combines elements from theories based upon common denominators, Giddens picks and mixes from incompatible theories (philosophical conservatism, socialism, and neo-liberalism), which generates an inconsistent political theoretical position. Yet as Anderson points out, "the history of political thought is a warning against any assumption that discrepant values cannot be coherently upheld by an effective ideology" (Anderson, 1994, p. 41). Consequently, Giddens's third way project might still prove to be a major success, since it can turn into an ideology with a strong impact on policy-makers and society as a whole.

Concluding Remarks: Giddens in a Theory-historical Perspective

Anthony Giddens is one of the most influential English sociologists since Herbert Spencer. While others may surpass Giddens as original thinkers, he is among the few who have made a major international impact. Giddens's sociology has become an industry (to which this book contributes), in which countless books and journal articles discuss or apply parts of his work. It is impossible to say what significance Giddens will have for sociology and social science in the future, but over the past ten years he has had an impact in several fields. He was among the first in the Anglo-Saxon world to integrate Marx as part of the classical sociological heritage (1971a), and early on he saw the need to rethink the classics as the basis for reformulating and modernizing sociological theory. In the early 1970s, other sociologists, including Jeffrey Alexander (1982–3), Randall Collins (1975), Alvin Gouldner (1970), and Jürgen Habermas (1971, 1973, 1984, 1987), also began to revive the classical thinkers. Giddens was thus part of the wave of theorists who returned to the classics in order to "start over again." Here could be found the foundation for building a new synthesis between subject and object, actor and structure, individual and society, and micro- and macrosociology. Giddens's structuration theory is thus in line with the Frenchman Pierre Bourdieu, the American Jeffrey Alexander, and the German Jürgen Habermas, all of whom attempt to transcend the dualism mentioned above. Giddens's structuration theory, while not the only attempt at synthesis, is nevertheless unique in its scope. Giddens applies the entire spectrum of classical and modern social theory as the basis of his grandiose attempt at reconstruction. No one other than Giddens has been able to combine elements from Marx, Weber, Durkheim, Mead, Goffman, Parsons, Merton, Schutz, Offe, Heidegger, the Swedish geography of time, Freud, Eriksson, Foucault, etc. into an apparently coherent theoretical approach. It is precisely the enormous, ambitious character of the project which is also Giddens's weakness, creating flaws and gaps in his argumentation. Giddens is like a tightrope walker who attempts a backwards flip while balancing in a high wind with water below. This is too ambitious, even for Giddens!

Giddens's work on the theory of the state can also be seen as a part of a larger breakthrough within sociology, where several theorists, such as Michael Mann, Brian Downing, Charles Tilly, Martin Shaw, and John Hall, have over the past decade or so placed the problem of the state and war on the agenda. With *A Contemporary Critique of Historical Materialism* and *The Nation-State and Violence*, Giddens situated himself as a central actor in this debate. With these books, he succeeded in conceptualizing the relations between state and society, pointing out the importance of the external relations of the state for societal development, and most of all emphasizing the importance of war and violence for societal development. The problem of violence, always a sensitive topic in sociology, had been overlooked for many years. Therefore, it has been liberating that someone has had the courage to take up the problem again in a time where war, civil war, gang warfare, and street violence belong to the order of the day.

The diagnosis of contemporary society and modernity, the ability to grasp the central trends in society (*Zeitdiagnose*), occupied Giddens in the 1990s. Four of his books demonstrate his exceptional ability to observe processes of change which characterize both societal institutions as well as single individuals and their self-identity (1990a, 1991a, 1992b, 1994b). His books on the condition of self, sexuality, and intimacy in modern society are pathbreaking works. Here, too, he has succeeded in setting the agenda for the sociology of the future and in pulling sexuality and intimacy out of the shadows and making them acceptable fields of study.

His recent move into politics and political theory demonstrates his ability to be at the center of current concerns (1994a, 1998a). There has never been a clear-cut division between sociology and politics in Giddens's work, but in these works, for the first time, he positively formulates and concentrates on political issues. It is an interesting development of his project, and it places him among many other contemporary sociologists who took the same step during the 1990s.

In general, Giddens is important because he breaks down the narrow disciplinary boundaries which have characterized the social and human sciences for years. Giddens allows the field of study to govern the choice of discipline, the theory, and the method instead of the reverse. With no respect for classical disciplinary boundaries, Giddens cuts across psychology, sociology, history, anthropology, ethnology, linguistics, political science, economics, and law. He picks, chooses, and applies the most useful elements to his own approach. This break with the narrow disciplinary boundaries can only be applauded. Notwithstanding the fact that his project is breathtaking and transcends disciplinary boundaries, it contains many problems and flaws. The inability to bridge the gap between actors and structures in his analysis of modernity is a serious problem, and perhaps it indicates that the 1980s and 1990s were the decades which saw the rise and fall of structuration theory. Much work needs to be done to save the theory and make it fruitful to base a genuine sociological analysis upon this perspective. We still have to wait and see if Giddens or others can elaborate the theory in order to provide an analysis of contemporary society and a political theory which contains a better balance in the actor–structure problem. Another conspicuous problem is that of culture and a more elaborated political theory. Time will tell if Giddens is able to overcome these problems and challenges. Notwithstanding these critical and unsolved aspects of his work, no one will be surprised if Giddens moves on to new unconquered areas where he will continue to give inspiration to sociologists in the new millennium.

Note

1 An idealtype is a conceptual abstraction which can be employed in trying to come to grips with the complexities of the social world. Max Weber, who can be considered the father of the idealtype method, developed among others an idealtype to characterize Protestantism in *The Protestant Ethic and the Spirit of Capitalism* (1920).

Epilogue
Giddens's Defense of Sociology: Stepping into Politics

In 1996, Giddens published a collection of essays, interpretations and rejoinders with the title *In Defence of Sociology*. In his introduction, he discusses problems and prospects for sociology. He is fairly optimistic, as long
as sociology regains self-confidence and redirects its focus toward more policy
and practical matters. It is interesting, however, to see that this collection of
essays ends with three chapters on politics: "T. H. Marshall, the state and
democracy," "Brave New World: the new context of politics," and "The
Labour Party and British politics." In other words, in order to defend sociology, his own response has been to step into politics – at least to tie
sociological analysis closer to politics and policy. This is not a unique step.
It is a more general trend, after some years of separation between sociology
and politics. After the decline of critical theory and Marxism in the late
1970s and 1980s, we saw a decline in the involvement of sociology in more
political matters. Over the past decade, several journals and books completely irrelevant to practical political matters have been published. A lot of
research has concentrated on methodological issues or pure theoretical discussions. Other brilliant British scholars, such as David Held, Paul Hirst,
and Barry Hindess, left a sociological focus long ago, and their work became anchored in political theory. The works of Jürgen Habermas have
been closely linked to political theory and even the late Michel Foucault,
with his work on governability, became more interested in politics. Clearly,
we cannot talk about a unitary movement within sociology stepping into
politics, but it is significant that during the 1990s high-profile sociologists
such as Ulrich Beck and Pierre Bourdieu followed this path.

Giddens's analysis of the development of the nation-state led him to
politics. Despite the fact that he returned to sociology by his focus on
modernity and the transformation of intimacy in the first part of the 1990s,

his ideas in *The Nation-State and Violence* remained important. When he became more interested in practical politics, his old ideas became reactualized and developed further into a more comprehensive political understanding. In other words, Giddens sees clearly, as other former sociologists did before him, that a move toward state and politics is necessary if you want more than just to interpret the world. Therefore, in order to change the world, or at least to have an impact, he has if not replaced then at least supplemented society and economy with state and politics.

Giddens and the Liberal Tradition in British Sociology

In this book, I have followed Giddens's development from critical commentator on the sociological classics, contemporary social theory, and philosophy, to his analysis of modernity and its institutions and his more recent contribution to politics. Giddens's endeavor and work are remarkable, but how can we assess his project and position within British social science in particular?

Within British sociology, Giddens can be compared with some of his predecessors with an institutional link to Cambridge and the London School of Economics and Political Science (LSE): Leonard T. Hobhouse (1864–1929), Morris Ginsberg (1889–1970), and T. H. Marshall (1893–1982) (Studholme, 1997; Smith, 1998). Recently, Studholme has demonstrated many parallels between Hobhouse and Giddens (Studholme, 1997). First, there is the institutional continuity: Hobhouse was affiliated with the LSE and influenced the development of sociology there. When Hobhouse died in 1929, Morris Ginsberg became his successor as sociology professor until he retired in 1954. Sociology spread as an academic discipline from the LSE to other departments such as those at Leicester and Hull – two universities which Giddens attended. Here Giddens became familiar with Hobhousian sociology, which he took with him in his fusion between the more heavy continental sociology and social philosophy and American sociology. Some of Giddens's colleagues at Leicester – Norbert Elias, Ilya Neustadt, and Percy Cohen – were influenced by Ginsberg, who became a communicator between the Hobhousian tradition and the new sociology departments in the postwar UK.

Another similarity between Hobhouse and Giddens concerns the content of their sociology: Giddens's interest in social psychology and his ideas of the reflexive agent and the emergence of the post-traditional global order are very much in line with Hobhouse's thinking (Studholme, 1997, p. 538). Studholme claims that Giddens's sociology functions to bolster a political theory in which the "good society" is one where (provided with the right sort of "institutions" and "therapy") even the poorest and most materially deprived social agents can reflexively choose "how to be," and in which radical redistributive measures become redundant if we can only define the "life values" appropriate to a "post-scarcity" order. This is Hobhousian Ethical sociology all over again. (Studholme, 1997, p. 545)

Giddens is the heir of Hobhousian liberal sociology. As an heir of Hobhouse and as an extremely influential sociologist in the postwar years, T. H. Marshall was also very important to Giddens. Being an important contributor to the liberal tradition going back to Hobhouse or perhaps even J. S. Mill, he influenced Giddens in the liberal direction. Marshall's interest in citizenship and social class and the continuous focus on the welfare state have been essential to Giddens's work on class and power, his interest in rights and obligations, and his redefinition of the welfare state (1974a, 1982a, c, 1985a, 1994a, 1998a). Giddens added a new ontological and epistemological basis, a touch of Marxism, and his whole baggage of continental sociology, not least Weber and Durkheim. One of the conspicuous denominators in Marshall's and Giddens's sociology is the strong belief "in the need for energetic and creative individualists" (Smith, 1998, p. 667). Similar to the Hobhouse parallel, the institutional affiliations between Marshall and Giddens are another denominator. Marshall, like Giddens, had a connection with Cambridge, the LSE, Leicester University, and the Labour Party (Smith, 1998, p. 667).

It is interesting that Hobhouse, Marshall, and Giddens share a common project. They are all concerned about the decay of social institutions and the welfare state. In particular, Giddens continues many of Marshall's tasks. Marshall pointed out the tension between capitalism and democracy. Citizenship, and the extension of social rights in particular, was Marshall's response to the inherent conflict. Giddens deals with this problem in *The Third Way* (1998a). He appreciates the dynamic forces of capitalism as necessary, since they create jobs, enable people to become risk-takers, and are very innovative forces which benefit society. He cannot accept, however, the increasing social inequality, because it undermines social cohesion and solidarity. Thus Giddens is stuck in the same dilemma as Marshall, but Giddens attempts to come up with new solutions, including a redefinition of welfare and Marshall's conception of rights. Giddens stresses responsibility and obligations, and suggests a new type of positive welfare and generative politics.

This attempt to situate Giddens in a broader context in British sociology clearly demonstrates that he is a part of a longer liberal tradition, and also that his institutional affiliations are important to his career and thinking.

To claim that Giddens's way of thinking and his basic ideas have their origin in Hobhouse or Marshall only, as indicated especially by Studholme, is not reasonable. It is to simplify a much more complex pattern of interchange of ideas between many schools of thought. Even if Giddens shares some common ideas with Hobhouse and tends to stress the agent at the expense of structures and material conditions, this cannot alone be taken as evidence of Giddens's close connection to Hobhouse. Partly, Giddens has picked up these ideas from other traditions as well (such as Heidegger, Wittgenstein, Goffman, Garfinkel, and perhaps Weber), and partly it is embedded in British social theory going further back than Hobhouse. In other words, Giddens is a replicate of neither Hobhouse nor Marshall, but there can be no doubt that they share some common ideas and have many similar institutional affiliations.

Giddens and the Future

Giddens has become a phenomenon – an intellectual star. In 1999, he received the honor of giving the Reith Lectures at the BBC. He lectured in London, Hong Kong, Washington DC, and Delhi, concentrating on his favorite themes: globalization, the family, risk, tradition, and democracy. Since taking up a position as director at the LSE, he has regularly lectured for all students and faculty – the so-called "The Director's Lectures" with the theme "politics after socialism." He is widely read, in many languages, and he has without doubt been one of the most important ambassadors for sociology during the past two decades. His latest shift of focus from social theory and sociology to politics could indicate that he might be lost for sociology. His shift from Professor to Director, from doing research to concentrating on administrative work, might suggest that he has said what he needs to say in the sociological area. I doubt that this is true. Giddens will probably reinvent himself as a sociologist. A book on media, religion, or the family would be appropriate and might appear in the future.

Other questions remain to be answered. How influential will Giddens be in the future? Which part of his work will stand as the most original? These are obviously difficult questions. However, my guess is that despite the many problems of the theory of structuration, this part will stand as Giddens's most important contribution to social theory. Next, his ideas on globalization, detraditionalization, and social reflexivity will be remembered, perhaps not for their originality, but because he put them on the agenda. How he will be assessed in the future compared to the classical sociologists (Marx, Weber, Durkheim, and Simmel) is difficult to predict, but his work will probably only be regarded as parenthetical and as an indication of his time.

Compared with such contemporary thinkers as Bourdieu, Luhmann, and Habermas, he might be regarded as slightly "lighter," but I am not sure this is a fair assessment of his work. There is no doubt that compared to these thinkers Giddens is less methodologically cogent. Compared to the other three, his concepts are more loose and less clearly defined. However, his theories contain more potential than is often realized. Moreover, we cannot know what he will come up with in the future. He could produce a number of important works which will strengthen his project and make it even more comprehensive. His political contribution will hardly be regarded as a significant one to political theory, but it will be remembered for two reasons: here, for the first time, he reveals his political position and attempts to contribute actively to changing the world; second, he will be remembered for his attempt to provide some intellectual substance to the Blair project.

The final questions to be raised but not answered are: Does Giddens's shift from sociology to politics and more policy-oriented issues represent a general trend in social sciences? Does it symbolize the failure of sociology? Or is it, on the contrary, a sign of a reinvention and strengthening of the discipline? These questions can hardly be answered from scrutinizing Giddens's work alone, but it is thought provoking that a prominent sociologist takes this step. At any rate, Giddens's move can be seen as a challenge to sociology in general.

Sociology under Transformation?

Before I close this epilogue, an attempt at answering the following question is appropriate: why are some scholars becoming less involved in sociology? Here we need to look into the heart of sociology and see the ambivalence of the discipline. I shall argue that while sociology, as Giddens claims, in some respects has been a success, it can be seen from another perspective as a failure. As Giddens argues, and rightly in my opinion, the discipline has provided an enormous amount of knowledge which has become a part of common knowledge among people. For example, we know that modern societies have a higher divorce rate compared to previous societies, or that work, family, and leisure structures have changed considerably over the past 100 years. This is knowledge generated by sociologists in various contexts. Also, concepts and terms such as deviance, charisma, and social status, and their implications, have been introduced by sociologists and used by lay people to understand their own world.

Another strength but also a weakness of sociology relates to the very core of the discipline and its development. Sociology developed as a sci-

ence during the eighteenth but mainly the nineteenth century as a response
to enormous social changes, including industrialization, expanding capitalism, and the rise of the nation-state. In the mid- and late nineteenth century economics as the dominating social science ran into problems conceiving
and explaining these social changes. Sociology as a discipline arose in opposition to unsatisfactory explanations and propositions about society, its
institutions, and its evolution brought forward mainly by economists such
as Adam Smith, David Ricardo, the older historical school, and classical
and neo-classical economists. Marx himself was a response to inconsistent
economic theory (Adam Smith and David Ricardo), while Weber and
Durkheim both responded to problems in economic theories in the late
nineteenth century. Marx, Weber, and Durkheim developed alternative
theories and explanations because they found economic theories deeply
unsatisfactorily. The three classical thinkers provided us with new concep-
tions of society and the social, and new attempts to overcome dichotomies
such as micro versus macro, agent versus structure and nometetic versus
idiographic explanations. Nevertheless, they remained in some respects
within a framework generated by economics. Their theories focus on the
problems of industrialization, the increasing division of labor and its implications, the rise and expansion of capitalism, and the development of a new
ethic, formal rationalization, and alienation. They stressed explanations and
reasons for the rapid change in the eighteenth and nineteenth centuries
that were different from those of the economists. In general they were
much more sophisticated and comprehensive in their theories and explanations than economists, but they still responded to changes mainly related
to economic issues in the broad sense of the term.

This economic framework has kept a major part of sociology embedded
in a societal thinking where society has been the center of the discipline.
This concern with societal matters and society as a point of departure for
most theorizing within sociology can be seen as a strength and a weakness
at the same time. No doubt, as already indicated, sociology, by concentrating on society and the social, has contributed to new and important knowledge. Yet the societal focus also involves some problems for sociology.

First, most sociological theories take for granted that society is identical
to the nation-state. This problem has been pointed out by several scholars
during the past fifteen years or so (Giddens, 1985a; Mann, 1986; Tilly,
1992). To overcome this problem requires a sociology which among other
things takes history and politics, including interstate relations, warfare, and
geopolitics, into account. Otherwise, it is difficult to understand how and
why a single form of political organization – the nation-state – ended up
being the dominant state form in the European state system. From the
Middle Ages on various political organizations coexisted and competed in

a life-and-death struggle which, eventually, led to the emergence of the territorial sovereign state and later the nation-state as dominant state forms. Consequently, the correspondence between a demarcated society and the nation-state developed as a result of a long historical process. This cannot be explained by traditional sociological theory in any satisfactorily way. This is again related to other problems of sociology: the problem of demarcation of society, the concept of the state and the state–society relationship.

Most theories conceive state and society in very similar terms. Often society is seen as preceding the state, as a result of a group of individuals or classes merging or fusing into a single entity – a society. Then the state is installed as a political and administrative superstructure necessary to maintain law and order, protection, administration, and infrastructure. The state and its society are demarcated entities. Other demarcated states/societies coexist next to them. Why state and societies are demarcated and how this has happened are two questions that are never addressed and never theoretically explained by most sociological theories. An example is the Hobbesian model of society and state, in which a group of individuals enter into a contract and transfer power to the state. Why don't all individuals of the world, however, make one single contract with one world state? The logical consequence of Hobbes's model would be a global contract with one Leviathan, but not even Hobbes anticipated that as a possibility. Why is the world divided into several societies and states? Hobbes and most thinkers since the late Renaissance, including the whole sociological tradition, never question this problem. All theories simply presuppose that the globe is covered by multiple states and societies separated by borders or frontiers. What determines this division is hardly ever questioned.

Thus this conception of state and society has two major problems. First, it cannot account for the problem of separation of societies. Why is the world divided into separate states and societies? Why not one single contract between all people in the world? The second problem concerns the theoretical implications of this theory. If the state is a result of an internal fusion, the state and society are conceived as entities prior to the system of states and societies. The state (and society) is taken as a given, and only at this stage can relations between states or societies be understood.

> States form *systems* to the extent that they interact, and to the degree that their interaction significantly affects each party's fate. Since states always grow out of competition for control of territory and population, they invariably appear in clusters, and usually form systems. . . . States form a *system* to the extent that they interact with each other regularly, and to the degree that their interaction affects the behavior of each state. (Tilly, 1992, pp. 4, 162; emphasis in original)

As demonstrated in this quotation, the conception of a fusion model of state and society implies that the fundamental features of the state system is a result of interacting states. A conception of states based on the fusion of individuals, classes, modes of production, etc. implies that social change is mainly regarded as a consequence of internal processes; for example, class struggle, rationalization, technological changes, individual agency, or social movements fighting for rights. Warfare, too, is considered as a result of action of the states. Usually peace is regarded as the normal and dominant feature of the state system, but occasionally war breaks out following changes within a state leading to a threat of other states.

In other words, this conception of state and state system has some inherent flaws in explaining social change and social reproduction. The processes of change and reproduction, derived from the very state *system* itself (the relations between states) and with immense consequences for states and their internal relations, cannot be explained or understood adequately from a fusion perspective. In the latter, external relations between states are regarded as a result of the conduct and action performed by states, and not as a consequence of the *relation between states*. Moreover, warfare, with its implications for social change, is often ignored or at best only underrated by most of the traditional social theories, such as Marxism, functionalism/liberalism, and theories of social interaction.

This endogenous perspective on state and society, the embeddedness in a fusion conception of state and society, is an obstacle to sociology. It prevents sociology from moving toward a genuinely relational social theory in which the very *relation* between entities (states, societies, social groups, individuals) are seen as the point of departure. To understand the relationship between states as constituting these states is crucial to the conception of some fundamental aspects of politics, state, and state–society relations. Only by taking a relational perspective incorporating the interstate relationship can we reconceptualize the state, society, and their relationship, and, therefore, provide sociology with a stronger theoretical framework to understand past, current, and future developments. Only by such a step can sociology respond more appropriately to contemporary challenges.

Some sociologists focus on these problems, but few have come up with solutions. Giddens himself made an attempt with *The Nation-State and Violence* (1985), but he failed to come up with convincing theoretical solutions that can transcend the society-centered approach inherited from classical sociology. Even Giddens remains anchored in a fusion conception of state and society, although he clearly demonstrates in his empirical analysis that the state is constituted through its relations with other states and politics, and in the last instance war as the *ultimo ratio* is the essence of the state. Politics and war are key means of survival as a state – of remaining recognized by other states. Giddens also observes the changes in warfare in the twentieth century, especially in recent years, but without a stronger theory of the state, politics, and warfare, he is not capable of producing an analysis where the implications for state and society are clearly demonstrated.

At least Giddens has realized the problems of sociology and its limitations. Thus he has taken the step and faced the challenge from contemporary politics. Some sociologists have turned their back on this strategy and instead stepped into cultural sociology or cultural studies, while others have returned to economics. Unfortunately, these sociologists have not reinvented sociology as a discipline attempting to overcome poor economic theory. On the contrary, these scholars have returned to economic theory (mainly classical and neo-classical economics) in the shape of rational choice theory, which in its essence developed before the rise of modern sociology.

My answer to the question raised at the beginning of this section must be that many sociologists have realized that only a closer link to politics can bring sociology further. Remaining embedded in traditional sociological thinking, with its constraining conception of state and society, partly prevents the discipline from producing more appropriate and plausible analyses of and stronger explanations for the many contemporary challenges, and partly is an obstacle to the development of more visionary ideas on what constitutes a good society. Consequently, I can only endorse Giddens and others stepping into politics, although a more appropriate reconceptualization of the state is a necessity, if we are to strengthen not only sociology but also social theory in general to meet contemporary and future challenges. A forthcoming book takes up this challenge (Kaspersen, forthcoming).

Bibliography

Works by Anthony Giddens

A complete listing of books published by Giddens is included. It includes both his own work and edited books. The listed journal articles have been selected by the author. Book reviews by Giddens are included only when they have been cited in the text.

Books

Giddens, A. (1971a) *Capitalism and Modern Social Theory*. Cambridge: Cambridge University Press.

Giddens, A. (ed.) (1971b) *The Sociology of the Suicide*. London: Cassier.

Giddens, A. (1972a) *Politics and Sociology in the Thought of Max Weber*. London: Macmillan.

Giddens, A. (ed.) (1972b) *Emile Durkheim – Selected Writings*. Cambridge: Cambridge University Press.

Giddens, A. (1973) *The Class Structure of the Advanced Societies*. London/New York: Hutchinson.

Giddens, A. and Stanworth, P. (eds) (1974a) *Elites and Power in the British Society*. Cambridge: Cambridge University Press.

Giddens, A. (ed.) (1974b) *Positivism and Sociology*. London: Heineman.

Giddens, A. (1976a) *New Rules of Sociological Method*. London: Hutchinson.

Giddens, A. (1977a) *Studies in Social and Political Theory*. London: Hutchinson.

Giddens, A. (1978a) *Durkheim – Modern Masters*. London: Fontana.

Giddens, A. (1979a) *Central Problems in Social Theory*. London: Macmillan.

Giddens, A. (1981a) *A Contemporary Critique of Historical Materialism*. London: Macmillan.

Giddens, A. and Mackenzie, G. (eds) (1982a) *Social Class and the Division of Labour: Essays in Honour of Ilya Neustadt*. Cambridge: Cambridge University Press.

Giddens, A. and Held, D. (eds) (1982b) *Classes, Power, and Conflict*. London: Macmillan.

Giddens, A. (1982c) *Sociology – a Brief but Critical Introduction*. London: Macmillan.

Giddens, A. (1982d) *Profiles and Critique in Social Theory*. London: Macmillan.

Giddens, A. (1984a) *The Constitution of Society*. Cambridge: Polity Press.

Giddens, A. (1985a) *The Nation-State and Violence*. Cambridge: Polity Press.

Giddens, A. (ed.) (1986a) *Durkheim on Politics and The State*. Cambridge: Polity Press.

Giddens, A. (1987a) *Social Theory and Modern Sociology*. Cambridge: Polity Press.

Giddens, A. and Turner J. (eds) (1987b) *Social Theory Today*. Cambridge: Polity Press.

Giddens, A. (1989a) *Sociology*. Cambridge: Polity Press.

Giddens, A. (1990a) *The Consequences of Modernity*. Cambridge: Polity Press.

Giddens, A. (1991a) *Modernity and Self-Identity*. Cambridge: Polity Press.

Giddens, A. (ed.) (1992a) *Human Societies*. Cambridge: Polity Press.

Giddens, A. (1992b) *The Transformation of Intimacy*. Cambridge: Polity Press.

Giddens, A. (1994a) *Beyond Left and Right – the Future of Radical Politics*. Cambridge: Polity Press.

Giddens, A. (1995a) *Politics, Sociology and Social Theory: Encounters with Classical and Contemporary Social Thought*. Cambridge: Polity Press.

Giddens, A. (1996a) *In Defence of Sociology: Essays, Interpretations, and Rejoinders*. Cambridge: Polity Press.

Giddens, A. (1998a) *The Third Way – a Renewal of Social Democracy*. Cambridge: Polity Press.

Giddens, A. and Pierson, C. (1998b) *Conversations with Anthony Giddens. Making Sense of Modernity*. Cambridge: Polity Press.

Giddens, A. (2000a) *The Third Way and Its Critics*. Cambridge: Polity Press.

Giddens, A. and Hutton, W. (2000b) *On the Edge*. London: Jonathan Cape.

Journal Articles, Contributions to Books, etc.

Giddens, A. (1960) Aspects of the social structure of a university hall of residence. *The Sociological Review*, 8, 97–108.

Giddens, A. (1964a) Notes on the concepts of play and leisure. *The Sociological Review*, 12(1), 73–89.

Giddens, A. (1964b) Suicide, attempted suicide, and the suicidal threat. *Man: a Record of Anthropological Science*, 64,115–16.

Giddens, A. (1965a) Theoretical problems in the sociology of suicide. *Advancement of Science*, 21, 522–6.

Giddens, A. (1965b) The suicide problem in French sociology. *The British Journal of Sociology*, 16(1), 365–72.

Giddens, A. (1965c) The present position of social psychology. *British Journal of Sociology*, 1, 365–72.

Giddens, A. (1965d) Georg Simmel. *New Society*, 4(112), 24–5.

Giddens, A. and Holloway, S. W. F. (1965e) Profiting from a comprehensive school: a critical comment. *British Journal of Sociology*, 16, 365–72.

Giddens, A. (1965f) Suicide. *British Journal of Sociology*, 16, 164–5.

Giddens, A. (1966a) Personal and social identity. *Common Factor Monographs*, 2.

Giddens, A. (1966b) A typology of suicide. *Archives européennes*, 7, 276–95.

Giddens, A. (1968a) Power in the recent writings of Talcott Parsons. *Sociology*, 2, 257–72.

Giddens, A. (1968b) Founding fathers of sociology: Georg Simmel. In T. Raison (ed.), *Founding Fathers of Sociology*. London: Penguin.

Giddens, A. (1970a) Durkheim as a review critic. *The Sociological Review*, 18, 171–96.

Giddens, A. (1970b) Recent works on the history of social thought. *Archives européennes de sociologie*, 11, 130–42.

Giddens, A. (1970c) Recent works on the position and prospects of contemporary sociology. *Archives européennes de sociologie*, 11, 143–54.

Giddens, A. (1970d) Introduction. In Thomas Masaryk, *Suicide and the Meaning of Civilization*. Chicago: Chicago University Press.

Giddens, A. (1970e) Marx, Weber and the development of capitalism. *Sociology*, 4, 289–310.

Giddens, A. (1971c) Marx and Weber: a reply to Mr Watson. *Sociology*, 5, 395–7.

Giddens, A. (1971d) Durkheim's political sociology. *Sociological Review*, 19, 477–519.

Giddens, A. (1971e) The 'individual' in the writings of Emile Durkheim. *Archives européenes de sociologie*, 12, 210–28.

Giddens, A. (1972c) Four myths in the history of social thought. *Economy and Society*, 1, 357–85.

Giddens, A. (1972d) Elites in the British class structure. *Sociological Review*, 2, 345–72.

Giddens, A. (1972e) Elites, Article 7 in a series on social stratification. *New Society*, 22 (258), 389–92.

Giddens, A. and Stanworth, P. (1975a) The modern corporate economy: interlocking directorships in Britain 1960–70. *The Sociological Review*, 23, 5–23.

Giddens, A. (1975b) The high priest of positivism: Auguste Comte. *The Times Literary Supplement*, 14 November.

Giddens, A. (1975c) American sociology today. *New Society*, 33 (676), 633–4.

Giddens, A. (1976b) Ethnometodology, hermeneutics, and the problems of interpretive analysis. In L. Coser and O. Larsen (eds), *The Uses of Controversy in Sociology*. New York: Basic Books.

Giddens, A. (1976c) Excerpts from 1975 address to the American Sociological Association in San Francisco. *Phenomenological Sociology Newsletter*, 4, 5–8.

Giddens, A. (1976d) Classical social theory and the origins of modern sociology. *American Journal of Sociology*, 81.

Giddens, A. (1976e) Functionalism: apres la lutte. *Social Research*, 23, 325–66.

Giddens, A. (1976f) The rich. *New Society*, 38 (732), 63–6.

Giddens, A. (1977b) Habermas's social and political theory. *American Journal of Sociology*, 82, 198–212.

Giddens, A. (1977c) Introduction to Max Weber: *The Protestant Ethic and the Spirit of Capitalism*. London: Allen and Unwin.

Giddens, A. and Stanworth, P. (1978b) Elites and privilege. In P. Abrams (ed.),

UK Society Today. London: Weidenfeld and Nicolson.

Giddens, A. (1978c) Positivism and its critics. In T. Bottomore and R. Nisbet (eds), *A History of Sociological Analysis.* New York: Basic Books.

Giddens, A. (1978d) Class and classless society. *Partisan Review,* 45, 133–45.

Giddens, A. (1979b) An anatomy of the British ruling class. *New Society,* 50, 8–10.

Giddens, A. (1979c) Habermas's critique of hermeneutics. In T. Freiburg (ed.), *Critical Sociology, European Perspectives.* New York: Irvington.

Giddens, A. (1979d) Prospects for social theory today. *Berkeley Journal of Sociology,* February, 201–23.

Giddens, A. (1979e) Literature and society: Raymond Williams. *Times Higher Education Supplement,* 14 December.

Giddens, A. (1979f) Schutz and Parsons: problems of meaning and subjectivity. *Contemporary Sociology,* 8, 682–5.

Giddens, A. (1980) Review essay: classes, capitalism, and the state – a discussion of Frank Parkin, Marxism and class theory: a bourgeois critique. *Theory and Society,* 9, 877–90.

Giddens, A. (1981b) Agency, institution and time–space analysis. In K. Knorr-Cetina and A. Cicourel (eds), *Advances in Social Theory and Methodology: Toward an Integration of Micro- and Macro-Sociologies.* London: Routledge.

Giddens, A. (1981c) Modernism and postmodernism. *New German Critique,* 22 (winter), 15–18.

Giddens, A. (1981d) Time and space in social theory: critical remarks on functionalism. *Current Perspectives in Social Theory,* 2, 3–13.

Giddens, A. (1981e) Durkheim, socialism and Marxism. In A. Izzo et al. (eds), *Durkheim.* Rome: Institute of Sociology.

Giddens, A. (1981f) Sociology and philosophy. In P. Secord (ed.), *Action Theory and Structural Analysis.* Oxford: Blackwell.

Giddens, A. (1981g) Trends in the philosophy of social sciences. In D. Lawton (ed.), *Current Perspectives in Education.* London: Methuen.

Giddens, A. (1981h) Labour and interaction. In J. Thompson and D. Held (eds), *Habermas, Critical Debates.* London: Macmillan.

Giddens, A. (1982e) A reply to my critics. *Theory, Culture and Society,* 1(2), 107–13.

Giddens, A. (1982f) Reason without revolution? *Praxis International,* 4, 318–38.

Giddens, A. (1982g) European society in the 1980s: class division, conflict and citizenship rights. In S. Vea (ed.), *Perspectives on Europe Today.* Milan: Feltrinelli.

Giddens, A. (1982h) Functionalism: commentary on the debate. *Theory and Society,* 11, 527–39.

Giddens, A. (1982i) On the relation of sociology and philosophy. In P. Secord (ed.), *Explaining Human Behavior: Consciousness, Human Action and Social Structure.* Beverly Hills, CA: Sage.

Giddens, A. (1982j) Mediator of meaning. *Times Literary Supplement,* 4118, 240.

Giddens, A. (1982k) Action, structure and power. In P. Secord (ed.), *Explaining Human Behavior.* Beverly Hills, CA: Sage.

Giddens, A. (1982l) Hermeneutics and social theory. In A. Sica and S. McNall (eds), *Hermeneutics.* Amherst: University of Massachusetts Press.

Giddens, A. (1982m) Historical materialism today. An interview with A. Giddens. *Theory, Culture and Society*, 1, 63–77.

Giddens, A. (1982n) Space, time and politics in social theory: an interview with A. Giddens. *Society and Space*, 2, 123–32.

Giddens, A. (1982o) Review Symposium – Ulf Himmelstrand et al., Beyond Welfare Capitalism. *Acta Sociologica*, 25(3), 301–20.

Giddens, A. (1983a) Four theses on ideology. *Canadian Journal of Social and Political Theory*, 7, 18–21.

Giddens, A. (1983b) Comments on the theory of structuration. *Journal for Theory of Social Behaviour*, 13, 75–80.

Giddens, A. (1983c) Klassenspaltung, Klassenkonflikt and Burgerrechte. *Soziale Welt*, Supplement 1, 15–31.

Giddens, A. (1984b) The nation-state and violence. In W. W. Powell and R. Robbins (eds), *Conflict and Consensus, Essays in Honour of Lewis Coser*. New York: Praeger.

Giddens, A. (1984c) The body, reflexivity, social reproduction: Erving Goffman and social theory. *Rassegna Italiana di Sociologia*, 25(3), 369–400.

Giddens, A. (1985b) Marx's correct views on everything. *Theory and Society*, 14, 167–74.

Giddens, A. (1985c) Review essay: liberalism and sociology. *Contemporary Sociology*, 14, 320–2.

Giddens, A. (1985d) Jürgen Habermas. In Q. Skinner (ed.), *The Return of Grand Theory in the Human Sciences*. Cambridge: Polity Press.

Giddens, A. (1985e) Time, space and regionalization. In D. Gregory and J. Urry (eds), *Social Relations and Spatial Structures*. London: Macmillan.

Giddens, A. (1985f) The end of the working class? In J. Goldthorpe and H. Strasser (eds), *Stratification and Inequality*. Opladen.

Giddens, A. (1985g) Time, history and sociology. *Society and Space*, 4.

Giddens, A. (1986b) Action, subjectivity, and the constitution of meaning. *Social Research*, 53(3), 529–45.

Giddens, A. (1987c) Time and space in social theory. *Social Science*, 72(2–4), 99–103.

Giddens, A. (1988) Globalisation and modern social development. In E. Bartocci (ed.), *Social Change and Social Conflict in Neo-Industrial Society*, Rome.

Giddens, A. (1989b) A Reply to my critics. In D. Held and J. Thompson (eds), *Social Theory of Modern Societies: Anthony Giddens and His Critics*. Cambridge: Cambridge University Press.

Tonkin, B. and Giddens, A. (1989c) States of Emergency. *New Statesman and Society*, 2(49), 14–15.

Giddens, A. (1989d) R. K. Merton on structure and function. In J. Clark et al. (eds), *Robert K. Merton: Consensus and Controversy*. Brighton: Falmer Press.

Giddens, A. (1990b) Socialism, modernity and utopianism. *New Statesman and Society*, 3, 125.

Giddens, A. (1990c) Modernity and utopia. *New Statesman and Society*, 3 (125), 20–2.

Giddens, A. (1990d) Structuration theory and sociological analysis. In J. Clark, C. Modgil, and S. Modgil (eds), *Consensus and Controversy: Anthony Giddens*. London: Falmer Press.

Giddens, A. (1990e) Introduction to Thomas Scheff, *Microsociology*. Chicago: University of Chicago Press.

Giddens, A. (1991b) Structuration theory: past, present and future. In C. G. A. Bryant and D. Jary (eds), *Giddens' Theory of Structuration*. London: Routledge.

Giddens, A. (1991c) Rejoinder to MacKenzie and Spinardi. *Sociology*, 25(3), 473–5.

Giddens, A. (1992c) Commentary on the reviews. *Theory, Culture and Society*, 9(2), 171–4.

Giddens, A. (1993) Review essay: modernity, history, democracy. *Theory and Society*, 22, 289–92.

Giddens, A. (1994b) Living in the post-traditional society. In U. Beck, A. Giddens, and S. Lash, *Reflexive Modernization*. Cambridge: Polity Press.

Giddens, A. (1994c) What's left for Labour? *New Statesman and Society*, 30 September, 37–40.

Giddens, A. (1994d) Agenda change. *New Statesman and Society*, 7 October, 23–5.

Giddens, A. (1994e) Out of the red. *New Statesman and Society*, 14 October, 22–4.

Giddens, A. (1994f) Brave New World? The new context of politics. In D. Miliband (ed.), *Reinventing the Left*. Cambridge: Polity Press.

Giddens, A. (1994g) Rough and Tough. *New Statesman and Society*, 7 (284), 37–8.

Giddens, A. (1995b) What's he up to? *New Statesman and Society*, 8 (342), 21–4.

Giddens, A. (1995c) In defence of sociology. *New Statesman and Society*, 8 (347), 18–21.

Giddens, A. (1996b) There is a radical centre-ground. *New Statesman*, 125 (3412), 18–20.

Giddens, A. (1996c) Centre left at centre stage. *New Statesman*, 126 (4332), 37–40.

Giddens, A. (1996d) Affluence, poverty and the idea of a post-scarcity society. *Development and Change*, 27(2), 365–77.

Seldon, A. (1996e) Interview: the influence of sociology in post-war Britain. *Contemporay British History*, 10(1), 144–51.

Giddens, A. and Soros, G. (1997) Beyond chaos and dogma . . . : dialogue on need for global polity to regulate world economy. *New Statesman*, 31 October, 24–31.

Giddens, A. (1998c) After the left's paralysis: the third way can provide a framework for political and economic thought that cuts across the old divides of social democracy and neoliberalism. *New Statesman*, 127 (4383), 18–22.

Giddens, A. (1999a) Better than warmed over porridge. *New Statesman*, 12 February, 25–6.

Giddens, A. (1999b) Director's Lectures, London School of Economics.

Giddens, A. (1999c) *BBC Reith Lectures 1999*. (Published under the title *Runaway World* by Profile Books, London.)

Debate and Critique of Giddens's Work

Most of the works included are in English. Key contributions are marked with an asterisk.

Agger, B. (1990) Review: Giddens/Turner, Social Theory Today. *Social Forces*, 69(2), 647–9.

Albrow, M. (1990) English Channel. *Times Higher Education Supplement*, 991 (April).

Anderson, Perry (1994) Power, politics, and the Enlightenment. In D. Miliband (ed.), *Reinventing the Left*. Cambridge: Polity Press.

*Archer, M. S. (1982) Morphogenesis versus structuration: on combining structure and action. *British Journal of Sociology*, 33(4), 455–83.

Archer, M. S. (1985) Structuration versus morphogenesis. In S. Eisenstadt and H. Helle (eds), *Macro-sociological Theory: Perspectives on Sociological Theory, 1*. London: Sage.

Archer, M. S. (1990) Human agency and social structure: a critique of Giddens. In J. Clark, C. Modgil, and S. Modgil (eds), *Consensus and Controversy: Anthony Giddens*. London: Falmer Press.

Arnason, J. P. (1987) Review essay: the state and its contexts. *Australian and New Zealand Journal of Sociology*, 23(3), 433–42.

Ashley, D. (1982) Historical materialism and social evolutionism. *Theory, Culture and Society*, 2(2), 89–91.

Baber, Z. (1991) Beyond the structure/agency dualism: an evaluation of Giddens' theory of structuration. *Sociological Inquiry*, 61(2), 219–30.

Badham, R. (1984) The sociology of industrial and post-industrial societies. *Current Sociology*, 32, 1–14.

*Bagguley, P. (1984) Giddens and historical materialism. *Radical Philosophy*, 38, 18–24.

Bang, H. P. (1987a) Politics as praxis. A new trend in political science. *Statsvetenskaplig Tidsskrift*, 90(1), 1–20.

Bang, H. P. (1987b) The reawakening of a slumbering tradition. A reply. *Statsvetenskaplig Tidsskrift*, 90(4), 303–13.

Barbalet, J. M. (1987) Power, structural resources, and agency. *Current Perspectives in Social Theory*, 8, 1–24.

Barbalet, J. M. (1990) Review: Giddens and Turner (eds), Social Theory Today. *Theory, Culture and Society*, 7(1), 163–6.

Barnes, B. (1980) Review: central problems in social theory. *Sociological Review*, 28, 674–6.

Barrett, J. C. (1988) Fields of discourse: reconstituting a social archeology. *Critique of Anthropology*, 7, 5–16.

*Bauman, Z. (1989) Hermeneutics and modern social theory. In D. Held and J. Thompson (eds), *Social Theory of Modern Societies: Anthony Giddens and His Critics*. Cambridge: Cambridge University Press.

Bauman, Z. (1993) Review: the transformation of intimacy: sexuality, love and eroticism in modern societies. *The Sociological Review*, 41(2), 363–8.

*Beck, U. (1992) How modern is modern society? *Theory, Culture and Society*, 9(2), 163–70.

Beck, U., Giddens, A. and Lash, S. (1994b) *Reflexive Modernization*. Cambridge: Polity Press.

Berger, J. (1977) Handlung und Struktur in der soziologishen Theorie. *Das Argu-*

ment, 19, 55–6.

Berger, J. (1984) Review of Giddens, 'A Contemporary Critique of Historical Materialism', vol. 1. *Kölner Zeitschrift für Soziologie und Socialpsychologie*, 36, 175–7.

*Bernstein, R. J. (1986) Structuration theory as critical theory. *Praxis – a Philosophical Journal*, 6 (2), 235–49.

Bernstein, R. J. (1989) Social theory as critique. In D. Held and J. Thompson (eds), *Social Theory of Modern Societies: Anthony Giddens and His Critics*. Cambridge: Cambridge University Press.

*Bertilsson, M. (1984) The theory of structuration: prospects and problems. *Acta Sociologica*, 27(4), 339–53.

Bertilsson, M. (1987) Replik: Struktureringsteorin – en teori utan praxis? *Statsvetenskaplig Tidskrift*, 90(4), 298–302.

Bertilsson, M. (1988) Recensionsartikel: Giddens mot Giddens – med hjälp av Hegel. *Sociologisk Forskning*, 4, 64–71.

Betts, K. (1986) The conditions of actions, power and the problem of interests. *Sociological Review*, 34, 39–64.

Bhaskar, R. (1983) Beef, structure and place: notes from a critical naturalist perspective. *Journal for Theory of Social Behaviour*, 13, 81–95.

*Bleicher, J. and Featherstone, M. (1982) Historical materialism today: an interview with Anthony Giddens. *Theory, Culture and Society*, 1(2), 63–77.

Boland, R. J. (1993) Accounting and the interpretative act. *Accounting, Organizations and Society*, 18(2/3), 125–46.

Bologh, R. W. (1994) Review: the transformation of intimacy. *Contemporary Sociology*, 23, 845–6.

Bottomore, T. (1990) Giddens' view of historical materialism. In J. Clark, C. Modgil, and S. Modgil (eds), *Consensus and Controversy: Anthony Giddens*. London: Falmer Press.

Boyne, R. (1991) Power-knowledge and social theory: the systematic misrepresentation of contemporary French social theory in the work of A. Giddens. In C. G. A. Bryant and D. Jary (eds), *Giddens' Theory of Structuration*. London: Routledge.

Boynton, R. S. (1997) The two Tonys: why is the prime minister so interested in what Anthony Giddens thinks? *New Yorker*, 73(30), 66–75.

Brante, T. (1989) *Anthony Giddens och samhällsvetenskapen*. Stockholm: Symposion.

Braun, J. (1996) Review: reflexive modernization – politics, tradition and aesthetics in the modern social-order. *Theory and Society*, 25(5), 752–60 .

Breuilly, J. (1990) The nation-state and violence: a critique of Giddens. In J. Clark, C. Modgil, and S. Modgil (eds), *Consensus and Controversy: Anthony Giddens*. London: Falmer Press.

Bromley, Simon (1991) The politics of postmodernism – review article. *Capital and Class*, 45 (autumn), 129–50.

Bryant, C. G. A. (1987a) Developing theories – review of social theory and modern society. *Times Higher Education Supplement*, 24 April.

Bryant, C. G. A. (1987b) The constitution of society: Elias, Bhaskar and Giddens compared. Paper presented to the Faculty of Social Sciences, University of Utrecht, mimeo.

Bryant, C. G. A. (1989) Review article: Towards post-empiricist sociological theorising – review of Giddens/Turner, Social Theory Today. *The British Journal of Sociology*, 40(2), 319–27.

Bryant, C. G. A. (1990) Sociology without epistemology? The Case of Giddens' structuration theory. Unpublished paper presented to XII World Congress of Sociology, Madrid.

Bryant, C. G. A. (1991a) Review: Clark et al., A. Giddens – Consensus and Controversy. *Sociology*, 25(1), 151–2.

Bryant, C. G. A. (1991b) Review: A. Giddens, Sociology. *Theory, Culture and Society*, 8(2), 191–3.

Bryant, C. G. A. (1991c) The dialogical model of applied sociology. In C. G. A. Bryant and D. Jary, *Giddens's Theory of Structuration*. London: Routledge.

Bryant, C. G. A. (1992) Sociology without philosophy? The case of Giddens' structuration theory. *Sociological Theory*, 10(2), 137–49.

Bryant, C. G. A. (1993) Anthony Giddens, Hon. D.Litt., Salford. *Network: Newsletter of the British Sociological Association*, 57, 7.

Bryant, C. G. A. (1998) The uses of Giddens' structuration theory. *International Sociological Association*, paper.

*Bryant, C. G. A. and Jary, D. (1991a) *Giddens's Theory of Structuration: a Critical Appreciation*. London: Routledge.

Bryant, C. G. A. and Jary, D. (1991b) Introduction: coming to terms with Anthony Giddens. In C. G. A. Bryant and D. Jary, *Giddens's Theory of Structuration*. London: Routledge.

*Bryant, C. G. A. and Jary, D. (eds) (1996) *Anthony Giddens: Critical Assesments*. New York: Routledge.

Caccama, R. (1998) The transition to late modern society: a conversation with Anthony Giddens. *International Sociology*, 13(1), 117–133.

*Callinicos, A. (1984) Anthony Giddens – a contemporary critique. *Theory and Society*, 14, 133–66.

Callinicos, A. (1987) *Making History: Agency, Structure and Change in Social Theory*. Cambridge: Polity Press.

Carlstein, T. (1981) The sociology of structuration in time and space: a time geographic assesment of Giddens's theory. *Swedish Geographical Yearbook*, 41–57.

Cassell, P. (ed.) (1993) *The Giddens Reader*. London: Macmillan.

Clark, J. (1990) Anthony Giddens, sociology and modern social theory. In J. Clark, C. Modgil, and S. Modgil (eds), *Consensus and Controversy: Anthony Giddens*. London: Falmer Press.

*Clark, J., Modgil, C., and Modgil, S. (eds) (1990) *Consensus and Controversy: Anthony Giddens*. London: Falmer Press.

Clegg, S. (1992) Review article: how to become an internationally famous British social theorist. *The Sociological Review*, 40(3), 576–98.

Cohen, I. (1983) Breaking new ground in the analysis of capitalism. *Contemporary Sociology*, 12, 363–5.

Cohen, I. (1986) The status of structuration theory: a reply to McLennan. *Theory, Culture and Society*, 3 (1), 123–34.

Cohen, I. (1987) Structuration theory and social praxis. In A. Giddens and J. Turner (eds), *Social Theory Today*. Cambridge: Polity Press.

*Cohen, I. (1989) *Structuration Theory – Anthony Giddens and the Constitution of Social Life*. London: Macmillan.

Cohen, I. (1990) Structuration theory and social order: five issues in brief. In J. Clark, C. Modgil, and S. Modgil (eds), *Consensus and Controversy: Anthony Giddens*. London: Falmer Press.

Cohen, I. (1991) Review: D. Held and J. B. Thompson, *Social Theory of Modern Societies: Anthony Giddens and His Critics*; and Giddens, *The Consequences of Modernity*. *British Journal of Sociology*, 42, 638–41.

Cohen, I. (1998) Anthony Giddens. In R. Stones (ed.), *Key Sociological Thinkers*. London: Macmillan.

Collins, R. (1983) Society as timetraveller. *Contemporary Sociology*, 12, 365–7.

Collins, S. L. and Hoopes, J. (1995) Anthony Giddens and Charles Sanders Peirce: history, theory and a way out of the linguistic cul-de-sac. *Journal of the History of Ideas*, 56(4), 625–51.

Coser, L. A. (1990) Giddens on historical materialism. In J. Clark, C. Modgil, and S. Modgil (eds), *Consensus and Controversy: Anthony Giddens*. London: Falmer Press.

Craib, I. (1986) Back to Utopia: Anthony Giddens and modern social theory. *Radical Philosophy*, 43, 17–21.

Craib, I. (1992a) Review: Ira Cohen, Structuration Theory. Held and Thompson (eds), Social Theory of Modern Societies. *Theory, Culture and Society*, 9(2), 175–8.

*Craib, I. (1992b) *Anthony Giddens*. London: Routledge.

Dahrendorf, R. (1975) Review: the class structure of the advanced societies. *Sociology*, 9, 134–7.

Dallmayr, F. R. (1982a) Agency and structure. *Philosophy of the Social Science*, 12, 427–38.

Dallmayr, F. R. (1982b) The theory of structuration: a critique. In A. Giddens (ed.), *Profiles and Critique in Social Theory*. London: Macmillan.

Dandeker, C. (1990) The nationstate and the modern world system. In J. Clark, C. Modgil, and S. Modgil (eds), *Consensus and Controversy: Anthony Giddens*, London: Falmer Press.

Dickie-Clark, H. F. (1984) Anthony Giddens' theory of structuration. *Canadian Journal of Political and Social Theory*, 8, 92–110.

Dickie-Clark, H. F. (1986) The making of a social theory: Anthony Giddens' theory of structuration. *Sociological Focus*, 19(2), 159–76.

Dickie-Clark, H. F. (1990) Hermeneutics and Giddens' theory of structuration. In J. Clark, C. Modgil, and S. Modgil (eds), *Consensus and Controversy: Anthony Giddens*. London: Falmer Press.

Dupuis, A. and Thorns, D. C. (1998) Home, home ownership and the search for ontological security. *The Sociological Review*, 46(1), 24–47.

Eide, M. and Knapskog, K. (1994) Samfunnsforsking mellem Cambridge og Dikemark. *Sociologi i dag*, 24(1), 53–66.

Elchardus, M. (1988) The rediscovery of chronos: the new role of time in sociological theory. *International Sociology*, 3, 35–59.

Elster, J. (1983) Reply to comments. *Theory and Society*, 12(1), 111–20.

Fallding, H. (1991) Review: Held, D. and Thompson, J. 1989, *Social Theory of Modern Societies: Anthony Giddens and His Critics* and Giddens, A. 1990, *The Consequences of Modernity*. *Social Forces*, 70(2), 529–32.

Fauske, H. (1994) Sosialteori for det neste århundre? En sammenligning av Giddens og Parsons. *Sociologi i dag*, 24(1), 67–96.

Fontana, B. (1994) Plastic sex and the sociologist: a comment on The Transformation of Intimacy by A. Giddens. *Economy and Society*, 23(3), 374–83.

Franzén, M. (1992) Anthony Giddens and his critics. *Acta Sociologica*, 35(2), 151–6.

Friedland, R. (1987) Review essay: Giddens' golden gloves. *Contemporary Sociology*, 16(1), 40–2.

*Fuller, T. (1996) 'Beyond Left and Right': the future of radical politics – a review. *American Political Science Review*, 90(1), 174–5.

Gadacz, R. R. (1987) Agency, unlimited. *Canadian Journal of Political and Social Theory*, 11(3), 158–63.

Gane, M. (1983) Anthony Giddens and the crisis of social theory. *Economy and Society*, 12, 368–98.

Gottlieb, R. (1986) Three contemporary critiques of historical materialism. *Philosophy and Social Criticism*, 11, 87–101.

Graves, C. P. (1989) Social space in the English medieval parish church. *Economy and Society*, 18, 297–322.

Green, Simon (1989) Anthony Giddens's project for a new sociology: a critique. *Critical Review*, 3(2), 186–205.

Gregory, D. (1984) Space, time, and politics in social theory: an interview with Anthony Giddens. *Environment and Planning D: Society and Space*, 2, 123–32.

Gregory, D. (1989) Presences and absences: time–space relations and structuration theory. In D. Held and J. Thompson (eds), *Social Theory of Modern Societies – Anthony Giddens and His Critics*. Cambridge: Cambridge University Press.

Gregory, D. (1990) 'Grand maps of history': structuration theory and social change. In J. Clark, C. Modgil and S. Modgil, *Consensus and Controversy: Anthony Giddens*. London: Falmer Press.

Gregory, D. and Urry, J. (eds) (1985) *Social Relations and Spatial Structures*. London: Macmillan.

Gregson, N. (1986) On duality and dualism: the case of structuration and time geography. *Progress in Human Geography*, 10, 184–205.

Gregson, N. (1987) Structuration Theory: Some Thoughts on the Possibilities for empirical Research. *Environment and Planning D: Society and Space*, 5, 73–91.

*Gregson, N. (1989) On the (ir)relevance of structuration theory to empirical research. In D. Held and J. Thompson (eds), *Social Theory of Modern Societies: Anthony Giddens and His Critics*. Cambridge: Cambridge University Press.

Gross, D. (1982) Time–space relations in Giddens' social theory. *Theory, Culture and Society*, 1(2), 83–8.

Hall, J. A. (1987) A contemporary critique of historical materialism: The Nation-State and Violence. Review. *The Sociological Review*, 35, 430–4.

Hammond, P. E. (1993) Review: Giddens, A. Modernity and Self-Identity. *Ameri-

can Journal of Sociology, 98(5), 1198–9.

Harris, C. (1990) Review: I. Cohen, Structuration Theory and Held and Thompson (eds), Social Theory of Modern Societies. *Sociology*, 24(4), 729–31.

Hartland, N. G. (1995) Structure and system in Garfinkel and Giddens. *The Australian and New Zealand Journal of Sociology*, 31(3), 23–36.

Hay, C., O'Brian, M., and Penna, S. (1993–4) Giddens, modernity and self-identity: "the hollowing out" of social theory. *Arena*, 2, 45–75.

Hechter, M. (1987) Review: a contemporary critique of historical materialism. *American Journal of Sociology*, 93(2), 516–18.

*Hekman, S. (1990) Hermeneutics and the crisis of social theory: a critique of Giddens' epistemology. In J. Clark, C. Modgil, and S. Modgil (eds), *Consensus and Controversy: Anthony Giddens*. London: Falmer Press.

Held, D. (1982) Review article on Giddens, A., Contemporary Critique of Historical Materialism, vol. 1 (1981). *Theory, Culture and Society*, 1, 98–102.

Held, D. (1989) Citizenship and autonomy. In D. Held and J. Thompson (eds), *Social Theory of Modern Societies: Anthony Giddens and His Critics*. Cambridge: Cambridge University Press.

Held, D. (1993a) Liberalism, Marxism, and democracy. Review essay. *Theory and Society*, 22, 249–81.

Held, D. (1993b) Anything but a dog's life? Further comments on Fukuyama, Callinicos, and Giddens. *Theory and Society*, 22, 293–304.

*Held, D. and Thompson, J. (eds) (1989) *Social Theory of Modern Societies: Anthony Giddens and His Critics*. Cambridge: Cambridge University Press.

Hewitt, J. N. (1996) Review of Giddens, Anthony et al., The Polity Reader in Social Theory. *Australian and New Zealand Journal of Sociology*, 32(1), 111–13.

Hindess, B. (1977) Review: new rules of sociological method. *British Journal of Sociology*, 28, 510–12.

Hirst, P. Q. (1972) Recent tendencies in sociological theory. (Review of A. Giddens, "Capitalism and Modern Social Theory," 1971). *Economy and Society*, 1, 216–28.

*Hirst, P. Q. (1982) The social theory of Anthony Giddens: a new syncretism? *Theory, Culture and Society*, 1(2), 78–82.

*Hirst, P. Q. (1998b) Not for the faint-hearted. *New Times*, 153.

Højrup, T. (1995) *Omkring livsformsanalysens udvikling*. Copenhagen: Museum Tusculanums Forlag.

Holmer-Nadesan, M. (1997) Essay: dislocating (instrumental) organizational time. *Organization Studies*, 18(3), 481–510.

Holmwood, J. M. and Stewart, A. (1983) The role of contradictions in modern theories of social stratification. *Sociology*, 17, 234–54.

Horne, J. (1983) Review article: profiles and critiques in social theory (1982). *Sociological Review*, 31, 769–72.

Horne, J. (1992) Review: I. Craib, Anthony Giddens. *The Sociological Review*, November, 776–8.

Innes, M. (1979) The objective and subjective components of class in relation to schooling in industrial societies: the contribution of Giddens and Parkin. *Educational Theory*, 29(4), 297–310.

Jary, D. (1984) Review: A. Giddens, Profiles and Critiques in Social Theory. *Political Studies*, 32, 167–8.

Jary, D. (1991a) Review: the consequences of modernity. *Sociological Review*, 39(2), 365–7.

Jary, D. (1991b) "Society as a time-traveller": Giddens on historical change, historical materialism and the nation-state in world society. In C. G. A. Bryant and D. Jary (eds), *Giddens' Theory of Structuration*. London: Routledge.

Jary, D. and Jary, J. (1995) The transformations of Anthony Giddens – the continuing story of structuration theory. *Theory, Culture and Society*,12(2), 141–60.

Jerdal, E. (1994) Anthony Giddens – kritisk sociolog eller samfunnsfilosof? *Sociologi i dag*, 24(1), 27–52.

Jessop, B. (1986) Review: A. Giddens, The Nation-State and Violence. *Capital and Class*, Summer, 216.

Jessop, B. (1989) Capitalism, nation-states and surveillance. In D. Held and J. Thompson (eds), *Social Theory of Modern Societies: Anthony Giddens and His Critics*. Cambridge: Cambridge University Press.

Jessop, B. (1993) Review: I. Craib, Anthony Giddens. *Sociology*, 27(3), 556–8.

Joas, H. (1986) Giddens' Theorie der Strukturbildung: Einführende Bemerkungen zu einer soziologischen Transformation der Praxisphilosophie. *Zeitschrift für Soziologie*, 15, 237–45.

Joas, H. (1987) Giddens' theory of structuration. *International Sociology*, 2(1), 13–26.

Joas, H. (1990) Giddens' critique of functionalism. In J. Clark, C. Modgil, and S. Modgil (eds), *Consensus and Controversy: Anthony Giddens*. London: Falmer Press.

Johnson, D. P. (1990) Security versus autonomy motivation in Anthony Giddens' concept of agency. *Journal for the Theory of Social Behaviour*, 20(2), 111–30.

Kaspersen, L. B. (1991) Anthony Giddens og strukturationsteorien: en løsning på sociologiens dualisme? *Dansk Sociologi*, 2(2), 51–66.

Kaspersen, L. B. (1992a) Forholdet mellem filosofi og sociologi i A. Giddens' strukturationsteori. *GRUS*, 36, 83–97.

Kaspersen, L. B. (1992b) Moderne teorisynteser. In H. Andersen (ed.), *Sociologi – En grundbog til et fag*. Copenhagen: Hans Reitzels Forlag.

Kaspersen, L. B. (1993) Strukturationsteori og empirisme. *GRUS*, 40, 144–19.

Kaspersen, L. B. (1994) Samfunds og statsbegrebet i sociologien. *Dansk Sociologi*, 1, 24–43.

*Kiessling, B. (1988a) *Kritik der Giddenshen Sozialtheorie*. Frankfurt: Lang.

Kiessling, B. (1988b) Die Theorie der Strukturierung. *Zeitschrift für Soziologie*, 17, 286–95.

Kilminster, R. (1991) Structuration theory as a world-view. In C. G. A. Bryant and D. Jary (eds), *Giddens' Theory of Structuration*. London: Routledge.

Kimmerling, B. and Moore, D. (1997) Collective identity as agency and structuration of society: The Israeli example. *International Review of Sociology*, 7(1), 25–49.

Knobl, W. (1993) Nation-state and social theory. Nationalstaat und Gesellschaftstheorie. Anthony Giddens, John A. Halls und Michael Manns Beitrage zu einer notwendigen Diskussion. *Zeitschrift fur Soziologie*, 22(3), 221–35.

Kreckel, R. (1989) Anthony Giddens' Sozialontologie als Zeitkritik gelesen.

Soziologische Revue, 12(4), 339–45.

Lackey, Chad (1992) Giddens' modernity and selfidentity. *Berkeley Journal of Sociology*, 37, 181–5.

Lash, Scott (1993) Reflexive modernization: the aesthetic dimension. *Theory, Culture and Society*, 10(1), 1–23.

Laursen, P. F. (1992) Adgang til videregående uddannelser i Danmark. *Dansk Sociologi*, 3(3), 18–35.

Layder, D. (1981) *Structure, Interaction and Social Theory*. London: Routledge and Kegan Paul.

Layder, D. (1982) Contemporary critique of historical materialism. *The Sociological Review*, 30, 518–20.

Layder, D. (1985) Power, structure and agency. *Journal for the Theory of Social Behavior*, 15(2), 131–49.

*Layder, D. (1987) Key issues in structuration theory: some critical remarks. *Current Perspectives in Social Theory*, 8, 25–46.

Layder, D. (1989) The macro/micro distinction, social relations and methodological bracketing: unresolved issues in structuration theory. *Current Perspectives in Social Theory*, 9, 123–41.

Layder, D., Ashton, D., and Sung, J. (1991) The empirical correlates of action and structure: the transition from school to work. *Sociology*, 25 (3), 447–64.

Lazar, J. (1992) La compétence des acteurs dans la "Théorie de la Structuration." *Cahiers internationaux de Sociologie*, 93, 399–416.

Lee, R. L. M. (1992) The structuration of disenchantment: secular agency and the reproduction of religion. *Journal for the Theory of Social Behaviour*, 22, 381–402.

Livesay, J. (1985) Normative grounding and praxis: Habermas, Giddens and a contradiction within critical theory. *Sociological Theory*, 3, 66–76.

Livesay, J. (1989) Structuration theory and the unacknowledged conditions of action. *Theory, Culture and Society*, 6, 263–92.

Lloyd, J. (1996) Interview: Anthony Giddens. *New Statesman*, 126(4316), 18–20.

*Lloyd, J. (1997a) Portrait: Anthony Giddens. *Prospect*, April, 40–4.

Lloyd (1997b) The LSE should be a powerhouse for a different kind of politics, addressing the crisis in conservatism and socialism, says its new director. *New Statesman*, 10 January, 18–19.

Lovering, J. (1987) Militarism, capitalism, and the nation-state: towards a realist synthesis. *Environment and Planning D: Society and Space*, 5, 283–302.

Lukes, S. (1972) Review: capitalism and modern social theory. *Sociology*, 6, 466–7.

Macintosh, N. and Scapens, R. (1987) Giddens' structuration theory: its implications for empirical research in management accounting. Working Papers in Accountancy, no. 10, Queens University, Kingston, Canada.

Macintosh, N. and Scapens, R. (1990) Structuration theory in management and accounting. *Accounting, Organizations and Society*, 15, 455–77.

MacKenzie, D. and Spinardi, G. (1991) A. Giddens on nuclear strategy: a comment. *Sociology*, 25 (3), 465–72.

*McLennan, G. (1984) Critical or positive theory? A comment on the status of Anthony Giddens' social theory. *Theory, Culture and Society*, 2(2), 123–9.

McLennan, G. (1985) Agency and totality. *Radical Philosophy*, 40, 33.

McLennan, G. (1988) Structuration theory and postempiricist philosophy: a rejoinder. *Theory, Culture and Society*, 5(1), 101–9.

McLennan, G. (1990) The temporal and the temporizing in structuration theory. In J. Clark, C. Modgil, and S. Modgil (eds), *Consensus and Controversy: Anthony Giddens*. London: Falmer Press.

McLennan, G. (1997) Review: reflexive modernization: politics, tradition and aesthetics in the modern social-order. *Australian and New Zealand Journal of Sociology*, 33(2), 258–60.

Manicas, Peter (1980) The concept of social structure. *Journal for the Theory of Social Behaviour*, 10(2), 65–82.

May, C. and Cooper, A. (1995) Personal identity and social change: some theoretical considerations. *Acta Sociologica*, 38(1), 75–85.

Mellor, P. A. (1993) Reflexive traditions: Anthony Giddens, high modernity, and the contours of contemporary religiosity. *Religious Studies*, 29, 111–27.

Mendoza, J. D. (1989a) Structuralism and the concept of structure. In J. D. Mendoza, *The Theory of Structuration of Anthony Giddens*. Leuven: Catholic University of Leuven.

Mendoza, J. D. (1989b) The duality of structure. In J. D. Mendoza, *The Theory of Structuration of Anthony Giddens*. Leuven: Catholic University of Leuven.

Mendoza, J. D. (1989c) Ontological security, routine, social reproduction. In J. D. Mendoza, *The Theory of Structuration of Anthony Giddens*. Leuven: Catholic University of Leuven.

Mestrovic, S. G. (1990) Review: I. Cohen, Structuration Theory: Anthony Giddens and the Constitution of Social Life. *Social Forces*, 69(1), 285–6.

*Mestrovic, S. G. (1998 *Anthony Giddens: the Last Modernist*. London: Routledge.

Mingers, J. (1996) A comparison of Maturana's autopoietic social theory and Giddens' theory of structuration. *System Research*, 13(4), 469–82.

Moos, A. I. and Dear, M. J. (1986) Structuration theory in urban analysis: 1. Theoretical exegesis. *Environment and Planning A*, 18, 231–52.

Mouzelis, N. (1989) Restructuring structuration theory. *Sociological Review*, 37(613), 35.

Mouzelis, N. (1997) Social and system integration: Lockwood, Habermas and Giddens. *Sociology*, 31(1), 111–19.

Mullan, B. (1987) Anthony Giddens. In B. Mullan, *Sociologists on Sociology*. London: Croom Helm.

Murgatroyd, L. (1989) Only half the story: some blinkering effects of "malestream" sociology. In D. Held and J. Thompson (eds), *Social Theory of Modern Societies: Anthony Giddens and His Critics*. Cambridge: Cambridge University Press.

*O'Brian, M., Penna, S., and Hay, C. (eds) (1998) *Theorizing Modernity: Reflexivity, Environment, and Identity in Giddens' Social Theory*. New York: Longman.

Ortmann, G. (1996) Rewalking the modern: Derrida, Giddens, and the ghost of the Enlightenment/Wiederganger der Moderne: Derrida, Giddens und die Geister der Aufklarung. *Soziologische Revue*, 19(1), 16–28.

Outhwaite, W. (1990) Agency and structure. In J. Clark et al. (eds), *Anthony Giddens – Consensus and Controversy*. London: Falmer Press.

Parker, N. (1983) State clusters. *Radical Philosophy*, 49, 44–5.

Parkin, F. (1980) Reply to Giddens. *Theory and Society*, 9, 891–4.

Pleasants, N. (1997) The epistemological argument against socialism. A Wittgensteinian critique of Hayek and Giddens. *Inquiry*, 40(1), 23–46.

Poggi, G. (1990) Anthony Giddens and "the classics." In J. Clark, C. Modgil, and S. Modgil (eds), *Consensus and Controversy: Anthony Giddens*. London: Falmer Press.

Pred, A. (1981) Power, everyday practice and the dicipline of human geography. In *Space and Time in Geography: Essays Dedicated to T. Hägerstrand*. Lund: Gleerup.

Pred, A. (1983) Structuration and place: on the becoming of sense of place and structure of feeling. *Journal for the Theory of Social Behaviour*, 13, 45–68.

Pred, A. (1990) Context and bodies in flux: some comments on space and time in the writings of A. Giddens. In J. Clark, C. Modgil, and S. Modgil (eds), *Consensus and Controversy: Anthony Giddens*. London: Falmer Press.

Rachlin, A. (1991) Rehumanizing dialectic: toward an understanding of the interpenetration of structure and subjectivity. *Current Perspectives in Social Theory*, 11, 255–69.

Rammert, W. (1997) New rules of sociological method: rethinking technology studies. *The British Journal of Sociology*, 48(2), 171–91.

Reichert, D. (1988) Möglichkeiten und Aufgaben einer kritischen Sozialwissenschaft: Ein Interview mit Anthony Giddens. *Geographica Helvetica*, 3, 141–7.

Roberts, J. and Scapens, R. (1985) Accounting systems and systems of accountability. *Accounting, Organizations and Society*, 10, 443–56.

Robertson, P. (1992) Globality and Modernity. *Theory, Culture and Society*, 9(2), 153–62.

Roche, M. (1987) Social theory and the lifeworld. *British Journal of Sociology*, 38(2), 283–7.

*Rose, Nikolas (1999) Inventiveness in politics. *Economy and Society*, 28, 467–93.

Rosenberg, J. (1990) A non-realist theory of sovereignty? Giddens' The Nation-State and Violence. *Millennium: Journal of International Studies*, 19(2), 249–59.

Roudometof, V. (1997) Review: The Consequences of Modernity. *Sociological Forum*, 12(4), 661–70.

Runciman, W. G. (1974) Review: The Class Structure of the Advanced Societies. *British Journal of Sociology*, 25, 108–11.

Rustin, M. (1995) The future of post-socialism. *Radical Philosophy*, 74 (Nov/Dec), 17–27.

Rønning, G. O. (1994) Handling og struktur hos Anthony Giddens. *Sociologi i dag*, 24(1), 3–26.

Saunders, P. (1989) Space, urbanism and the created environment. In D. Held and J. Thompson (eds), *Social Theory of Modern Societies: Anthony Giddens and His Critics*. Cambridge: Cambridge University Press.

Sayer, D. (1990) Reinventing the wheel: A. Giddens, Karl Marx and social change. In J. Clark, C. Modgil, and S. Modgil (eds), *Consensus and Controversy: Anthony Giddens*. London: Falmer Press.

Schatzki, T. R. (1997) Practices and actions – a Wittgensteinian critique of Bourdieu and Giddens. *Philosophy of the Social Sciences*, 27(3), 283–308.

*Seidman, S. (1998) *Contested Knowledge: Social Theory in the Postmodern Era*. Albany: State University of New York Press.

Seldon, A. (1996) Interview: the influence of sociology in post-war Britain. *Contemporary British History*, 10(1), 144–51.

Sewell, W. H. Jr (1992) A theory of stucture: duality, agency, and transformation. *American Journal of Sociology*, 98(1), 1–29.

Shaw, M. (1989) War and the nation-state in social theory. In D. Held and J. Thompson (eds), *Social Theory of Modern Societies: Anthony Giddens and His Critics*. Cambridge: Cambridge University Press.

Shaw, M. (1993) There is no such thing as society: beyond individualism and statism in international security studies. *Review of International Studies*, 19, 159–75.

Shilling, C. (1992) Reconceptualising structure and agency in the sociology of education: structuation theory and schooling. *British Journal of Sociology of Education*, 13, 69–87.

Shilling, C. and Mellor, P. A. (1996) Embodment, structuration theory and modernity: mind/body dualism and the repression of sensuality. *Body and Society*, 2(4), 1–15.

Shotter, J. (1983) "Duality of structure" and "intentionality" in an ecological psychology. *Journal for the Theory of Social Behavior*, 13, 19–43.

Sica, A. (1983) A contemporary critique of historical materialism. *Social Forces*, 61(4), 1260–2.

Sica, A. (1986) Locating the 17th book of Giddens. *Contemporary Sociology*, 15, 344–6.

Sica, A. (1991) The California–Massachusetts strain in structuration theory. In C. G. A. Bryant and D. Jary (eds), *Giddens' Theory of Structuration*. London: Routledge.

Skocpol, T. (1987) Review: The Nation-State and Violence. *Social Forces*, 66(1), 294–6.

Smart, B. (1982) Foucault, sociology, and the problem of human agency. *Theory and Society*, 11(2).

Smart, C. (1997) Wishful thinking or harmful tinkering? Sociological reflections on family policy. *Journal of Social Policy*, 26(3), 301–21.

Smith, C. W. (1983) A case study of structuration: the pure-bred beef business. *Journal for the Theory of Social Behaviour*, 13, 3–17.

*Smith, D. (1982) "Put not your trust in princes" – a commentary upon Anthony Giddens and the absolute state. *Theory, Culture and Society*, 1(2), 93–9.

Smith, D. (1992) Review article: modernity, postmodernity and the new middle ages. *Sociological Review*, November, 754–71.

Smith, D. (1998) Review article: Anthony Giddens and the liberal tradition. *British Journal of Sociology*, 49(4), 661–9.

Smith, J. W. and Turner, B. S. (1986) Constructing social theory and constitution society. *Theory, Culture and Society*, 3(2), 125–33.

Soja, E. W. (1990) Spatializations: a critique of the Giddensian version. In E. W. Soja, *Postmodern Geographies*. London: Verso.

Spybey, T. (1984) Traditional and professional frames of meaning in management.

Sociology, 18(4), 550–62.

Spybey, T. (1987) Some problems on Giddens' structuration theory. Paper given at Uppsala University.

Stant, M. (1977) Review of new rules. *British Journal of Sociology*, 11, 369–73.

Steele, J. (1997) Centre forward. *The Guardian*, 3 November, 6–7.

Stinchcombe, A. (1990) Milieu and structure updated: a critique of the theory of structuration. In J. Clark, C. Modgil, and S. Modgil (eds), *Consensus and Controversy: Anthony Giddens*. London: Falmer Press.

Stones, R. (1991) Strategic context analysis: a new research strategy for structuration theory. *Sociology*, 25(4), 673–95.

Storper, M. (1985) The spatial and temporal constitution of social action: a critical reading of Giddens. *Environment and Planning D: Society and Space*, 3, 407–24.

Studholme, M. (1997) From Leonard Hobhouse to Tony Blair: a sociological connection? *Sociology*, 31(3), 531–47.

Swanson, G. E. (1992) Modernity and the postmodern. *Theory, Culture and Society*, 9(2), 147–52.

Sydow, J. and Windeler, A. (1996) Managing inter-firm networks: a structurationist perspective. In C. G. A. Bryant and D. Jary (eds), *Anthony Giddens: Critical Assesments*. London: Routledge.

*Theory, Culture and Society (1992) Review symposium: Anthony Giddens on modernity. *Theory, Culture and Society*, 9(2).

Thompson, J. B. (1984a) The theory of structuration: an assessment of the contribution of Anthony Giddens. In J. B. Thompson, *Studies in the Theory of Ideology*. Cambridge: Polity Press.

Thompson, J. B. (1984b) Rethinking history: for and against Marx. *Philosophy of the Social Sciences*, 14, 543–51.

Thompson, J. B. (1989) The theory of structuration. In D. Held and J. Thompson (eds), *Social Theory of Modern Societies: Anthony Giddens and His Critics*. Cambridge: Cambridge University Press.

Thompson, J. B. (1995) *The Media and Modernity*. Cambridge: Polity Press.

Thompson, K. (1979) Review: A. Giddens, Studies in Social and Political Theory. *British Journal of Sociology*, 30, 375–6.

Thrift, N. J. (1983) On the determination of social action in space and time. *Environment and Planning D: Society and Space*, 1, 23–57.

Thrift, N. J.(1984) A. Giddens, 1981: A contemporary critique of historical materialism. Review, *Progress in Human Geography*, 8, 139–42.

Thrift, N. J. (1985) Bear and mouse or bear and tree? Anthony Giddens' reconstitution of social theory. *Sociology*, 19 (4), 609–23.

Thrift, N. J. (1993) The arts of the living, the beauty of the dead: anxieties of being in the work of Anthony Giddens. *Progress in Human Geography*, 17(1), 111–21.

Tomlinson, J. (1994) A phenomenology of globalization – Giddens on global modernity. *European Journal of Communication*, 9(2), 149–72.

Tucker, Kenneth H. Jr (1993) Aesthetics, play, and cultural memory: Giddens and Habermas on the postmodern challenge. *Sociological Theory*, 11(2), 194–211.

Tucker, Kenneth H. Jr (1998) *Anthony Giddens and the Modern Social Theory*. London: Sage.

Turner, B. S. (1992a) Weber, Giddens and modernity. *Theory, Culture and Society*, 9(2), 141–6.

Turner, B. S. (1992b) The absent body in structuration theory. In B. S. Turner, *Regulating Bodies: Essays in Medical Sociology*. London: Routldge.

Turner, J. H. (1986) Review essay: the theory of structuration. *American Journal of Sociology*, 91(4), 969–77.

Turner, J. H. (1990) Giddens's analysis of functionalism: a critique. In J. Clark, C. Modgil, and S. Modgil (eds), *Consensus and Controversy: Anthony Giddens*. London: Falmer Press.

Urry, J. (1977) Review of Giddens, New Rules of Sociological Method (1976). *The Sociological Review*, 25, 911–15.

Urry, J. (1982) Duality of structure: some critical issues. *Theory, Culture and Society*, 1(2), 100–6.

Urry, J. (1986) Review: A. Giddens, "The Constitution of Society." *The Sociological Review*, 34, 434–7

Urry, J. (1987) Survey 12: society, space, and locality. *Environment and Planning D: Society and Space*, 5, 435–44

Urry, J. (1990) Giddens on social class: a critique. In J. Clark, C. Modgil, and S. Modgil (eds), *Consensus and Controversy: Anthony Giddens*. London: Falmer Press.

Urry, J. (1991) Time and space in Giddens's social theory. In C. G. A. Bryant and D. Jary (eds), *Giddens' Theory of Structuration*. London: Routledge.

Wacquant, L. J. D. (1992) Au chevet de la modernité: le diagnostic du docteur Giddens. *Cahiers internationaux de Sociologie*, 93, 389–97.

Wagner, G. (1993) Giddens on subjectivity and social order. *Journal for the Theory of Social Behaviour*, 23, 139–55.

Wagner, P. (1996) Review: reflexive modernization – politics, tradition and aesthetics in the modern social-order. *Berliner Journal für Soziologie*, 6(3), 419–27.

*Wallace, R. A. (1991a) Structuration theory: Anthony Giddens. In R. A. Wallace, *Contemporary Sociological Theory*. Englewood Cliffs, NJ: Prentice Hall.

Wallace, R. A. (1991b) Women administrators of priestless parishes: constraints and opportunities. *Review of Religious Research*, 32 (4), 289304.

Warde, A. (1994) Consumption, identity-formation and uncertainty. *Sociology*, 28(4), 877–98.

Weaver, G. R. and Gioia, D. A. (1994) Paradigms lost: incommensurability vs structurationist inquiry. *Organization Studies*, 15(4), 565–90.

Whittington, R. (1992) Putting Giddens into action: social systems and managerial agency. *Journal of Management Studies*, 29, 693–712.

Willmott, H. C. (1986) Unconscious sources of motivation in the theory of the subject: an exploration and critique of Giddens's dualistic models of action and personality. *Journal for the Theory of Social Behaviour*, 16, 105–21.

Wilson, D. (1995) Review: excavating the dialectic of blindness and insight – Giddens, Anthony structuration theory. *Political Geography*, 14(3), 309–18.

Woodiwiss, A. (1997) Against "modernity": a dissident rant. *Economy and Society*, 26(1), 1–21.

*Wright, E. O. (1983) Giddens's critique of Marxism. *New Left Review*, 138, 11–35.

Wright, E. O. (1984) Review essay: is marxism really functionalist, class reductionist, and teleological? *American Journal of Sociology*, 89(2), 452–9.

Wright, E. O. (1989) Models of historical trajectory: an assessment of Giddens' critique of Marxism. In D. Held and J. Thompson (eds), *Social Theory of Modern Societies: Anthony Giddens and His Critics*. Cambridge: Cambridge University Press.

Wrong, D. (1990) Giddens on classes and class structure. In J. Clark, C. Modgil, and S. Modgil (eds), *Consensus and Controversy: Anthony Giddens*. London: Falmer Press.

Yates, J. and Orlikowski, W. J. (1992) Genres of organizational communication: a structurational approach to studying communication and media. *Academy of Management* Review, 17, 299–326.

Yates, J. and Orlikowski, W. J. (1982) A contemporary critique of historical materialism. *Theory, Culture and Society*, 1(1), 99–101.

Supplementary Literature

Alexander, J. (1982–3) *Theoretical Logic in Sociology*. 4 volumes. Berkeley: University of California Press.

Althusser, L. (1976) *Marxisme og klassekamp – kritik og selvkritik*. Copenhagen: Aurora.

Appelbaum, R. (1988) *Karl Marx*. Newbury Park, CA: Sage.

Bhaskar, R. (1978) *A Realist Theory of Science*. Hemel Hempstead: Harvester Wheatsheaf.

Bhaskar, R. (1996) *Scientific Realism and Human Emancipation*. London: Verso.

Blair, T. (1998) *The Third Way – New Politics for a New Century*. Fabian Pamphlet 588. London: Fabian Society.

Collins, R. (1975) *Conflict Sociology: towards an Explanatory Science*. New York: Academic Press.

Ertmann, T. (1997) *Birth of the Leviathan*. Cambridge: Cambridge University Press.

Galbraith, J. K. (1992) *The Culture of Contentment*. Boston: Houghton-Mifflin.

Garfinkel, H. (1967) *Studies in Ethnomethodology*. Englewood Cliffs, NJ: Prentice Hall.

Gouldner, A. (1970) *The Coming Crisis of Western Sociology*. New York: Basic Books.

Gurevitch, M., Benneth, T., Curran, J., and Woolacott, J. (1982) *Culture, Society, and the Media*. London: Methuen.

Habermas, J. (1971) *Knowledge and Human Interests*. Boston: Beacon Press.

Habermas, J. (1973) *Theory and Practice*. Boston: Beacon Press.

Habermas, J. (1984) *The Theory of Communicative Action. Vol. 1*. Boston: Beacon Press.

Habermas, J. (1987) *The Theory of Communicative Action. Vol. 2*. Boston: Beacon Press.

Hirst, P. (1994) *The Associative Democracy*. Cambridge: Polity Press.

Hirst, P (1998a) *From Statism to Pluralism*. London: UCL Press.

Hirst, P. and Hindess, B. (1975) *Pre-capitalist Modes of Production*. London:

Routledge and Kegan Paul.

Hirst, P. and Thompson, G. (1992) The problem of "globalization": international economic relations, national economic management and the formation of trading blocs. *Economy and Society*, 21(4), 357–96.

Hirst, P. and Thompson, G. (1999) *Globalization in Question*, rev. edn. Cambridge: Polity Press.

Hjelmslev, L. (1961) *Prolegomena to a Theory of Language*. Madison: University of Wisconsin Press (first published 1943).

Højrup, Thomas (1983) *Det glemte folk*. Statens Byggeforskningsinstitut.

Kaspersen, L. B. (forthcoming) *From a Theory of Fusion to a Thoery of Fission* of the State – *an Analysis of Postwar Europe*.

Mann, M. (1986) *The Sources of Social Power, Vol. 1*. Cambridge: Cambridge University Press.

Mann, M. (1993) *The Sources of Social Power, Vol. 2*. Cambridge: Cambridge University Press.

Marx, K. (1954) *The Eighteenth Brumaire of Louis Bonaparte*. London: Lawrence and Wishart.

Marx, K. and Engels, F. (1970) *The German Ideology*. London: Lawrence and Wishart.

Merton, R (1968) *Social Theory and Social Structure*. New York: Free Press (originally published in 1949).

Mortensen, N. (1993) Interaktionisme, fænomenologi og social samhandling. In H. Andersen (ed.), *Sociologi – en grundbog til et fag*. Copenhagen: Hans Reitzels Forlag.

Østerberg, D. (1984) *Sociologiens nøkkelbegreber*. Trondheim: Cappelen.

Outhwaite, W. (1983) Toward a realist perspective. In G. Morgan (ed.), *Beyond Method*, London: Sage.

Outhwaite, W. (1987) *New Philosophies of Social Sciences*. London: Macmillan.

Outhwaite, W. (1990) Realism, naturalism and social behaviour. *Journal for the Theory of Social Behaviour*, 20(4), 365–77

Tilly, C. (1992) *Coercion, Capital, and European States*. Oxford: Blackwell.

Turner, J. H. and Maryanski, A. (1979) *Functionalism*. Menlo Park, CA: Benjamin/Cummings Publishing Company.

Weber, M. (1930) *The Protestant Ethic and the Spirit of Capitalism*. London: Allen and Unwin.

Willis, P. (1977) *Learning to Labour*. Farnborough: Saxon House.

Index